By the Book

By the Book

Writers on Literature and the Literary Life
from *The New York Times Book Review*

Edited and with an introduction by
Pamela Paul

Foreword by
Scott Turow

Illustrations by
Jillian Tamaki

A New York Times Book   Henry Holt and Company   New York

Henry Holt and Company, LLC
Publishers since 1866
175 Fifth Avenue
New York, New York 10010
www.henryholt.com

Henry Holt ® and 🅗® are registered trademarks of Henry Holt and Company, LLC.

Library of Congress Cataloging-in-Publication Data
By the book : writers on literature and the literary life from the New York Times Book Review / edited and with
an introduction by Pamela Paul ; foreword by Scott Turow ; illustrations by Jillian Tamaki. — First edition.
   pages cm
  Includes index.
 "A New York Times book"
  ISBN 978-1-62779-145-8 (hardback) — ISBN 978-1-62779-146-5 (electronic copy) 1. Authors —Interviews. 2.
Books and reading. 3. Authorship. I. Paul, Pamela editor. II. Tamaki, Jillian, 1980– illustrator. III. New York
Times book review.
 PN452.B9 2014
 809—dc23
 [B]
                        2014009601

Henry Holt books are available for special promotions and premiums.
For details contact: Director, Special Markets.

First Edition 2014

Designed by Meryl Sussman Levavi

Printed in the United States of America

10 9 8 7 6 5 4 3 2 1

Teddy, this one's for you.

Contents

Scott Turow

I arrived at Amherst College as a freshman in 1966, possessed by the dream of becoming a novelist, which was immediately when I learned that there were no classes in creative writing in the curriculum. (Naturally, I could have discovered the same thing by paying more attention to the course catalog rather than to the splendid physical setting that had made me fall in love with the school. But I was seventeen.) In time, English professors explained to me that instruction in fiction or poetry writing was worthless, offering no more intellectual content than auto shop or basket weaving.

Eventually, the college relented and hired its first visiting writer, the fine English poet Tony Connor, in 1968. I consulted him eagerly, but he shook his head as soon as he heard me out.

"Scott, I know noo-thing about writing noovels," he said in the potent accent of his native Manchester, "but if I wanted to be a noovelist, I'd stoof myself with noovels."

I didn't need Tony's encouragement to read. I remember lying in bed for two weeks as a freshman, enthralled with *The Alexandria Quartet*, by Lawrence Durrell, whose four volumes I tore through to the detriment of my classes and assignments.

Yet Tony's remark was a mandate to read another way. Novels, he was telling me, were going to be my best teacher. From the work of other novelists I'd learn to define my taste, to judge what authorial strategies worked or didn't, to figure out how good sentences and paragraphs and stories were constructed. For years after that, I didn't merely read, I reread, then read again, writers and passages that filled me with wonder. Tillie Olsen. James Joyce. Robert Stone. I must have read Updike's *Rabbit, Run* five times and Bellow's *Herzog* even more than that, thinking about the choices that governed every word, each chapter. Over time, the comparison with my own work also made me recognize what was sadly out of reach.

To some degree, reading is an instrumental activity for all of us. While most readers don't try to mine the secrets of craft in the determined way I did, all of us experience a minute, incremental intellectual bonus every time our eyes cross a page. Neuroscientists almost certainly will be researching for decades how our sense for the nuances of language and syntax expands, how we gather and contrast constellations of ideas from what we consume as readers.

Yet for most of us, writers and readers, the passion for books goes in the category of an enigmatic and sui generis desire. Even for those of us who have made our way by putting words on paper, the commitment to literature has almost always preceded the urge to write. In my own By the Book interview (p. 242), I recount how my will to be a novelist began to form the first time I was totally captured by a novel. That was at age ten when I read *The Count of Monte Cristo*, by the older Alexandre Dumas. If it was that exciting to read a book, I reasoned, then it had to be even more thrilling to write one, to feel the story come to life inside you over an extended period of time. But it was a long while, with many more novels taking hold of me, before I actually tried writing fiction myself.

I read most of these columns as they appeared, because they have become my favorite part of *The New York Times Book Review*. I relish the company of other writers, maybe for the same reason dogs love other dogs. Yet over the years I've come to realize that what an individual writer has to say about his or her creative process will tell me as much about how to write as the body styling on a car is liable to reveal about how its engine runs. On the other hand, what someone reads is almost always telling. One of the saddest parts of the portended decline of physical books is losing the self-revelation that people casually—or sometimes with great calculation—make with the volumes they place in view on their shelves.

When the reader is a writer I admire, there is even more news contained in her or his reading habits. At a minimum, I'm likely to hear about or recall a book I think I should read, an opinion that gathers force when the suggestion repeats what I've heard before. More subtly, a fine writer's reading passions are often a window into his or her mind and the deeper process of literary taste and judgment that may not be visible on the page.

Because Pamela Paul, who edited these columns for the *Book Review*, often put the same questions to a number of participants, I couldn't help being struck by certain answers. When I responded that among writers living or dead, I'd choose to hang around with Shakespeare, I knew I wasn't being particularly original, just honest. Yet I was cheered to realize that my fantasy was shared by at least ten other respondents, each of whom I greatly admire.

Even more interesting to me were the answers to the *Book Review*'s question about the works individual writers found particularly remarkable or disappointing, especially the varied responses about James Joyce's *Ulysses*. One thing I thought I'd learned as a college freshman was that *Ulysses* held the number one ranking in the race for the title of Greatest Novel Ever Written. Outsized reverence for Joyce's work seemed to have begun decades before with T. S. Eliot's pronouncement, "I hold this book to be the most important expression which the present age has found." Even a novelist as seemingly different from Joyce as Hemingway had named *Ulysses* as the last book that had influenced his writing.

The summer after my freshman year I found myself working as a substitute mail carrier in one of the tony North Shore suburbs outside Chicago. The post office was an intriguing place (just see short stories by Eudora Welty and Herman Melville). I discovered, after a steep learning curve, that I could sort and deliver the mail on my route in less than the eight hours allotted for the job, but I made the mistake of returning to the post office early only once. I received a very colorful lecture from the chief clerk, who dragged me down to the employee lunchroom in the basement and explained how poorly my colleagues would regard me if I dared show up again before 3:15 p.m., when I was scheduled to punch out.

As a result, I hid in the only air-conditioned public building in town: the library. With an hour or two to spare each afternoon, I decided to improve myself by reading the Greatest Novel Ever Written. During my six weeks with *Ulysses*, I had a number of observations. First, I swooned over many of the most gorgeous sentences I'd ever encountered. Second, unlike other works by Joyce that I'd adored, like *Portrait of the Artist as a Young Man* or "The Dead" in *Dubliners*, *Ulysses* didn't seem to be a novel in the narrow way I thought of that form, that is, as a story which would carry me along because of my emotional connection with one or more characters. I had to work at *Ulysses*, so much so that it seemed somewhat fitting that the taxpayers of the United States were paying me $2.52 an hour while I read it. Finally, it was startling but instructive that in an affluent community with a sky-high educational level, the library's lone copy of *Ulysses* was on the shelf every time I went to find it. I spent many years after that wondering whether Joyce's book could really be the greatest novel ever written if no one else in town wanted to read it.

As the frequent mentions of *Ulysses* in the pages that follow reveal, the novel is no longer the object of universal admiration within the literary community. It retains many fans, but there are also more than a few very fine writers who have their qualms—take a look at what Richard Ford says, for instance. The contrast with the continued reverence for Shakespeare from so many writers is striking. As I like to say, all literature is contemporary literature. It is read and preserved by those to whom it continues to speak. And the Bard's unique genius has stirred yet another generation, while Joyce's experiments seem to some experienced readers to be modernist failures.

But whether a given writer likes or abhors a given book, all writers probably would concede that, to an extent infinitesimal or great, they are who they are because of every one of the books with which they've "stoofed" themselves during their lifetimes.

Introduction by
Pamela Paul

We all want to know what other people are reading. We peer at strangers' book covers on an airplane and lean over their e-books on the subway. We squint at the iPhone of the person standing in front of us in the elevator. We scan bestseller lists and customer reviews and online social reading sites. Asking someone what she's read lately is an easy conversational gambit—and the answer is almost bound to be more interesting than the weather. It also serves an actual purpose: we may find out about something *we* want to read ourselves.

When I launched By the Book in *The New York Times Book Review*, it was an effort to satisfy my own genuine, insatiable desire to know what others—smart people, well-read people, people who are good writers themselves—were reading in their spare time. The idea was to stimulate a conversation over books, but one that took place at a more exalted level than the average watercooler chat. That meant starting big, and for me that meant David Sedaris. Who wouldn't want to know which books he thinks are funny? Or touching or sad or just plain good?

In coming up with the questions for David Sedaris, and then for those who followed, I decided to keep some consistent—What book would you recommend to the president to read?—while others would come and go. If you're going to find out what books John Grisham likes, you've got to ask about legal thrillers. When talking to P. J. O'Rourke, you want to know about satire.

Similarly, the range of writers for By the Book had to sweep wide, to include relative unknowns and new voices alongside the James Pattersons and Mary Higgins Clarks. That meant poets and short story writers and authors of mass market fiction. And while the most obvious, and often most desirable, participants would be authors themselves, I didn't want to limit the conversation to book people.

For that reason, I went to Lena Dunham (not an author at the time) next. I asked musicians like Pete Townshend and Sting, scientists and actors, the president of Harvard, and even an astrophysicist. Cross-pollination between the arts—and the sciences—is something many of us haven't experienced since our college days, and I wanted to evoke some of that excitement of unexpected discovery—in the subjects, in the questions, and in the answers.

Once the ball got rolling, an unexpected discovery on my part was the full-throttle admiration our most respected public figures have for one another. Colin Powell marveled over J. K. Rowling's ability to endure the spotlight. Michael Chabon, Jeffrey Eugenides, and Donna Tartt were all consumed by the Patrick Melrose novels of Edward St. Aubyn. (He, in turn, was reading Alice Munro.) Writer after writer extolled the reportorial prowess of Katherine Boo. And then Boo, who told me she read the column religiously, praised Junot Díaz and George Saunders and Cheryl Strayed when it was her turn.

When I'd meet writers at book parties or literary lunches, they'd thrill over what other By the Book subjects had said about their work. In her interview, Donna Tartt told me how much she looked forward to reading Stephen King's new novel—before he'd raved about *The Goldfinch* on our cover. In a world that can feel beset by cynicism, envy, and negative reviews, By the Book has become a place for accomplished peers to express appreciation for one another's art.

Then there are the humanizing foibles. The books we never finished or are embarrassed never to have picked up, the books we hated, the books we threw across the room. It's not just us. Many writers confess here to unorthodox indulgences (Hilary Mantel adores self-help books) and "failures" of personal taste (neither Richard Ford nor Ian McEwan has much patience for *Ulysses*).

Reading the interviews gathered together for the first time, I found myself flipping back and forth between pages, following one author to another, from one writer's recommendation to another's explication of plot, like browsing an endlessly varied, annotated home library in the company of thoughtful and erudite friends. I learned about mutual loves, disagreements, surprise recommendations, unexpected new voices, forgotten classics. Let the conversation begin.

By the Book

David Sedaris

What book is on your night stand now?

I was a judge for this year's Scholastic Art and Writing Awards, so until very recently I was reading essays written by clever high school students. Now I've started Shalom Auslander's *Hope: A Tragedy*. His last book, *Foreskin's Lament*, really made me laugh.

When and where do you like to read?

Throughout my twenties and early thirties—my two-books-per-week years—I did most of my reading at the International House of Pancakes. I haven't been to one in ages, but at the time, if you went at an off-peak hour, they'd give you a gallon-sized pot of coffee and let you sit there as long as you liked. Now, though, with everyone hollering into their cellphones, it's much harder to read in public, so I tend to do it at home, most often while reclining.

What was the last truly great book you read?

I've read a lot of books that I loved recently. *Nothing to Envy: Ordinary Lives in North Korea*, by a woman named Barbara Demick, was a real eye-opener. In terms of "great," as in "This person seems to have reinvented the English language," I'd say Wells Tower's *Everything Ravaged, Everything Burned*. What an exciting story collection it is, unlike anything I've ever come across.

David Sedaris is the author of *Me Talk Pretty One Day*, *Naked*, *When You Are Engulfed in Flames*, and *Let's Explore Diabetes with Owls*, among other books.

Do you consider yourself a fiction or a nonfiction person? What's your favorite literary genre? Any guilty pleasures?

I like nonfiction books about people with wretched lives. The worse off the subjects, the more inclined I am to read about them. When it comes to fictional characters, I'm much less picky. Happy, confused, bitter: if I like the writing I'll take all comers. I guess my guilty pleasure would be listening to the British audio versions of the Harry Potter books. They're read by the great Stephen Fry, and I play them over and over, like an eight-year-old.

What book had the greatest impact on you? What book made you want to write?

I remember being floored by the first Raymond Carver collection I read: *What We Talk About When We Talk About Love*. His short, simple sentences and familiar-seeming characters made writing look, if not exactly easy, then at least possible. That book got me to work harder, but more important it opened the door to other contemporary short story writers like Tobias Wolff and Alice Munro.

If you could require the president to read one book, what would it be?

I would want him to read *Is There No Place on Earth for Me?*, Susan Sheehan's great nonfiction book about a young schizophrenic woman. It really conveys the grinding wheel of mental illness.

What are your reading habits? Paper or electronic? Do you take notes? Do you snack while you read?

I sometimes read books on my iPad. It's great for traveling, but paper versions are easier to mark up, and I like the feeling of accomplishment I get when measuring the number of pages I've just finished—"Three-quarters of an inch!" I like listening to books as well, as that way you can iron at the same time. Notewise, whenever I read a passage that moves me, I transcribe it in my diary, hoping my fingers might learn what excellence feels like.

What is your ideal reading experience? Do you prefer a book that makes you laugh or makes you cry? One that teaches you something or one that distracts you?

Yes, all the above.

What were your favorite books as a child? Do you have a favorite character or hero from one of those books? Is there one book you wish all children would read?

There was a series of biographies with orange covers in my elementary school library, and I must have read every one of them. Most of the subjects were presidents or founding fathers, but there were a few heroes thrown in as well: Daniel Boone, Davy Crockett. I loved reading about their early years, back when they were chopping firewood and doing their homework by candlelight, never suspecting that one day they would be famous. I wish all children would read *Is There No Place on Earth for Me?* That way they'd have something to talk about when they meet the president.

Disappointing, overrated, just not good: What book did you feel as if you were supposed to like, and didn't? Do you remember the last book you put down without finishing?

Boy, did I have a hard time with *Moby-Dick*. I read it for an assignment ten years ago and realized after the first few pages that without some sort of a reward system I was never going to make any progress. I told myself that I couldn't bathe, shave, brush my teeth, or change my clothes until I had finished it. In the end, I stunk much more than the book did.

What's the funniest book you've ever read?

The staff of *The Onion* put out an atlas that gives me a stomachache every time I read it. I can just open it randomly, and any line I come upon makes me laugh. For funny stories it's Jincy Willett, Sam Lipsyte, Flannery O'Connor, and George Saunders. Oh, and I love Paul Rudnick in *The New Yorker*.

What's the one book you wish someone else would write?

I'd love to read a concise, nonhysterical biography of Michael Jackson. I just want to know everything about him.

If you could meet any writer, dead or alive, who would it be? What would you want to know? Have you ever written to an author?

I'm horrible at meeting people I admire, but if I could go back in time, I'd love to collect kindling or iron a few shirts for Flannery O'Connor. After I'd finished, she'd offer to pay me, and I'd say, awestruck, my voice high and quivering, that it was on me.

If somebody walked in on you writing one of your books, what would they see? What does your work space look like?

When stuck, I tend to get up from my desk and clean, so if someone walked in they'd most likely find me washing my windows, or dusting the radiator I'd just dusted half an hour earlier.

Do you remember the last book that someone personally recommended you read and that you enjoyed? Who recommended you read it, and what persuaded you to pick it up?

My sister Amy and I have similar tastes in nonfiction, and on her recommendation I recently read and enjoyed *Tiger, Tiger*, by Margaux Fragoso.

What do you plan to read next?

I'm looking forward to the new Michael Chabon book. I loved *The Yiddish Policemen's Union*.

Childhood Inspiration

C. S. Lewis was the first writer to make me aware that somebody was writing the book I was reading—these wonderful parenthetical asides to the reader. I would think: "When I am a writer, I shall do parenthetical asides. And footnotes. There will be footnotes. I wonder how you do them? And italics. How do you make italics happen?"
—**Neil Gaiman**

What really made me want to be a writer was the Hardy Boys series, and also daily newspapers. My mom says I learned to read on the sports pages of the *Miami Herald*.
—**Carl Hiaasen**

Lewis Carroll's *Alice in Wonderland* and *Through the Looking-Glass*, which my grandmother gave me when I was nine years old and very impressionable. These were surely the books that inspired me to write, and Alice is the protagonist with whom I've most identified over the years. Her motto is, like my own, "Curiouser and curiouser!"
—**Joyce Carol Oates**

The truth is that the most beloved and the most formative books of my childhood were comic books, specifically Marvel Comics. Fantastic Four and Spider-Man, The Mighty Thor and The Invincible Iron Man; later came Daredevil and many others. These combinations of art and writing presented to me the complexities of character and the pure joy of imagining adventure. They taught me about writing dialect and how a monster can also be a hero. They lauded science and fostered the understanding that the world was more complex than any one mind, or indeed the history of all human minds, could comprehend.
—**Walter Mosley**

Lena Dunham

What book is on your night stand now?

Right now I'm looking right at Mary Gaitskill's *Bad Behavior*; the new Diane Keaton autobiography; *Having It All*, by Helen Gurley Brown (research); and *The Consolations of Philosophy*, by Alain de Botton—all in various states of having-been-read-ed-ness.

When and where do you like to read?

On the big couch by sunlight in the afternoon when I should be working. While I get my hair and makeup done on set. In bed. Always in bed.

What are your reading habits? Paper or electronic? Do you take notes? Do you snack while you read?

I loved my Kindle, but then I broke it, so I am back to my first love, paperbacks. And you know what? I don't miss that little machine, even though it was saving me pounds in my luggage. That leaning tower of books by my bed pleases me to no end to look at and rearrange. I snack while I do most things. I like gluten-free crackers and soy cheese, even though I'm not allergic to the traditional version of either.

What was the last truly great book you read? Do you remember the last time you said to someone, "You absolutely must read this book"?

I am obsessed with *The Private Diaries of Catherine Deneuve*, in which we learn intimate details about working with titans of the French New Wave *and* she talks smack about Bjork. Her prose is elegant and defiant and very, very French.

Lena Dunham is the creator, producer, and star of HBO's *Girls* and the author of *Not That Kind of Girl*.

What's your favorite literary genre? Any guilty pleasures?

I love biographies and autobiographies, especially of famous (and famously complicated) women. Barbra Streisand, Leni Riefenstahl, Edna St. Vincent Millay. *Minor Characters*, by Joyce Johnson, with all that Beat generation gossip told from the eyes of a sweet 'n' sour teen. Spiritually leaning self-help is obviously my guilty pleasure (not that guilty: I like Ram Dass, Deepak Chopra, and especially Mark Epstein's Buddhist psychology books). I also like extremely speculative books in which psychics explain what happens before we're born/after we die (Sylvia Browne, master psychic). I have to read *Eloise* once a month or I'll perish.

Have you ever read a book about girls or women that made you angry or disappointed or just extremely annoyed?

I don't have a taste for airport chick-lit, even in a guilty-pleasure way. Any book that is motored by the search for a husband and/or a good pair of heels makes me want to move to the outback. If there is a cartoon woman's torso on the front or a stroller with a diamond on it, I just can't.

And what's the best book about girls you've ever read?

Catherine, Called Birdy, by Karen Cushman. *Lolita*, by Vladimir Nabokov.

If you could require the president to read one book, what would it be?

The *Guide to Getting It On!* seems like it would have something to offer anyone, although if Obama's singing is any indication he's got it covered.

One of the movies you included in your BAM film festival is *Clueless*, which was based on *Emma*. What's your all-time favorite movie based on a book? The worst?

The Group is a favorite adaptation. It's gaudy and sexy and a mess in the best way. I can't watch the *Eloise* movie or I will also perish.

What book makes you laugh?

Without Feathers, by Woody Allen, makes me giggle like a baby. *Holidays on Ice*, by David Sedaris. *How to Have a Life-Style*, by Quentin Crisp.

What were your favorite books as a child? Do you have a favorite character or hero from one of those books? Is there one book you wish all children would read?

I have tattoos from children's books all over my arms and torso. The biggest one is of Ferdinand the bull, which Elliott Smith also had, but his was a different page. What a good message that book has! Just be yourself and don't gore anyone with your horns if you don't feel like it.

Disappointing, overrated, just not good: What book did you feel as if you were supposed to like, and didn't? Do you remember the last book you put down without finishing?

This question is so up my alley because my history is dotted with shameful unfinisheds. *The Great Gatsby*? I put it down in eighth grade and haven't picked it up again. Should I not be saying this? Will I be sent away somewhere awful? I often don't finish books, even ones that I like.

Would you like to write a book? If you could write a book about anything, what would it be?

Who doesn't want to write a book? I wish it were a mystery novel set in a quietly seething college town, but alas it would likely be memoir.

What's the one book you wish someone else would write?

I wish my mom would let me type and edit her journals from when she was my age, but she doesn't trust me that they're a fascinating account of the inner life of a young artist in 1970s SoHo. I also wouldn't mind reading Bill Murray's memoirs or an instructional guide to getting dressed by Chloë Sevigny.

If you could meet any writer, dead or alive, who would it be? What would you want to know? Have you ever written to an author?

This is not exactly an answer to your question, but I wonder fairly often how Anne Sexton and Sylvia Plath would be doing in the age of better living through chemistry. I love both their work dearly. I wrote a letter to Nikki Giovanni in middle school, care of her publisher, using many different-colored pens. I didn't hear back but do not hold a grudge.

What do you plan to read next?

I am woefully unread in the areas of history and politics and have a grand plan to read *A People's History of the United States*, *The Power Broker: Robert*

Moses and the Fall of New York, and some other books that might hack away at my ignorance. I am also looking forward to David Stockman's upcoming book on the financial crisis, because I met him at a party and thought he was a very compelling character. I am going to go back and read *The Triumph of Politics: Why the Reagan Revolution Failed* (I am not a libertarian, but I will read a book by one). I just pre-ordered Sheila Heti's book *How Should a Person Be?* and *Love, an Index*, poetry by Rebecca Lindenberg, because I read excerpts of both and found them stunning in different ways. If you couldn't tell, I mostly like confessional books by women.

On *Ulysses*

Every few years, I think, "Maybe now I'm finally smart enough or sophisticated enough to understand *Ulysses*. So I pick it up and try it again. And by page ten, as always, I'm like, "What the HELL . . . ?"
—**Elizabeth Gilbert**

I know I don't love *Ulysses* as much as I am supposed to—but then again, I never cared even one-tenth so much for the *Odyssey* as I do for the *Iliad*.
—**Donna Tartt**

Overrated . . . Joyce's *Ulysses*. Hands down. A professor's book. Though I guess if you're Irish it all makes sense.
—**Richard Ford**

I'd swap the last dozen pages of "The Dead" for any dozen in *Ulysses*. As a form, the novel sprawls and can never be perfect. It doesn't need to be, it doesn't want to be. A poem can achieve perfection—not a word you'd want to change—and in rare instances a novella can too.
—**Ian McEwan**

James Joyce's *Ulysses*. In June of this year I reread this ever astonishing classic with my neuroscientist husband, who had not read it before, in preparation for a trip to Dublin, which overlapped, just barely, with the annual Bloomsday celebration. (And my favorite chapter? "Ithaca.")
—**Joyce Carol Oates,**
on the last great book she's read

I bet it's great, but I wasn't smart enough to make it through James Joyce's *Ulysses*.
—**Penn Jillette**

Neil Gaiman

What book is on your night stand now?

There are a few. My current audiobook (Yes, they count; of course they count; why wouldn't they?) is *The Sisters Brothers*, by Patrick deWitt. It was recommended by Lemony Snicket (through his representative, Daniel Handler), and I trust Mr. Snicket implicitly. (Or anyway, as implicitly as one can trust someone you have never met, and who may simply be a pen name of the man who played accordion at your wedding.) I'm enjoying it—such a sad, funny book about family, framed in a Wild West of prospectors and casual murder.

My "make this last as long as you can" book is *Just My Type: A Book About Fonts*. It's illuminated a subject I thought I understood, but I didn't, and its chapter on the wrongnesses of Comic Sans came alive for me recently visiting a friend at a Florida retirement community, in which every name on every door was printed in Comic Sans. The elderly deserve more respect than that. Except for the lady I was visiting, widow of a comics artist. For her, it might have been appropriate. On the iPad there are several books on the go, but they are all by friends, and none of them is actually published yet, so I will not name them.

When and where do you like to read?

When I can. I read less fiction these days, and it worries me, although my recent discovery that wearing reading glasses makes the action of reading more pleasurable is, I think, up there with discovering how to split the atom or America. Neither of which I did. (I clarify this for readers in a hurry.)

Neil Gaiman is the author of *Coraline, The Graveyard Book, Odd and the Frost Giants, The Wolves in the Walls,* and *The Ocean at the End of the Lane,* among other books.

What was the last truly great book you read?

The Sorcerer's House, by Gene Wolfe, amazed me. It was such a cunning book, and it went so deep. A foxy fantasy about a house that grows, with chapters that are the Greater Trumps of a tarot deck.

The latest graphic novel I read was *Dotter of Her Father's Eyes,* by Mary M. Talbot, drawn by Bryan Talbot. I have known the Talbots for thirty years—Bryan drew some Sandman comics—and admired Bryan's work for almost forty years. (How old *is* he? How old am I?) I wasn't expecting such a beautiful, personal mingling of biography (of Lucia, James Joyce's daughter) and autobiography (Mary's father was a Joycean scholar) told so winningly and wisely. It's short but is, I think, truly great.

Are you a fiction or a nonfiction person? What's your favorite literary genre? Any guilty pleasures?

My guiltiest pleasure is Harry Stephen Keeler. He may have been the greatest bad writer America has ever produced. Or perhaps the worst great writer. I do not know. There are few faults you can accuse him of that he is not guilty of. But I love him.

How can you not love a man who wrote books with names like *The Riddle of the Traveling Skull?* Or *The Case of the Transposed Legs?*

I get into arguments with Otto Penzler, of the Mysterious Bookshop in New York, when I say things like that. "No, Neil!" he splutters. "He was just a bad writer!"

Otto still takes my money when I buy Keeler books like *The Skull of the Waltzing Clown* from him. But the expression on his face takes some of the fun out of it. And then I read a paragraph like:

> For it must be remembered that at the time I knew quite nothing, naturally, concerning Milo Payne, the mysterious Cockney-talking Englishman with the checkered long-beaked Sherlockholmesian cap; nor of the latter's "Barr-Bag," which was as like my own bag as one Milwaukee wienerwurst is like another; nor of Legga, the Human Spider, with her four legs and her six arms; nor of Ichabod Chang, ex-convict, and son of Dong Chang; nor of the elusive poetess, Abigail Sprigge; nor of the Great Simon, with his 2,163 pearl buttons; nor of—in short, I then knew quite nothing about anything or anybody involved in the affair of which I had now become a part, unless perchance it were my Nemesis, Sophie Kratzenschneiderwümpel—or Suing Sophie!

And then I do not give a fig for Otto's expression, for as guilty pleasures go, Keeler is as strangely good as it gets.

What book had the greatest impact on you? What book made you want to write?

I don't know if any single book made me want to write. C. S. Lewis was the first writer to make me aware that somebody was writing the book I was reading—these wonderful parenthetical asides to the reader. I would think: "When I am a writer, I shall do parenthetical asides. And footnotes. There will be footnotes. I wonder how you do them? And italics. How do you make italics happen?"

These days kids understand fonts and italics, and computers mean that the days of literary magic are done. But back then, we had to hand-carve our own fonts . . . well, more or less. I did have to learn the mysteries of copy-editing symbols, when I was a young journalist.

P. L. (Pamela) Travers, who wrote the Mary Poppins books, made me want to tell stories like that. Ones that seemed like they had existed forever, and were true in a way that real things that had actually happened could never be.

There were a handful of other authors who made me want to be a writer. And I think what they all had in common was that they made it look like fun. G. K. Chesterton, who delighted in painting pictures in sentences, like a child let loose with a paint box. Roger Zelazny, who reshaped myth and magic into science fiction. Harlan Ellison and Michael Moorcock, Samuel R. Delany, Ursula K. Le Guin (although she intimidated me), and Hope Mirrlees, who only wrote one good book, *Lud-in-the-Mist*. But if you write a book that good you do not need to do it again.

If you could require the president to read one book, what would it be?

One of mine. Preferably on a day when he gets asked a really awkward question at a press conference he'd rather not answer. So he'd distract them by going, "The economy? Bombing Iran? Wall Street? You know . . . I read this really great book the other day by Neil Gaiman. Has anyone here read it? *American Gods*? I mean, that scene at the end of chapter one . . . What the heck was going on there?"

Look, JFK made the James Bond franchise by talking about how much he liked the books. I can dream.

What are your reading habits? Paper or electronic? Do you take notes?

I like reading. I prefer not reading on my computer, because that makes whatever I am reading feel like work. I do not mind reading on my iPad. I have a Kindle, somewhere, but almost never use it, and a Kindle app on my phone, my iPad, and on pretty much everything except the toaster, and I use that, because I am besotted by Kindle's ability to know where I am in a book. I've been using it to read Huge Books of the kind I always meant to read, or to finish, but didn't, because carrying them around stopped being fun. Books like *The Count of Monte Cristo*.

Do you prefer a book that makes you laugh or makes you cry? One that teaches you something or one that distracts you?

Yes.

Wait, do you think those things are exclusive? That books can only be one or the other? I would rather read a book with all of those things in it: a laughing, crying, educating, distracting book. And I would like more than that, the kind of book where the pages groan under the weight of keeping all such opposites apart.

Disappointing, overrated, just not good: What book did you feel you were supposed to like, and didn't? Do you remember the last book you put down without finishing?

No. Perhaps because there have been few books in recent years I actually broke up with, realizing we were not right for each other. There are instead books I have stopped seeing, and vaguely intend to finish one day, the next time I run into them, but they are vaguer, more general things.

I remember the first book I didn't finish, though. It was *Mistress of Mistresses*, by E. R. Eddison. I was around seventeen, and I'd finished every book I'd started before then. It was inconceivable to me not to. I'd read and mostly enjoyed Eddison's *The Worm Ouroboros*, a fantasy epic written in a lush, thick, cod-Elizabethan style that started off irritating and then became part of the fun. I bought *Mistress of Mistresses* and abandoned it a third of the way through. It was gloriously liberating, the idea that I didn't have to finish every book.

But mostly, I did. If I started it, I'd read it to the end: until I found myself a judge of the Arthur C. Clarke Awards in the UK, and obliged to read every science-fiction book published in the UK in the year of eligibility. I was a judge for two years. The first year, I read everything. The second year, I read a lot of first chapters and took delight in hurling books across the room if I knew I would not be reading the second chapter.

Then I'd go and pick them up again, because they are books, after all, and we are not savages.

If you could meet any writer, dead or alive, who would it be? What would you want to know? Have you ever written to an author?

As a teenager I wrote to R. A. Lafferty. And he responded, too, with letters that were like R. A. Lafferty short stories, filled with elliptical answers to straight questions and simple answers to complicated ones.

He was a sui generis writer, the oddest and most frustratingly delightful of American tall-tale tellers. Not a lot of people have read him, and even fewer like what he wrote, but those of us who like him like him all the way. We never met.

The last time I wrote to Lafferty, he had Alzheimer's and was in a home in Oklahoma, shortly before his death, and I do not believe he read or understood the letter, but it made me feel like I was doing something right by writing it and sending it.

What's the best comic book you've ever read? Graphic novel?

Ow. That's hard. I think I love Eddie Campbell's *ALEC: The Years Have Pants* best of everything, but it's a hard call.

Alan Moore and Eddie Campbell's *From Hell* is pretty wonderful, after all. *Watchmen* had a bigger influence on me than anything else, reading and rereading it a comic at a time as it was published, as did the *High Society* and *Church and State* sequences of Dave Sim's Cerebus.

And Will Eisner's The Spirit is funny and sad, educational and entertaining (read the books, ignore the movie).

I'm about to start building giant lists of comics and graphic novels here, so I will stop. (Quick! Read anything by Lynda Barry!)

There. I stopped.

What do you plan to read next?

The Night Circus, by Erin Morgenstern. I have so many proof copies of the book, given to me by people certain that if I read it I would love it, that I feel guilty. They stare at me from all over the house. I resisted when Audrey Niffenegger told me I had to read it, but when my daughter Holly told me how much she loved it, I knew I would have to succumb.

The Gift of a Book

When I was nine, I was given a set of slightly abridged classics for Christmas, and the same again when I was ten. My mother got them from a mail-order catalog. We weren't a household that owned many books so it was a novelty to fill a whole shelf. There were plain cloth bindings and no pictures. (That's just the way I like it; I make my own pictures, thanks.) That's when I became enthralled by Robert Louis Stevenson, and failed to like Dickens, and met the Brontës. They were clever abridgments, too, as I came to realize when I read the full texts later. (Imagine, *Jane Eyre* without the embarrassing bits.)—**Hilary Mantel**

Gender Outlaw, by Kate Bornstein. I got it for my birthday last year from my daughter after a family discussion on the merits of transgender surgery. It's a fascinating and illuminating memoir by a transgender playwright.—**Caroline Kennedy**

A copy of *Libra*, with a nice inscription, that Don DeLillo sent me in 1989. I must have asked my publisher to send him a finished copy of my first novel; there's no way to explain the gift otherwise. But after spending my twenties working in near-total isolation and revering DeLillo from afar, I couldn't believe that I had something signed to me in his own human hand. At some level, I still can't believe it.—**Jonathan Franzen**

I'm not currently teaching, but it's a wonderful feeling when a former student gets a book published and sends me a copy. This happened last year with a woman named Bianca Zander, whose terrific first novel is called *The Girl Below*. It's about a young woman who returns to London after a decade in New Zealand and confronts strange events from her past—**Curtis Sittenfeld**

Peter the Great, by Robert Massie. It kicked off my obsession with Russian history.—**Jeannette Walls**

Not long ago, I had an amusing experience meeting the author of a book I received as a gift nearly two decades ago—a book that in many ways changed my life. Almost twenty years ago, I was halfway through writing my first novel, *Digital Fortress*, when I was given a copy of *Writing the Blockbuster Novel*, by the legendary agent Albert Zuckerman. His book helped me complete my manuscript and get it published. Two months ago, by chance, I met Mr. Zuckerman for the first time. I gratefully told him that he had helped me write *Digital Fortress*. He jokingly replied that he planned to tell everyone that he had helped me write *The Da Vinci Code*.—**Dan Brown**

On December 7, 1999, I left the bedside of my editor Faith Sale, just before she was removed from life support. We had been like sisters. Two hours later, Stephen King called and asked my husband, Lou, and me to meet him at his hotel room. It was his first public foray after being nearly killed by a van six months before. He gave me an advance reading copy of *On Writing*. A couple of years before, we had talked about the question no one asks us in interviews: language. He had been thinking of doing a book on writing, and I had said, "Do it." He now asked me to look at the dedication. It was for me. We then went to see the premiere of *The Green Mile*, about a man on death row who can heal people, including those dying of cancer. That night was both enormously sad and gloriously uplifting.
—**Amy Tan**

Mary Higgins Clark

What book is on your night stand now?

Dante to Dead Man Walking: *One Reader's Journey Through the Christian Classics*, by Raymond A. Schroth.

When and where do you like to read?

I like to read anywhere. I never go to a doctor or dentist without a book in my bag. At home I used to love to read in bed but fall asleep too easily. So my favorite spot is a roomy wing chair with a footstool in the family room. If I'm working on my own book, I'll be reading background material in my third-floor office at home in Saddle River.

What was the last truly great book you read?

After many years, I just reread *Pride and Prejudice* and understand why it is, and always will be, a classic.

Are you a fiction or a nonfiction person? What's your favorite literary genre? Any guilty pleasures?

Fiction or nonfiction: honestly, both. I love to read historical biographies, and of course I cut my teeth on suspense, starting with *The Bobbsey Twins and Baby May*, in which an infant is left on the doorstep. The babysitter had been in a daze because a can of tomato soup had fallen on her head, and she keeps trying to steal the baby back. After that it was the Nancy Drew series, and I was hooked.

Mary Higgins Clark has written suspense novels, collections of short stories, a historical novel, children's books, and a memoir.

You once worked as a stewardess, and presumably you have traveled quite a bit. Any observations about what people read on airplanes and how that's changed over the years? What do you like to read on the plane?

When I was a flight stewardess with Pan American a thousand years ago, everyone was carrying a book. Now everyone seems to be carrying a computer or looking at the television. A few years ago, I got on the plane and smiled to see a woman deeply engrossed in one of my books. I settled myself and a few minutes later glanced back. She was in a dead sleep. On a plane, I like to catch up with what my suspense writer friends are up to and grab their latest on the way to the plane.

If you could require the president to read one book, what would it be?

The Constitution, with emphasis on the First Amendment.

What is your ideal reading experience? Do you prefer a book that makes you laugh, or makes you cry? One that teaches you something, or one that distracts you?

I want to be emotionally involved with the characters, to laugh or cry with them, to yearn for things to turn out right for them. I don't think there is any book that can't teach you something, even if it is how not to tell a story.

What were your favorite books as a child? Did you have a favorite character or hero?

The Good Earth, *A Girl of the Limberlost*, *The Secret Garden*, *A Tree Grows in Brooklyn*. Favorite character was Jane Eyre after I saw the first movie and before I read the book.

Disappointing, overrated, just not good: What book did you feel you were supposed to like, and didn't?

Honestly not fair to answer. If I start a book that I'm supposed to like and don't like, I put it down. Maybe if I gave it a longer shot I might have loved it. We'll never know.

If you could meet any writer, dead or alive, who would it be? What would you want to know? Have you ever written to an author?

For years I admired Morris West from afar. Then I met him briefly at a cocktail party. His agent, a personal friend of mine, called the next morning: "Mary, where did you go? After the cocktails, Morris said, 'Let's collect

Mary Clark and go to dinner.'" I wanted to kill myself. I had slipped away to a teacher's retirement dinner. But later, on a publicity trip to Australia, I visited him and his family at home. Years later he asked me for a blurb for his new book. I was thrilled.

What are your reading habits? Are you a fast or slow reader? Do you take notes? Do you read print or electronic?

I'm a fast reader. I only take notes if it's for research purposes. I love the convenience of electronic, especially when I'm traveling, but love best the feel and smell of a print book.

What book made you want to become a writer?

I was writing from the time I could put words in a sentence. My one gift has been to be a storyteller.

Which of the books you've written is your favorite?

That would be like asking me which of my children is my favorite.

What's your favorite movie based on one of your books?

Sadly, I'm still waiting.

What's the best suspense novel you've ever read?

The Woman in White, by Wilkie Collins. Runner-up, *Rebecca*, by Daphne du Maurier.

What do you plan to read next?

The latest P. D. James. She's a marvelous writer and at age ninety-one gives me hope for my own future of continuing to be a storyteller.

José Martí, because he lived so many lives and because he was such a fantastic writer and because, damn it, he was José Martí (he also lived in the New York City area, so that will help the conversation). Octavia Butler because she's my personal hero, helped give the African diaspora a future (albeit a future nearly as dark as our past), and because I'd love to see her again. And Arundhati Roy because I'm still crushing on her mind and on *The God of Small Things*.

—**Junot Díaz**

Sappho, for a bit of ancient gender politics; Aphra Behn for theater gossip; and George Eliot because everyone who knew her said she was fascinating. All women, because they know how to get talking about the nitty-gritty so quickly and are less prone to telling anecdotes. I'd have gone for Jane Austen if I weren't convinced she'd just have a soft-boiled egg and leave early.

—**Emma Thompson**

Well, I eat dinner with writers a lot, and—like eating with children—the experience can really go both ways. I'd probably make it potluck, and then invite the best cooks who are (or were) also good company. If you were to assign writers an Invitability Score (prose style × kitchen chops × congeniality at the table), Ben Marcus (*The Flame Alphabet*) is always going to rate pretty high.

—**Michael Chabon**

First I call Shakespeare. "Who else is coming?" Shakespeare asks. "Tolstoy," I answer. "I'm busy that night," Shakespeare says. Next I call Kafka, who agrees to come. "As long as you don't invite Tolstoy." "I already invited Tolstoy," I tell him. "But Kundera's coming. You like Milan. And you guys can speak Czech." "I speak German," Kafka corrects me. When Tolstoy hears that Kundera's coming, he drops out. (Something about an old book review.) So finally I call Joyce, who's always available. When we get to the restaurant, Kafka wants a table in back. He's afraid of being recognized. Joyce, who's already plastered, says, "If anyone's going to be recognized, it's me." Kundera leans over and whispers in my ear, "People might recognize us too if we went around with a cane." The waiter arrives. When he asks about food allergies, Kafka hands him a written list. Then he excuses himself to go to the bathroom. As soon as he's gone, Kundera says, "The problem with Kafka is that he never got enough tail." We all snicker. Joyce orders another bottle of wine. Finally, he turns and looks at me through his dark glasses. "I'm reading your new book," he says. "Oh?" I say. "Yes," says Joyce.

—**Jeffrey Eugenides**

I know I should use my time machine to go deep-canonical, but the prospect of trying to navigate a dinner party with Herman Melville, Charlotte Brontë, and Honoré de Balzac—figuring out what I could say to them, or what they could say to each other—is beyond my capacities as a bon vivant. Instead, I think I'd want to hang out with three guys I just missed out on knowing, a group more "relatable" to twentieth-century me—Don Carpenter, Philip K. Dick, and Malcolm Braly. They're all, as it happens, semi-outlaw types with Marin County connections, so they'd probably have a good time if thrown together. And I could flatter myself and claim I've been implicated in the revival of each of their posthumous careers, so we'd have something to raise a glass or spark a joint to. I'd be thrilled to let them know they're in print.

—**Jonathan Lethem**

Drew Gilpin Faust

What book is on your night stand now?

Alan Hollinghurst's *The Stranger's Child*, Daniel Kahneman's *Thinking, Fast and Slow*, Katherine Boo's *Behind the Beautiful Forevers*, *The Civil War: The Second Year Told by Those Who Lived It* (Library of America). I always seem to be reading several books at once.

Where and when do you like to read?

Everywhere and anywhere—but always at night before I go to sleep.

What was the last truly great book you read?

Not having read *Huckleberry Finn* since high school, I returned to it last summer—ordering it on my Kindle on a bit of a whim. I was astonished to find how much of what I had been teaching and studying about race and slavery in American history was already there in a book published in 1884. The book offers as well striking—and eerily modern, or perhaps postmodern in their critical renderings of "reality"—insights into the masks and dissimulations that structure social order.

Are you a fiction or a nonfiction person? What's your favorite literary genre? Any guilty pleasures?

Both. I am a historian, so of course I read history. But now as Harvard president I have license and reason to read across the fields represented at the university. I also enjoy contemporary fiction, and I am a detective story addict.

My responsibilities as president include international travel, and for me, trip planning always includes reading. I have recently been immersed in books about India, which I visited in January. I have explored both

---

Drew Gilpin Faust is the president of Harvard University and the author of *Mothers of Invention*, among other books.

fiction and nonfiction: current affairs, history, art and architecture, and some wonderful novels—Mistry, Desai, Rushdie, Ghosh.

What was the best book you read as a student?

Albert Camus's *La Peste*—*The Plague*—had an enormous impact on me when I read it in high school French class, and I chose my senior yearbook quote from it. In college, I wrote a philosophy class paper on Camus and Sartre, and again chose my yearbook quote from *La Peste*. For a student during the 1960s, existentialism's emphasis on meaning as the product of action and engagement was very alluring.

What were your favorite books as a child? Did you have a favorite character or hero?

I have always loved animals, and as a child, I read a lot of horse books. I had a particular favorite called *Silver Snaffles* that my mother gave away. I looked for a copy for decades and won't soon forget the excitement I felt when I saw its familiar blue cover across the room in a bookcase of children's literature in G. Heywood Hill's legendary rare-book store in London just a few years ago. Now it is mine once again.

If you could meet any writer, dead or alive, who would it be? What would you want to know? Have you ever written to an author?

Emily Dickinson. She is such a puzzle. Her startling genius seems to have come from nowhere. She lived her life as a recluse; her work remained essentially unpublished and undiscovered until well after her death. Yet she turned language and poetry on end.

What are your reading habits? Do you take notes? Do you read electronic or paper?

I often read nonfiction with a pencil in hand. I love the feel, the smell, the design, the weight of a book, but I also enjoy the convenience of my Kindle—for travel and for procuring a book in seconds.

What is the best book you've read about academia? Or a book that prepared you for academic life in some way?

Amanda Cross's murderous take on academic life has provided me with a great deal of pleasure.

In a more serious vein, I much admire Clark Kerr's *The Uses of the University*, which was originally delivered as a series of lectures at Harvard in 1963 and has been amplified in several editions since. It remains the best explanation of how the American research university emerged and evolved, and why its commitment to the critical perspective and the long view is so important to our present and future.

Is there any book you wish all incoming freshmen at Harvard would read?

Kathryn Schulz's *Being Wrong* advocates doubt as a skill and praises error as the foundation of wisdom. Her book would reinforce my encouragement of Harvard's accomplished and successful freshmen to embrace risk and even failure.

What do you plan to read next?

After I finish the pile on my night stand, I may take up Karl Marlantes's *What It Is Like to Go to War*. My curiosity about that question has animated a great deal of my own research and writing about the Civil War. Ernest Hemingway once declared that war "is the best subject." It is certainly one that has engaged me as both author and reader.

My guiltiest pleasure is Harry Stephen Keeler. He may have been the greatest bad writer America has ever produced. Or perhaps the worst great writer. I do not know. There are few faults you can accuse him of that he is not guilty of. But I love him.—**Neil Gaiman**

Books about the Inquisition and the Crusades are a guilty pleasure because I feel guilty reading bad things about the Catholic Church—though it's hard to avoid these days. Biographies of famous horses and lives of the saints are among my favorite literary genres.—**Caroline Kennedy**

Listening to the British audio versions of the Harry Potter books. They're read by the great Stephen Fry, and I play them over and over, like an eight-year-old.—**David Sedaris**

Spiritually leaning self-help is obviously my guilty pleasure (not that guilty: I like Ram Dass, Deepak Chopra, and especially Mark Epstein's Buddhist psychology books). I also like extremely speculative books in which psychics explain what happens before we're born/after we die (Sylvia Browne, master psychic).—**Lena Dunham**

My (very) guilty pleasure is tabloid journalism. I hate to say it, but I know the names of all the celebrities' babies.—**Elizabeth Gilbert**

I don't believe in guilty pleasures, I only believe in pleasures. People who call reading detective fiction or eating dessert a guilty pleasure make me want to puke. Pedophilia is a pleasure a person should have guilt about. Not chocolate.—**Ira Glass**

I'm the guy in the waiting room flipping through *People*. Bellow said that fiction was "the higher autobiography," but really it's the higher gossip.—**Jeffrey Eugenides**

My guilty pleasures are the usual—crime and suspense. But my literary conscience doesn't bother me about Ruth Rendell, P. D. James, Elmore Leonard, and Alan Furst.—**P. J. O'Rourke**

When I was a teenager my guilty reading was, of course, erotic stuff. At fourteen, living in Lebanon, I discovered the irresistible mixture of eroticism and fantasy reading *One Thousand and One Nights* inside a closet with a flashlight. Nothing can be compared to the excitement of a forbidden book. Today nothing is forbidden to me, so there is no guilt. Too bad!—**Isabel Allende**

My guiltiest secret is that every Thursday, I buy *People* magazine, *Us Weekly*, and the *National Enquirer*. If anyone asks about this, I will lie and maintain that I just said it to be funny. If people call when I am reading the *Enquirer*, I say, "Oh, lah de dah, I'm just lying here reading the new *New Yorker*."—**Anne Lamott**

My guilty pleasure is tough-guy-loner action novels, like the Jack Reacher series, where the protagonist is an outwardly rugged but inwardly sensitive and thoughtful guy who, through no fault of his own, keeps having to beat the crap out of people.—**Dave Barry**

Carl Hiaasen

What book is on your night stand now?

Raylan, by Elmore Leonard, one of my writing heroes. There is nobody better at lowlife dialogue. And also, by the way, not a cooler guy on the planet.

When and where do you like to read?

Unfortunately, I don't get to read nearly as much as I want because I'm always working on my own stuff, either the novels or newspaper columns. So I do most of my reading when I travel, on airplanes, at least until the meds kick in.

What was the last truly great book you read? Do you remember the last time you said to someone, "You absolutely must read this book"?

I had that reaction to *Swamplandia!*, by Karen Russell. It just blew me away. Everybody's idea of a great book is different, of course. For me it's one that makes my jaw drop on every page, the writing is so original. I just reread *The Sporting Club*, by Tom McGuane, and it might be one of the funniest American novels ever. *Bonfire of the Vanities*, by Tom Wolfe, is still dazzling.

Do you consider yourself a fiction or a nonfiction person? What's your favorite literary genre? Any guilty pleasures?

When I'm working on a novel of my own, I try to read mostly nonfiction, although sometimes I break down and peek at something else. I'm probably biased toward contemporary fiction and satire because that's what I enjoy most, which is natural when you're coming from a journalism background. Vampires, wizards, dragon slayers—pretty tame stuff when you live in a place like Florida.

Carl Hiaasen is the author of numerous books for adults and children, including *Bad Monkey, Star Island, Nature Girl, Skinny Dip, Sick Puppy*, and *Lucky You.*

What book had the greatest impact on you? What book made you want to write?

I remember being greatly affected by several books—*Catcher in the Rye*, *Catch-22*, and Steinbeck's *Travels with Charley*, for starters. *Without Feathers*, a collection of Woody Allen's early short stories, was a prized possession. But long before that, what really made me want to be a writer was the Hardy Boys series, and also daily newspapers. My mom says I learned to read on the sports pages of the *Miami Herald*.

If you could require the president to read one book, what would it be?

The Monkey Wrench Gang, by Edward Abbey. It would definitely transport Obama out of the Beltway.

What are your reading habits? Paper or electronic? Do you take notes? Do you snack while you read?

I don't have an e-reader. One reason is that I like to dog-ear the page when I find a particularly good sentence or passage. Oddly, at recent book signings I've had readers ask me to autograph their Kindles or iPads. I even signed a few Nooks, I swear to God.

Do you prefer a book that makes you laugh or makes you cry? One that teaches you something or one that distracts you?

I don't want to read any book that makes me cry. I get all the gloom I can stand from newspaper headlines. Novels should be a sweeping distraction—entertainment, to put it simply, and there's no law against getting educated while you're getting entertained. For authors, the best books to read are the humbling ones. You should put it down when you're finished, thinking: "Geez, I'll never be able to write like that. Maybe I should try ceramics."

Disappointing, overrated, just not good: What book did you feel as if you were supposed to like, and didn't? Do you remember the last book you put down without finishing?

In seventh grade, for some perverse reason, I decided to read the entire *World Book Encyclopedia*. I got about fifty pages into the first volume before moss started growing on my eyelids.

If you could meet any writer, dead or alive, who would it be? What would you want to know? Have you ever written to an author?

I would have loved to have gone deep-sea fishing with Hemingway, as long as he didn't bring the Thompson submachine. He liked to shoot his initials into the heads of sharks. Seriously.

Which of the books you've written is your favorite? Your favorite character?

Novels are like your children—you've got deep affection for all of them, but there's always something you wished you'd done a bit differently, or better. *Tourist Season* is dear to me because it was my first solo try, and then *Hoot*, because it was my first book for young readers. In both cases I assumed the thing would bomb.

I suppose my favorite character is Skink, a totally unhinged, roadkill-eating ex-governor. He shows up in several novels, usually written during election years when I'm feeling especially torqued.

If somebody walked in on you writing one of your books, what would she see? What does your work space look like?

The first thing you see outside my office is a doormat that says: LEAVE. My wife got it for me, and it works pretty well. Inside, my so-called work space looks like it got tossed by burglars. Meanwhile, my prolific friend Mike Lupica has an office corkboard covered with colored index cards upon which he's meticulously plotted whatever novel he's writing. It's very disturbing.

Do you remember the last book someone personally recommended you read and that you enjoyed? Who recommended you read it and what persuaded you to pick it up?

My oldest son, Scott, recently sent me a novel about a pair of hired gunslingers called *The Sisters Brothers*, by Patrick deWitt. It was just terrific.

What was the last book you gave to someone as a gift? And to whom?

Last month I sent a wonderful British memoir called *Blood Knots* to Peter Solomon, a friend of mine who loves fishing like I do. (Technically it wasn't a gift—a friend sent it to me and I passed it along.)

What's the one book you wish someone else would write?

I'm waiting for the day when Rush Limbaugh's pharmacist writes a book.

What do you plan to read next?

The next thing I plan to read, for at least the hundredth time, is chapter nineteen of the novel I've been working on. Either that or volume two of the encyclopedia.

The Constitution, with emphasis on the First Amendment.—**Mary Higgins Clark**

The Best and the Brightest, by David Halberstam. Theories and grand ideas are important. But they seldom unfold as planned. People—it is all about people.—**Colin Powell**

The Best and the Brightest, by David Halberstam. Smart people make bad decisions about policy and then compound them by refusing to admit they were wrong. I wish George W. Bush had read it before invading Iraq.
—**Anna Quindlen**

The president—any president—could usefully acquaint him/herself with Walt Kelly's cartoon strip of Pogo Possum living in the swamps of Georgia. Very perspicacious about politics. The prime minister might revisit Geoffrey Willans's *Molesworth*, which is so illuminating about the character and habits of little boys. I am not being rude. Both president and prime minister have to deal with a great quantity of childish behavior.
—**Emma Thompson**

The president's already read *Team of Rivals*, and I can't think of anything better for him. I'd give our prime minister *Justice*, by Michael Sandel.—**J. K. Rowling**

Fifty Shades of Grey. Why should he miss all the fun? Plus, it might loosen him up a bit.
—**John Grisham**

The Road to Serfdom, no matter who is president. But a president is a busy man, and Hayek's syntax is heavy going. Being a native German speaker, Hayek strings together railroad sentences ending in train wreck verbs.
—**P. J. O'Rourke**

Your president is a complex case, a man of passion, courage, and oratory. And also, a diligent, prickly, practical law professor. I'd particularly keep him close to Whitman and Thoreau, those great American voices of openhearted humanity, daring, and liberty.—**Alain de Botton**

The Brothers Karamazov, by Dostoyevsky. I was required to read this book in English class during my freshman year at Haverford College, but I never finished it. I seriously doubt that Dostoyevsky ever finished it. So I figure if the president read it, he could tell me what happens.
—**Dave Barry**

I'm convinced that anyone who takes that job doesn't need advice from me on anything. It would only make their life worse. But if I had to force him to read something, it would be *My Way of Life*, a pocket-reader version (edited by Walter Farrell) of the *Summa Theologica* of St. Thomas. God's wisdom comes in handy when you're the leader of the free world. I got that as a gift from the late Lt. Gen. William J. McCaffrey. His son, Gen. Barry McCaffrey, was a leader of American forces in the Persian Gulf war. The father, Gen. William McCaffrey, was a commander in the all-black 92nd Division in Italy. He understood what it meant to send men into harm's way.
—**James McBride**

John Irving

What book is on your night stand now?

I don't read in bed, ever. As for the main character of my novel *In One Person*, Billy Abbott is a bisexual man; Billy would prefer having sex with a man or a woman to reading in bed.

Where, when, and how do you like to read? Paper or electronic?

I get up early. I like to read a little before anyone but the dog is up. I also like to read at night, not in bed but just before I go to bed. I don't read anything electronically. I don't write electronically, either—except e-mails to my family and friends. I write in longhand. I have always written first drafts by hand, but I used to write subsequent drafts and insert pages on a typewriter. Now (for the last two books) I write all my drafts by hand. It's the right speed for me—slow.

What was the last truly great book you read?

When I love a novel I've read, I want to reread it—in part, to see how it was constructed. The two novels I've reread this year are Michael Ondaatje's *The Cat's Table* and Edmund White's *Jack Holmes and His Friend*—a seamless use of time (most notably, the flash-forwards within the memory of the past) in the former, and a clarifying delineation of different sexual points of view in the latter. They are two terrific novels.

What's your favorite literary genre?

I hate the certainty with which literary works are categorized into one or another "genre"; this tempts me to say that my "favorite" genre is some-

---

John Irving is the author of *The World According to Garp*, *The Cider House Rules*, *In One Person*, and *A Prayer for Owen Meany*, among other books.

thing not easily categorized—such as same-sex foreplay in gardens, with dogs watching at a distance.

What book changed your life?

Great Expectations.

How old were you when you read it? And what changed?

I was fifteen. It made me want to be able to write a novel like that. It was very visual—I saw everything, exactly—and the characters were more vivid than any I had heretofore met on the page. I had only met characters like that onstage, and not just in any play—mainly in Shakespeare. Fully rendered characters, but also mysterious. I loved the secrets in Dickens— the contrasting foreshadowing, but not of everything. You both saw what was coming and you didn't. Hardy had that effect on me, too, but when I was older. And Melville, but also when I was older.

If you could require the president to read one book, what would it be?

I'm sure the president has read James Baldwin, but he may have missed *Giovanni's Room*—a short novel of immeasurable sadness. That is the novel he should read—or reread, as the case may be—because it will strengthen his resolve to do everything in his power for gay rights, and to assert that gay rights are a civil rights issue. The gay-bashing among the Republican presidential contenders may be born of a backlash against gay marriage; whatever it comes from, it's reprehensible.

What were your favorite books as a child?

My Father's Dragon, by Ruth Stiles Gannett.

Were you an early reader or did you come to it late? A fast or slow reader? Did you grow up around books?

I am a slow reader; when I'm tired, I move my lips. I almost read out loud. My grandmother read to me, and my mother—and my father. My father was the best reader; he has a great voice, a teacher's voice. Yes, I grew up around books—my grandmother's house, where I lived as a small child, was full of books. My father was a history teacher, and he loved the Russian novels. There were always books around.

You've often taught writing. What book do you find most useful to help teach aspiring writers?

There is no one book that students of writing "should" read. With young writers, I tried to focus on the choices you make before you write a novel. The main character and the most important character are not always the same person—you have to know the difference. The first-person voice and the third-person voice each come with advantages and disadvantages; it helps me to know what the story is, and who the characters are, before I choose the point-of-view voice for the storytelling. Two novels I taught a lot were *Cat and Mouse* (Grass) and *The Power and the Glory* or *The Heart of the Matter* (Greene). They were excellent examples of novels about moral dilemmas; I find that young writers are especially interested in moral dilemmas—they're often struggling to write about those dilemmas.

Disappointing, overrated, just not good: What book did you feel you were supposed to like, but didn't?

Everything by Ernest Hemingway.

What don't you like about Hemingway?

Everything, except for a few of the short stories. His write-what-you-know dictum has no place in imaginative literature; it's advice for a journalist, not for a novelist or a playwright. Imagine if Sophocles or Shakespeare or Dickens had heeded that advice! And Hemingway's sentences are short and simplistic enough for advertising copy. There is also the offensive tough-guy posturing—all those stiff-upper-lip, don't-say-much men! I like Melville's advice: "Woe to him who seeks to please rather than appall." I love Melville. Can you love Melville and also like Hemingway? Maybe some readers can, but I can't.

If you could meet any writer, dead or alive, who would it be? What would you want to know?

There's nothing I need or want to know from the writers I admire that isn't in their books. It's better to read a good writer than meet one.

Have you ever written to an author?

I've written to many authors; I love writing to writers.

And do they usually write back? What's the best letter you've received from another writer?

Yes, they write back. Gail Godwin writes exquisite letters. James Salter, too—and Salter uses an old typewriter and rewrites by hand. His handwriting is very good. He uses hotel stationery, some of it very exotic. Kurt Vonnegut was a very good letter writer, too. As you might imagine, he was very funny. Grass writes me in German and in English, which is how I write to him, but his English is much better than my German.

What book made you want to become a writer?

Great Expectations.

Which of the books you've written is your favorite? Your favorite character?

There are a lot of outsiders in my novels, sexual misfits among them. The first-person narrator of *A Prayer for Owen Meany* is called (behind his back) a "non-practicing homosexual"; he doesn't just love Owen Meany, he's probably in love with Owen, but he'll never come out of the closet and say so. He never has sex with anyone—man or woman. Dr. Larch, the saintly abortionist in *The Cider House Rules*, and Jenny Fields, Garp's mother in *The World According to Garp*, have sex only once and stop for life. The narrator of *The Hotel New Hampshire* is in love with his sister. The two most heroic characters in my new novel, *In One Person*, are transgender women—not the first time I've written about transgender characters. I love sexual outsiders; the world is harder for them.

What's your favorite movie adaptation of one of your books?

Lasse Hallstrom's *The Cider House Rules*. I loved working with Lasse. I wrote the screenplay, but it is Lasse's film; he is why it works. I also think Tod Williams's *The Door in the Floor* is an excellent adaptation of *A Widow for One Year*; he smartly adapted just the first third of that novel, when the character of Ruth (the eponymous widow) is still a little girl. He did a great job; he was the writer and director, but I enjoyed working with him—just giving him notes on his script, and then notes on the rough cut.

If somebody walked into the space where you do your writing, what would they see?

There are two big tables joined in an L-shaped fashion, so that I can move from one to the other in a chair on casters. There is a large dictionary stand with an unabridged dictionary. There are windows on two sides of my office—lots of books and papers around. My laptop is at a small desk in a far-off corner of the room, removed from the work tables—strictly for correspondence. There's a couch, and—usually—my dog, a chocolate Lab, is somewhere in my office.

What do you plan to read next?

I plan what I write, not what I read.

Elizabeth Gilbert

What book is on your night stand now?

Rome, by Robert Hughes. Though I'm finding it challenging to read about Rome without immediately wanting to run away to Rome.

When and where do you like to read?

When I am awake, and wherever I happen to be. If I could read while I was driving, showering, socializing, or sleeping, I would do it.

What was the last truly great book you read?

Nothing in the last few years has dazzled me more than Hilary Mantel's *Wolf Hall*, which blew the top of my head straight off. I've read it three times, and I'm still trying to figure out how she put that magnificent thing together. Now I'm on to its sequel, *Bring Up the Bodies*, which is nicely satisfying my need for more Thomas Cromwell.

Are you a fiction or a nonfiction person? What's your favorite literary genre? Any guilty pleasures?

I enjoy both, although I unfairly hold fiction to a far higher standard. With nonfiction, I figure I can glean something educational or interesting out of the book even if the writing is weak. But if the first chapter of a novel doesn't feel perfect and accurate to me, I simply can't read on; it's too painful. Meanwhile, my (very) guilty pleasure is tabloid journalism. I hate to say it, but I know the names of all the celebrities' babies.

Elizabeth Gilbert is the author of *Eat, Pray, Love*. Her other books include *The Last American Man*, *Committed*, and *The Signature of All Things*.

What was the best book you read as a student? What books over the years have most influenced your thinking?

It was a big deal for me in high school to be introduced to Hemingway. I already knew that I wanted to be a writer, but the deceptive simplicity of his voice made writing seem realistically attainable to me—as though all you had to do was get out of the way and let the story tell itself. Of course, Hemingway isn't simple, and writing isn't simple, and I certainly didn't end up thinking like him in any way. But he did open up for me a marvelous expanse of possibility and permission, and just at the right moment.

If you could require the president to read one book, what would it be?

My Life, by Bill Clinton—purely as a study guide for how to win a second term.

What is your ideal reading experience? Do you prefer a book that makes you laugh or makes you cry? One that teaches you something or one that distracts you?

Oh, I just want what we all want: a comfortable couch, a nice beverage, a weekend of no distractions, and a book that will stop time, lift me out of my quotidian existence, and alter my thinking forever. Either that, or the latest photos of celebrities' babies.

What were your favorite books as a child? Did you have a favorite character or hero?

The complete Wizard of Oz series, by L. Frank Baum. Over the course of those fourteen books, stalwart Dorothy Gale triumphs, step-by-step, through precisely what Joseph Campbell would later call "the hero's journey." I think Dorothy may be the only little Midwestern girl you could ever put in the same archetypal category as Odysseus or Siddhartha. She was absolutely totemic for me.

Disappointing, overrated, just not good: What book did you feel you were supposed to like, and didn't?

Every few years, I think, "Maybe now I'm finally smart enough or sophisticated enough to understand *Ulysses*." So I pick it up and try it again. And by page ten, as always, I'm like, "What the HELL . . . ?"

If you could meet any writer, dead or alive, who would it be? What would you want to know? Have you ever written to an author?

The poet Jack Gilbert. (No relation, sadly.) He's the poet laureate of my marriage: my husband and I have read him aloud to each other for years, and he exerts a subtle influence over the way we understand ourselves in love. I would like to thank him for that, but I've always been too shy to write him a letter.

What are your reading habits? Do you take notes? Electronic or paper?

If I'm reading for pleasure, I scrawl giant enthusiastic circles and exclamation points over particularly magical paragraphs. If I'm reading for research, it all goes neatly onto index cards and packed away into tidy shoeboxes.

What book made you want to become a writer?

Probably *Curious George.* Or one of the other first books I ever saw. I never recollect wanting to be anything else, is what I mean.

Read any good memoirs recently?

I lately discovered *A Three Dog Life*, by Abigail Thomas, and it's stunning.

What's the best movie based on a book you've seen recently?

Oh, come on, now—that's a setup! But since you asked, back in 2010 there was this nice movie with Julia Roberts and Javier Bardem that really meant a lot to me. . . .

What do you plan to read next?

Ulysses.

Gail Godwin writes exquisite letters. James Salter, too—and Salter uses an old typewriter and rewrites by hand. His handwriting is very good. He uses hotel stationery, some of it very exotic. Kurt Vonnegut was a very good letter writer, too. As you might imagine, he was very funny. Grass writes me in German and in English, which is how I write to him, but his English is much better than my German.

—**John Irving**

I've written to lots of authors—fan letters. From the heart.

—**Richard Ford**

I'm afraid that I squander as much as 90 percent of my time writing letters—e-mails—to authors, my writer-friends. The problem is that they write back, and so do I. And suddenly the morning has vanished irretrievably, or ineluctably (as Stephen Dedalus would say). And I certainly receive many letters, a goodly proportion of them beginning bluntly: "Our teacher has assigned us to write about an American writer and I have chosen you, but I can't find much information about you. Why do you write? What are your favorite books? Where do you get your ideas? I hope you can answer by Monday because my deadline is . . ."

—**Joyce Carol Oates**

I wrote to René Goscinny when I was seven or eight, a fan letter about Asterix. He wrote back, saying that he was very proud to have made a little English girl laugh.

—**Emma Thompson**

I've written to lots of writers. Laurie Colwin, after reading and foisting *Happy All the Time* many times. I saved her note for twenty years. Alice Adams wrote a sweet note to me after my first novel came out when I was twenty-six, and I was so blown away that I sent her a bunch of stamps by return mail. I have no idea what I was thinking. It was a star-struck impulse.

—**Anne Lamott**

I get hundreds of very sweet, heartfelt letters from parents thanking me for getting their kids reading. Each one absolutely makes my day—make that my week. Many, many women thank me for getting their husbands reading, or reading again. Occasionally, a husband thanks me for getting his wife reading, but that's rare.

—**James Patterson**

As a teenager I wrote to R. A. Lafferty. And he responded, too, with letters that were like R. A. Lafferty short stories, filled with elliptical answers to straight questions and simple answers to complicated ones. Not a lot of people have read him, and even fewer like what he wrote, but those of us who like him like him all the way. We never met.

—**Neil Gaiman**

An Italian reader wrote to describe how he met his wife. She was on a bus, reading one of my books, one that he himself had just finished. They started talking, they started meeting. They now have three children. I wonder how many people owe their existence to their parents' love of books.

—**Ian McEwan**

Richard Ford

What book is on your night stand now?

A Good Man in Africa, by William Boyd.

When and where do you like to read?

Not in bed. Long airplane rides are good. Early mornings before things get going.

What was the last truly great book you read?

A Writer at War, by Vasily Grossman. Grossman's diaries and journalism from the Eastern Front. Riveting and immensely humane.

Are you a fiction or a nonfiction person? What's your favorite literary genre? Any guilty pleasures?

I'm an equal opportunity reader—although I don't much read plays. And since I was raised a Presbyterian, pretty much all pleasures are guilty.

What book had the greatest impact on you? What book made you want to write?

Probably *Absalom, Absalom!*, Faulkner's masterpiece. I read it when I was nineteen. It embossed into my life the experience of literature's great saving virtue. Reading is probably what leads most writers to writing.

If you could require the president to read one book, what would it be?

A book of mine. What else? What am I, an altruist? He can choose which one.

What are your reading habits? Paper or electronic? Do you take notes?

I read "book" books—the ones between covers. And I mark 'em all up. They're mine, after all. Though I'm not opposed to e-books. It's not a moral issue for me.

Richard Ford is the author of *The Sportswriter, Independence Day, Canada,* and *The Lay of the Land,* among other novels.

Do you keep the books you read? Collect, store, shelve—or throw away, lend out, donate?

I mostly keep my books. I go back often to ones I've read, and so want them around. I've spent thousands of dollars just moving books here and there. Although . . . many books that come to me unasked-for I give to the library. I never sell books.

Do you prefer a book that makes you laugh or makes you cry? One that teaches you something or one that distracts you?

I'm not a tough cry under any circumstances. And like the saying goes, "stand-up's hard." I like to be taught things. Plus, I've got enough distracting me without my reading only doing that.

What was the last book that made you cry?

My own book *Canada* made me cry the last time I read it. If it was any good, it should've. Beyond that, the very last book that made me cry was more than one poem in James Wright's collected poems, *Above the River*.

What were your favorite books as a child? Is there one book you wish all children would read?

Rick Brant science mysteries. That said, being dyslexic, I wasn't a great reader when I was a kid. And since I don't have children, I don't know what they should read. Probably something their parents would disapprove of.

Disappointing, overrated, just not good: What book did you feel you were supposed to like, and didn't? Do you remember the last book you put down without finishing?

Overrated . . . Joyce's *Ulysses*. Hands down. A professor's book. Though I guess if you're Irish it all makes sense. I put down most books, unfinished. Most books aren't very good, and there's no reason they should be. Whatever "talent" may be, it isn't apportioned democratically. Happily, I don't remember the last not-very-good book I didn't finish. Although (which is why I don't review books) sometimes I return to a book I've left unfinished and discover—pleasurably—that it was I, not the book, that was unsatisfactory.

What is your favorite story collection? Do you tend to read more short fiction or novels?

I read both, undifferentiated. Probably high on my list (though I don't generally think of favorites) would be Cheever's *Collected* and Isaac Babel's *Collected*. Eudora Welty, too. If you asked me tomorrow, I might answer differently. William Trevor. Pritchett. *Dubliners*. Alice Munro. Deborah

Eisenberg. Ann Beattie. Donald Barthelme. Mavis Gallant. Chekhov. There are some awfully good story collections around.

If you could meet any writer, dead or alive, who would it be? What would you want to know? Have you ever written to an author?

I've written to lots of authors—fan letters. From the heart. And I suppose I'd love to have met Ford Madox Ford (no relation, alas). Such a big, messy, compelling, brilliant character. My kind of guy (though, of course, it would probably have turned out disastrously, as many things in his life did).

Which of the books you've written is your favorite? Your favorite character?

With all due respect, I wrote them all as hard as I could, did my best. That question is best left for readers—if I have any.

Any chance you'll return to Frank Bascombe?

I make notes for Frank all the time, carrying them (and "him") around with me daily. As of now, that seems like enough to do.

What's the best book about sports ever written?

Gee, I've read pretty few. *A Fan's Notes*, by Frederick Exley. *The Glory of Their Times*, by Lawrence S. Ritter. Pretty much any of Roger Angell's collections.

Do you think of yourself as a regional writer? Your books tend to be very much about place—whether it's New Jersey, the South, or the West. And do you enjoy reading regional literature?

Maybe I'm a serial regional writer. First here, then there, across the map. When I stopped thinking of setting books in the South—where I was born—I did it both because I didn't think I had anything new to tell about the South (Faulkner and Welty and Percy and Hannah and twenty other wonderful writers had already done it better than I could) and because I wanted to find a wider audience and take on different concerns from those the South seemed to invite—that is, invite me. And I don't really think about books as being "regional" or not. I just think of them as being either good or not good.

What do you plan to read next?

Bird Alone, by Sean O'Faolain.

When I was a kid, I drew a lot, so I gravitated to oversized books with a lot of artwork—books about giants, gnomes, Norse myths, and space travel. There was one called *21st Century Foss*, full of incredible imaginings of spaceships and future cities, all with radical and organic shapes. I hadn't seen it in thirty years and recently bought it on eBay. Looking at those pictures again was like reliving dreams I had when I was eight years old.
—**Dave Eggers**

I loved Encyclopedia Brown as a kid. Donald Sobol passed recently, and that really brought it all back to me, how important his books were to my little self. I didn't learn to read until I was seven, so I missed out on the early stuff, jumped right to chapter books, right to Encyclopedia Brown. What I loved about Boy Detective Leroy Brown was that (1) he was unabashedly smart (smart was not cool when and where I grew up) and (2) his best friend was a girl, tough Sally Kimball, who was both Leroy's bodyguard and his intellectual equal. Sobol did more to flip gender scripts in my head than almost anybody in my early years.—**Junot Díaz**

My sister and I loved Encyclopedia Brown, the fifth-grade nerd/observer who seldom took more than a day to unravel the nefarious conspiracies of childhood. Every child detective requires a sidekick, obviously, and I thought Encyclopedia's sidekick, Sally Kimball, was way cooler than any of Nancy Drew's. In addition to being smart, Sally was the only kid in town who could beat up Bugs Meany. But as a child I treasured the idea of this infinitely just place called Idaville. In Idaville the weak were rarely bullied for long, and the bad guys didn't get away.—**Katherine Boo**

I have tattoos from children's books all over my arms and torso. The biggest one is of Ferdinand the bull, which Elliott Smith also had, but his was a different page. What a good message that book has! Just be yourself and don't gore anyone with your horns if you don't feel like it.—**Lena Dunham**

The D'Aulaires' *Norse Gods and Giants. The Phantom Tollbooth. A Wizard of Earthsea. From the Mixed-Up Files of Mrs. Basil E. Frankweiler. Harriet the Spy*. John Christopher's Tripods trilogy. Bradbury's *R Is for Rocket. The Adventures of Sherlock Holmes*. I loved trickster heroes . . . and Holmes.—**Michael Chabon**

A Wrinkle in Time saved me because it so captured the grief and sense of isolation I felt as a child. I was eight years old when it came out, in third grade, and I believed in it—in the plot, the people, and the emotional truth of their experience. This place was *never* a good match for me, but the book greatly diminished my sense of isolation as great books have done ever since. I must have read it a dozen times.—**Anne Lamott**

We constantly read these terribly violent stories by the Grimm Brothers. I mean, the cleaned-up versions of these are nowhere near the horror stories we used to read. It's no wonder my brother was a total scaredy-cat and afraid to walk home alone after you realize he had been exposed to the tales of the Grimm Brothers.
—**Arnold Schwarzenegger**

I was a very unliterary child, which might reassure parents with kids who don't read. Lego was my thing, as well as practical books like *See Inside a Nuclear Power Station*. It wasn't till early adolescence that I saw the point of books and then it was the old stalwart, *The Catcher in the Rye*, that got me going.—**Alain de Botton**

Colin Powell

What book is on your night stand now?

The Summer of 1787, by David O. Stewart. As I grow older, I am increasingly fascinated by our founding fathers. The challenges they faced and the compromises they made, good and bad, to create a nation have inspired us and people around the world. I wish today's political leaders, especially in Washington, would show the courage and willingness to fight for what they believe in, but possess an understanding of the need to compromise to solve the nation's problems. They all need to go off and read *1787*.

When and where do you like to read?

On a plane. No phones, e-mails, or meetings to interfere. I used to read in bed, until I started to fall asleep after two minutes of reading anything.

What was the last truly great book you read?

Sorry, can't answer. I find some greatness in almost every book. It's like asking which is my greatest kid.

Are you a rereader? What book do you read over and over again?

It's a book I've had for over fifty years called *The Armed Forces Officer*. It was written by Brigadier S. L. A. (Slam) Marshall. After World War II he was commissioned to review the actions of our soldiers and provide a historically based book of guidance for army officers. It is one of the finest leadership books I've ever read and was given to every officer back then. It was always with me and is right in front of me now. It once went out of print, and I was able to persuade the Pentagon to reissue it with a new cover

---

Colin Powell is a former secretary of state, national security adviser, and chairman of the Joint Chiefs of Staff. His books include *My American Journey* and *It Worked for Me*.

and an update. The book has received more updates and can now even be found on Amazon.

Right next to it is *The Professional Soldier*, by Morris Janowitz. It was published in 1960, two years after I became an officer. It is a sociological analysis of the military officer at that time. I learned that the average senior army officer was white, a West Pointer, rural, and an Episcopalian from South Carolina. I nailed one out of five. In my early years in the army, my focus was on learning about and understanding my chosen profession. I was studying to be a good lieutenant. And, of course, the Bible.

What was the best book you read as a student? What books over the years have most influenced your thinking?

In high school, I finally was required to do serious reading. I don't recall how or why, but the first big, serious adult book I picked up was *Tales of the South Pacific*, by James Michener. Romance, mystery, geography, geology, culture, history, language, and fauna, all blended together in one hypnotic book. I couldn't wait for *Return to Paradise*. And I read every single one until there were no new ones. For most of my military career, my reading was historical, leadership, management theory, and military and political auto-biographies and biographies. Ulysses S. Grant's memoirs and Dean Acheson's were standards to be inhaled. *Street Without Joy*, by Bernard Fall, was a textbook for those of us going to Vietnam in the first wave of President Kennedy's advisers. *This Kind of War*, by T. R. Fehrenbach, was a classic history of the Korean War and the cost of unpreparedness.

If you could require the president to read one book, what would it be? What book would you require all heads of state to read?

The Best and the Brightest, by David Halberstam. Theories and grand ideas are important. But they seldom unfold as planned. People—it is all about people.

Do you tend to hold on to books or give them away?

We have hundreds of books in our home; my wife, Alma, is a voracious reader. We purge them once a year and give the purged ones to the annual book fair at the State Department conducted by the Associates of the American Foreign Service Worldwide. We purge until we have several empty bookshelves waiting for new books. I have a pretty good collection of books on African-American history, especially military history. I never purge those, and they will be sent to a library after I've passed on to the remainder table.

What were your favorite books as a child? Did you have a favorite character or hero?

There is only one that I remember vividly, *My Antonia*, by Willa Cather. Growing up in the South Bronx, the story of a couple of kids my age growing up on the great prairie of Nebraska was exciting and took me to a place far away from "Fort Apache, the Bronx." I loved the story of life in a full circle touching on love, adversity, tragedy, hope, and optimism.

Disappointing, overrated, just not good: What book did you feel you were supposed to like, and didn't?

Most contemporary political memoirs, including mine, *My American Journey*. Once you do the index search on yourself or a particular issue, they tend to become uninteresting. In my case, after telling the story of my growing up in New York and my early years in the army, it was time to tell the story of my chairmanship of the Joint Chiefs of Staff. As we worked our way through the end of the Cold War and the Soviet Union, the invasion of Panama and Desert Storm, my collaborator, Joe Persico, looked over at me one day and said: "Do you know how boring this stuff is? Let's drop it. It's becoming a 'Then I had lunch with . . .' book. Everyone knows this stuff, lived through it, and won't be interested."

I refused and wrote it all out for two hundred more pages. Joe was right. In the seventeen years since it was published, I've gotten very few questions about any of that stuff, but there is still a lot of interest in the first half of the book. It is still selling. I learned my lesson, and my new book, *It Worked for Me: In Life and Leadership*, consists of just stand-alone stories and is half the size of the usual political memoir. Unfortunately, I don't believe the genre has improved in recent years.

If you could meet any writer, dead or alive, who would it be? What would you want to know? Have you ever written to an author?

I would enjoy having lunch with J. K. Rowling. I'd probe her imagination and ask how she is dealing so well with her success and multimillionaire celebrity status. When I was chairman of the Joint Chiefs of Staff, I wrote a letter to Stephen Ambrose after I read his classic *Band of Brothers*, about E Company, 506th Infantry, in World War II. I complimented him on the book and shared with him my pride in having a battalion of the 506th Infantry under my brigade command in the 1970s. I also once wrote your language expert Bill Safire, disagreeing with one of his On Language pronouncements. He met me more than halfway.

Electronic or paper?

I do both.

What book made you want to become a writer?

My checkbook. After thirty-five years of military pay and educating three kids through college, I needed to improve my finances. I was also moved by the success of my buddy Gen. Norm Schwarzkopf's book, *It Doesn't Take a Hero*. But what really did it was my agent, Marvin Josephson, and editor, Harry Evans, convincing me I had a good story to tell. I still feel strange being called a writer. I'm mostly a speaker.

If somebody walked into your office while you were writing, what would they see?

Three computers running, paper strewn all about, a television on behind me, a sense of chaos.

If you had to recommend one book to a student of government, what would it be?

There is none, and I wouldn't want to mislead anyone. Government requires many disciplines and experiences. And even if you are widely read, it is still OJT, On-the-Job Training. Government is people, and until you know the people you can't follow, govern, or lead them.

What do you plan to read next?

Sigh. That's a problem. I keep sending new books to my e-reader, and I don't know which one I'll read next. Electronic books have become such an impulse and instinct purchase that I buy them constantly and can't remember what's on my e-shelf. When I do look, I often see titles I don't recognize or don't remember wanting or buying. I'll get to some of them.

Dave Eggers

What book is on your night stand now?

I'm reading a short story collection by Tom Barbash called *Stay Up with Me*. It's not out yet, and probably won't be for a year or so, but it's so good.

What was the last truly great book you read? Do you remember the last time you said to someone, "You absolutely must read this book"?

I'm in a weird position with that question, given we publish books at McSweeney's, and every one of them has to pass that "You must read this book!" test before we decide to publish it. I hope I can mention one recent book we put out called *Inside This Place, Not of It*, edited by Ayelet Waldman and Robin Levi. It's a book of oral histories from incarcerated women in the United States, and every story is shocking—women shackled to beds during childbirth, women given hysterectomies against their will, and the omnipresent sexual abuse at the hands of guards. Massive reform is needed immediately.

What's your favorite literary genre? Any guilty pleasures?

Lately I've been reading ghost stories and have been having a blast. At a yard sale, I found a collection Hitchcock edited called *Stories Not for the Nervous*; it's solid all the way through.

Take a moment to champion unheralded writers. Who do you think is egregiously overlooked or underrated?

I don't know if he's unheralded, but there's a writer named J. Malcolm Garcia who continually astounds me with his energy and empathy. He writes

---

Dave Eggers is the author of *A Heartbreaking Work of Staggering Genius*, *How We Are Hungry*, *You Shall Know Our Velocity*, *What Is the What*, *Zeitoun*, and *A Hologram for the King*, among other books.

powerful and lyrical nonfiction from Afghanistan, from Buenos Aires, from Mississippi, all of it urgent and provocative. I've been following him wherever he goes.

What were your most cherished books as a child? Do you have a favorite character or hero from children's literature?

When I was a kid, I drew a lot, so I gravitated to oversized books with a lot of artwork—books about giants, gnomes, Norse myths, and space travel. There was one called *21st Century Foss*, full of incredible imaginings of spaceships and future cities, all with radical and organic shapes. I hadn't seen it in thirty years and recently bought it on eBay. Looking at those pictures again was like reliving dreams I had when I was eight years old.

You cofounded 826 National, an organization dedicated to motivating young people to write. Was there a particular book that motivated you? A book that you find often motivates the children you work with?

The greatest motivator for a kid to write, I think, is having an encouraging and open-minded reader. At 826, we train our tutors to be encouraging of young writers, no matter how unusual the subject matter or where their writing skills are. The two things that stunt kids more than anything else are 1) the fear that whatever they want to write about won't be acceptable, or 2) that their first drafts have to be perfect. Kids have to know, without a doubt, that writing about anything, even flatulent hamsters, is OK, and that writing can and should be fun at that age. But when you say, your paper has to be five paragraphs long, this many sentences per paragraph, and about "appropriate" subject matter, then you're guaranteeing paralysis from young writers. You've got to remove the tethers to get them started. Then you can get at the grammar on the back end.

Is there one book you wish all kids would read?

For ten years I've been teaching a high school class that puts together the anthology *The Best American Nonrequired Reading*, and from these students I've learned that there's no one book or kind of writing that works for everyone. I'm always surprised at the range of reactions to just about anything. But for reluctant readers, the rule of thumb is that you have to meet them where they live. You probably shouldn't give a reluctant reader *The Scarlet Letter* or *Middlemarch*. You can work their way up to the canon, but start with something more immediately relevant to their lives.

Any bad book habits? Do you tend not to finish books? Skim? Scribble in margins? Fall asleep while reading?

All of the above. I put books down all the time. I mark them up, fold page corners. And I fall asleep, sure. Most of my books have gotten wet because I read in the tub.

Of the books you've written, which is your favorite?

I usually feel too close to whatever book I last wrote, but in this case I have to say that I like *A Hologram for the King* best. It's different than the book I thought I was writing, so I can look at it with some distance.

What's the one book you wish someone else would write?

I have to go back to the issue of women in American prisons. I really wish Michelle Alexander, who wrote *The New Jim Crow*, about African-American men in prisons, would write a sequel, focusing on the plight of women. (I'm being greedy here, given she wrote the intro to *Inside This Place*.) There are tens of thousands of women doing decades for nonviolent offenses, and the abuse they suffer behind bars is virtually a given. Given Alexander's skills and audience, an exposé on the subject would have a critical impact.

If you could meet any writer, dead or alive, who would it be? What would you want to know?

George Orwell. I would start by asking about the mustache.

And among authors you've met already, who most impressed you?

Christopher Hitchens was the most erudite and eloquent human I've ever met. He could speak on any topic, any hour of the day or night, at length, and captivate anyone in the room. I didn't agree with all of his politics, but he was always an extremely warm and generous man.

Is there a writer you consider to be a mentor or model in some way?

William T. Vollmann's range inspires me—and his empathy and curiosity. He gives absolutely everyone the benefit of the doubt, and I try to follow his lead on that.

Where do you get your books? Are you a downloader, online shopper, borrower, used-bookstore browser?

I'm a paper-only reader, and I get most of my books at the independent bookstores in the Bay Area. I like used books, too, so I raid the big used-book sales the libraries around here put on. That's where you can fill any holes in your collection for, say, a buck a book. Once I got a full Balzac set for twenty dollars. Not bad.

What do you plan to read next?

A few years ago a poet named Arif Gamal gave me his book, *Morning in Serra Mattu: A Nubian Ode*, and after reading and loving the first few pages, I lost it. I found it the other day while cleaning my office, and now am about halfway through it. It's an epic poem about growing up in northern Sudan, and it's really beautiful, unlike anything I can remember. I'm so glad I found it again. Feels like some kind of reunion.

My Library

At home we have floor-to-ceiling bookshelves of beautiful leather-bound editions of classic literature that my husband has bought for years. They are mostly decoration: they look smart. Personally, I have my own bookshelves for books in Spanish that I keep because they are hard to get in the United States. All the rest comes and goes. I don't collect anything, not even good novels. Once a year I gather all the books I have read already or will not read ever (several boxes) and give them away. I don't miss them, because if needed I can buy them again.
—**Isabel Allende**

My husband is a streamliner; I am a pack rat. I've even hung on to all my textbooks from college—you know, just in case I have the sudden urge to read Schopenhauer's *The World as Will and Representation*.
—**Sheryl Sandberg**

We had it organized by topic for nonfiction and alphabetically by author for fiction and poetry—but then the ceiling leaked and we had to paint the rooms and now it's every book for itself.
—**Caroline Kennedy**

Reference books in the dining room, older books needing and deserving protection in bookcases in the living room, theology and philosophy on shelves in the bedroom, classical and ancient Near Eastern literature in the study, modern history and Americana in the room that has only bookshelves in it, unclassifiable books in stacks on the stairs.
—**Marilynne Robinson**

I am proud to say that I give away or sell at little to no profit almost all of my books. I have mentioned a few favorites earlier, but as a rule I don't believe in keeping books. After I have read, reread, and reread a book it seems sinful to keep such a reservoir of fun and knowledge fallow on a shelf. Books are meant to be read, and if I'm not reading them then someone else should get the opportunity.
—**Walter Mosley**

Sylvia Nasar

What book is on your night stand now?

Two biographies of Frances Trollope, Anthony Trollope's mother; an Elizabeth Gaskell novel; and E. M. Delafield's *Diary of a Provincial Lady*. Some Cold War history.

When and where do you like to read?

In bed and in the car. I read page turners in bed and listen to more challenging books in the car.

What was the last truly great book you read? Do you remember the last time you said to someone, "You absolutely must read this book"?

The Widow Barnaby, by Frances Trollope, a deliciously witty satire about a vulgar, heartless, outrageously flirtatious widow of a village pharmacist who poses as a lady of great fortune. Beribboned and bedizened, Martha Barnaby drags her beautiful but penniless niece from watering hole to watering hole in her hunt for a rich second husband. The angelic Agnes dutifully complies when forced to wear the same hideous black gown every day for months, while acting as her aunt's personal maid. And I loved *Major Pettigrew's Last Stand*, by Helen Simonson, about two aging lovers whom children and relatives try to boss around.

Do you consider yourself a fiction or a nonfiction person? What's your favorite literary genre? Any guilty pleasures?

Before I wrote *A Beautiful Mind*, I never read anything but novels and plays for pleasure. For the next fifteen years I've mostly read history, biography, and economics. But when I was finishing *Grand Pursuit* I got into novels again.

Sylvia Nasar is the author of *A Beautiful Mind* and *Grand Pursuit*. She teaches at the Columbia University Graduate School of Journalism.

What book had the greatest impact on you? What book made you want to write?

I haven't thought about O. Henry in years, but I suppose his stories had a great influence on me. Also, Agatha Christie. Until I actually did it, I never had the idea of writing a book. I was particularly inspired by *Nora*, by Brenda Maddox, the biography of James Joyce's wife, and *The Man Who Knew Infinity*, about Ramanujan, the Indian mathematical genius, by Robert Kanigel.

If you could require the president to read one book, what would it be?

Grand Pursuit, of course.

What are your reading habits? Paper or electronic? Do you take notes? Do you snack while you read?

I love buying (cheap) first editions of books I use for research. I didn't see the point of a Kindle until my friend Trish Evans pointed out that I could carry the collected works of every nineteenth- and early-twentieth-century writer with me. Being able to travel with an entire library is amazing.

Do you prefer a book that makes you laugh or makes you cry? One that teaches you something or one that distracts you?

I like books that make me do both, which is one reason I adore Victorian fiction. All English novelists, it seems, have a deliciously wicked sense of humor, including Elizabeth Gaskell and Charlotte Brontë. I do also like novelists like Tolstoy who combine strong plots with philosophical or political musings.

What were your favorite books as a child? Do you have a favorite character or hero from one of those books? Is there one book you wish all children would read?

Grimms' fairy tales. My favorite was "The Bremen Town Musicians," about a dog, cat, donkey, and rooster, all over the hill, who learn that they are about to be discarded or worse. They decide to take matters into their own hands. I made my mother and grandmother read it to me so often that I could recite the whole story word for word.

Disappointing, overrated, just not good: What book did you feel you were supposed to like, and didn't? Do you remember the last book you put down without finishing?

The Marriage Plot, by Jeff Eugenides, and *The Stranger's Child*, by Alan Hollinghurst. I'd heard Jeff Eugenides on NPR and immediately wanted to read his novel. I adored the first two Hollinghursts. But I found both of these novels somewhat cold and inanimate. That said, there are so many books that I wasn't able to appreciate until I'd made two or three tries—*Middlemarch*, for example, or *Swann's Way*—and these may fall into that category. Reading is so contextual, like wine.

What's the best book about economics you've ever read? The worst?

There are so many great ones, but these are exquisite: *John Maynard Keynes*, by Robert Skidelsky. *Bankers and Pashas*, by David Landes. *The House of Rothschild*, by Niall Ferguson. *Economic Sentiments*, by Emma Rothschild. *Poverty and Compassion*, by Gertrude Himmelfarb.

Worst? To be worst it would have to have had a wide following, because otherwise who cares? I suppose *Das Kapital*, by Marx; *The Condition of the Working Class in England*, by Engels; and *Mein Kampf*, by Hitler.

If somebody walked in on you writing one of your books, what would they see? What does your work space look like?

Painted woodwork; tiled fireplace; a 1920s art-glass fixture; a ten-foot-long desk; nineteenth-century paintings of lighthouses and railroads; old globes; books, of course; and through the windows, my garden, currently a riot of orange and salmon-colored tulips and pink and white viburnums. I can look up and see whether I'm about to miss the garbage collection or Emma, the Labrador, is chasing the neighbor's cat.

Do you remember the last book someone personally recommended that you read and that you enjoyed? Who recommended it, and what persuaded you to pick it up?

Victoria Klein, my Anglophile interior designer friend, gave me *The Widow Barnaby*. Trish Evans, my Australian publicist/novelist best friend, introduced me to the Provincial Lady series, her favorites as a young girl. Christopher Potter, a London editor and writer friend, gave me *Cold Comfort Farm* and *The Diary of a Nobody* the Christmas before last. And Avinash Dixit, the Princeton economist, turned me on to P. G. Wodehouse and Patrick O'Brian. What convinced me? They all have slightly eccentric tastes and highly developed senses of humor, and they talk about books all the time.

Is there a book you wish you could write, but feel as if you can't or never will?

I'd love to write biographies of Frances Trollope; Elizabeth Gaskell; E. M. Delafield; Wilkie Collins; Frank Ramsey; John von Neumann; S. S. Chern and other Chinese and Japanese mathematical émigrés; Paul Krugman; and my father—as well as books about Cold War spies, the 1940s German economic miracle, the Chinese Cultural Revolution, medical hoaxes, do-gooders behaving badly. I hope to write more books, but since I'm always discovering new enthusiasms, I doubt I will be writing them all.

What is your favorite book to teach or otherwise ask your students of journalism to read?

Den of Thieves, by James B. Stewart; *Globalization: The Irrational Fear That Someone in China Will Take Your Job*, by Bruce Greenwald and Judd Kahn; *An Hour Before Daylight*, by Jimmy Carter; *Economics*, by Paul Krugman and Robin Wells.

What's the one book you wish someone else would write?

A great biography of John von Neumann, the most important mathematician of the twentieth century.

If you could meet any writer, dead or alive, who would it be? What would you want to know? Have you ever written to an author?

Henry James is my idea of the perfect friend. He was a brilliant talker, journalist, traveler, gardener, decorator, correspondent, as well as my favorite writer. He is not primarily an intellectual like Proust or Tolstoy, deeply interested in abstract ideas, but he is much warmer, sensitive and compassionate. I did write to an author once, but her reply was so chilly that I never did it again.

What do you plan to read next?

Anna Karenina.

Ira Glass

What book is on your night stand now?

Everything I'm reading right now is homework of one sort or another. That's pretty typical. I'm jumping around like a grad student, writing a paper on Mary Wingerd's history, *North Country: The Making of Minnesota*, for this big story we're doing on the show about the Dakota Uprising of 1862.

I just finished the manuscript of the new book *Love, Dishonor, Marry, Die; Cherish, Perish, a Novel*, by David Rakoff. It's a rhyming "novel," very funny and very sad, which is my favorite combination.

Were there any books that helped with the process of making your new movie?

I just got a copy of the screenwriting manual *Save the Cat!* to fact-check a thing I'm hoping to talk about while promoting this film we're putting out this month.

And I'm rereading Cameron Crowe's *Conversations with Wilder*. I first read it over a decade ago when screenwriters and studios started trying to convert stories from our show into films, and I was trying to understand the storytelling tricks you can use in a movie. I'm sure people who study film in school would have a different perspective, but for someone like me who's just a movie fan, scanning for quick insight, it was wonderful: anecdotal and fun to read.

Crowe was a reporter before he became a filmmaker, and you get both sides of him here. He's interviewing Billy Wilder, who made *Some Like It Hot* and *The Apartment* and *Sunset Boulevard* and *Double Indemnity*, and sometimes Crowe talks to him like a peer and sometimes like the best-informed fan in the world. In a typical bit of wisdom, Wilder is explaining to Crowe how director Ernst Lubitsch solved a story problem Wilder was having in

---

Ira Glass is the producer and host of the public radio program *This American Life*.

writing the screenplay for *Ninotchka*: How would they show Greta Garbo's evolution from hard-core Communist to fierce capitalist without a lot of cumbersome speechifying? They'd do it with a prop! A hat! At three spots in the film. Near the top, she's with her three Bolshevik comrades and spots the hat in a store window and sneers at this capitalist trinket: "She gives it a disgusted look and says, 'How can a civilization survive which allows women to wear this on their heads?' Then the second time she goes by the hat and makes a noise—*tch, tch, tch*. The third time, she is finally alone, she has gotten rid of her Bolshevik accomplices, opens a drawer and pulls it out. And now she wears it."

I spent a lot of my spare time over the last three years cowriting and coproducing a film—not a documentary but a comedy, with actors and all—and I'm having the pleasure of rereading the book and noticing completely different things now that I've gone through the process. That *Ninotchka* story was a complete revelation when I first read it, a totally new idea, that you'd illustrate out the turns in a story through a prop like that. Now I realize, that's the basics. The ABCs. Every move in a screenplay aspires to work like that, to illustrate the emotional beats and the plot turns with such simple visual gestures.

What was the last truly great book you read?

Michael Lewis's *The Big Short*. God knows he doesn't need the press: he's the greatest living nonfiction writer; Brad Pitt stars in the movie adaptations of his books. But *The Big Short* made me want to give up journalism it's so good. Scene after scene I felt like, how do you compete with this? He's telling the story of the mortgage crisis, and his angle couldn't be better: he follows the guys who knew it was coming and bet on it. This lets him explain how they knew and tell the story through these amazing contrarians and great funny scenes. It's crazy how funny the book is. And as a story it's got everything going against it. His characters are rich know-it-alls, but somehow Lewis makes you love them because he loves them. You know how it's all going to end, but somehow he creates suspense. When the market doesn't collapse as quickly as his characters think it should, some of them start to wonder: "Am I wrong? Is the whole world right and I'm wrong?" It all climaxes in this amazing, almost hallucinogenic set of scenes at this convention for the mortgage industry in Las Vegas, where our heroes have a series of encounters that make them all realize, no, no, no, they're not wrong. Everything's going to collapse. The economy will go to hell. And these people walking around are like zombies who just don't know they're doomed.

What's your favorite literary genre? Any guilty pleasures?

It's rare for me to read any fiction. I almost only read nonfiction. I don't believe in guilty pleasures, I only believe in pleasures. People who call reading detective fiction or eating dessert a guilty pleasure make me want to puke. Pedophilia is a pleasure a person should have guilt about. Not chocolate.

So many books began as segments on *This American Life*. Do you have a favorite?

Naked, by David Sedaris. I love it when Sedaris writes about his mom and his family, and I love when he writes about his boyfriend, Hugh. These stories are just as funny as anything he ever writes, but have all that extra emotional resonance. The story about his mom dying, "Ashes," is my favorite story of his, the barest thing in the book. I just wish the title essay weren't in the book. Doesn't really belong with all the biographical stuff.

Is there a *This American Life* segment that you wish would be made into a book?

Nah. If anything, I think too many of the ones that are made into books were better as twenty- to thirty-minute radio stories and should've stayed that way. Problem is, a thirty-minute radio piece, typed out, would total less than fifteen pages, and nobody publishes a book that short. But some of these stories are such important personal stories for the writers that once they finish the version of the story that goes on the radio, they feel sure that something else should be done with it. So they do books. Which feels more permanent to them, though as a radio person I feel differently about that.

Take a moment to champion unheralded writers. Who do you think is egregiously overlooked or underrated?

I don't know about egregious, but there's a book I loved called *When the Shooting Stops . . . the Cutting Begins*, by Ralph Rosenblum, that any fan of the early Woody Allen would like, and that nobody seems to know about. Rosenblum was Allen's editor on all those early classics, and explains how different the final cuts were from what was shot. It's well known, I guess, that *Annie Hall* was a radically different movie after the editing, and Rosenblum walks you through what they did. If I remember right, he also claims that he personally invented the falling-in-love montage, where you see the couple buy vegetables at the open-air market and get caught in the rain while a song plays. He says he invented it for the 1965 film *A Thousand Clowns*, and the song is one Jason Robards plays on a ukulele if I remember correctly. If he is the rightful inventor, where's the statue to the guy?

What were your most cherished books as a child?

A few years ago I reconnected with a close friend from childhood after not seeing him for two decades. His name's Maury Rubin, and he'd moved to New York from Baltimore, where we grew up. One of the first things he said to me was, "Can I ask you something?" I remember he leaned in close for this and his voice got low. "Did you read anything when we were growing up? Did anyone ever tell us to read?" He'd been dating women in New York and said it often came up, they'd ask him what his favorite books were as a kid. He always thought: "Books? Were we supposed to have favorite books?" I totally related. We weren't dumb kids. We were expected to get good grades and go to college. But reading was something you did for school. I was in college before the thought occurred to me that reading was something I could do for pleasure. Finally I met people (or maybe they were always around but I was too self-absorbed to notice) who enjoyed reading.

So all the books I loved as a kid were comic books; *Peanuts Treasury* as a little kid. It defined the emotional climate of my elementary years. I completely identified with the loneliness and melancholy of Charlie Brown. And *Doonesbury Chronicles* was a revelation to me when I was in middle school. I'd never met people like the ones in Doonesbury, or a world like that where the people were so smart and talked about politics and the stuff they talked about.

Do you have a favorite character or hero from children's literature?

Hermione. Harry Potter to me is a bore. His talent arrives as a gift; he's chosen. Who can identify with that? But Hermione—she's working harder than anyone, she's half outsider, right? Half Muggle. She shouldn't be there at all. It's so unfair that Harry's the star of the books, given how hard she worked to get her powers.

You studied semiotics at Brown. How has that informed the way you read novels?

I don't read novels, but my semiotics study influenced everything about the way I read and edit and write.

But the fact is, I don't read many books. I'm in production year-round. I work long hours, I have a dog and a wife. There's not a lot of available time for consuming any culture: TV, movies, books. When I read, it's generally magazines, newspapers, and Web sites.

What's the one book you wish someone else would write?

Could someone please write a book explaining why the Democratic Party and its allies are so much less effective at crafting a message and having a vision than their Republican counterparts? What a bunch of incompetents the Dems seem like. Most people don't even understand the health care policy they passed, much less like it. Ditto the financial reform. Or the stimulus. Some of the basic tasks of politics—like choosing and crafting a message—they just seem uninterested in.

I remember reading in the *Times* that as soon as Obama won, the Republicans were scheming about how they'd turn it around for the next election, and came up with the plan that won them the House, and wondered, did the House Dems even hold a similar meeting? Kurt Eichenwald! Mark Bowden! John Heilemann and Mark Halperin! I'll preorder today.

If you could meet any writer, dead or alive, who would it be? What would you want to know?

Edgar Allan Poe. I don't have a question, but dude just seems like he could use a hug.

What do you plan to read next?

I just started the manuscript of this book, *And Every Day Was Overcast*, by Paul Kwiatkowski, that's unlike any book I've ever read. He's a photographer, and the book is a mix of this clean, spare, unaffected prose about growing up near the swamps of South Florida—plus these incredible photos he's taken of that area. Seems like he spent his teenage years wandering from one trashy spot to another, drinking vodka, taking drugs, and messing around with girls. It's totally killing me. A completely original and clearheaded voice. Google him if you're curious. Last I heard he doesn't have a publisher because it's such an in-between sort of project—part pictures, part story.

Postwar, by the historian Tony Judt; David Finkel's account of US forces in Iraq, "The Good Soldiers"; and a proof of Nadeem Aslam's new book, *The Blind Man's Garden*, which I haven't started yet. Plus my notebook, in case a decent idea ambushes me after turning out the light.—**David Mitchell**

I'm halfway through *All the King's Men*, by Robert Penn Warren. I haven't read it since college.—**John Grisham**

Kearny's March, by Winston Groom. The author of *Forrest Gump* has become a wonderful military historian and tells us how, as a result of the Mexican War, we acquired not just Texas but New Mexico, Arizona, Colorado, Utah, Nevada and—every silver lining has its cloud—California.—**P. J. O'Rourke**

Three books: One is *Gypsy Boy*, by Mikey Walsh; a novel, *The Darlings*, by Cristina Alger; and a wonderful collection of stories by Alethea Black, *I Knew You'd Be Lovely*, which reminds me so much of the late, great Laurie Colwin.—**Anne Lamott**

Right now I'm reading a book called *Incognito*, by David Eagleman, about the human brain. I've always been interested in psychology, so learning about the things that influence our thinking is really important for me. In bodybuilding, I was known for "psyching" out my opponents with mind tricks. I wish I had this book then because the stuff I was doing was Mickey Mouse compared with what's in this book.
—**Arnold Schwarzenegger**

Pedantically, none, because I don't have a night stand. So my version of the question would be: What book is on your kitchen counter now, waiting to be picked up in the morning while the first pot of coffee brews? And today's answer is: *Live by Night*, by Dennis Lehane. I always read for an hour or two in the morning, before I do anything else. And Lehane was in my graduating class, so to speak, in that we came up together, and in some ways he's the best of us.—**Lee Child**

Sabine Kuegler, *Child of the Jungle*. This unique book is the autobiography of the daughter of a German missionary linguist couple, who moved when she was a child to live with a Fayu clan in a remote area of swamp forest in Indonesian New Guinea.—**Jared Diamond**

Rome, by Robert Hughes. Though I'm finding it challenging to read about Rome without immediately wanting to run away to Rome.—**Elizabeth Gilbert**

I'm currently reading *Ways of Going Home*, by the Chilean novelist and poet Alejandro Zambra. If it's only half as good as his novella, *Bonsai*, it'll still be a fine way to lose a weekend.
—**Katherine Boo**

I'm loving Adam Johnson's *The Orphan Master's Son*, set in North Korea. The novel won this year's Pulitzer but, more important, comes with the enthralled recommendations of writer friends. Like most readers, I'm inclined to rely on the word of people in my life whose tastes I respect.
—**Scott Turow**

Junot Díaz

You've just recovered from back surgery. What books helped you get through it?

Man, you guys have some good intel. I have family members who only found out after the neck brace came off. But definitely, I read like crazy while I was laid up; reading for me is proof against anything, but especially pain. These books in particular gave solace: Two superb collections of stories, from Krys Lee (*Drifting House*) and Tania James (*Aerogrammes*). Also Wasik and Murphy's *Rabid: A Cultural History of the World's Most Diabolical Virus*. But really, the book that most lifted me out of my bent clay was Ramón Saldívar's *The Borderlands of Culture: Américo Paredes and the Transnational Imaginary*. There's a reason Saldívar won the National Humanities Medal. His insights on Paredes's years reporting in Japan alone are priceless.

What's the last truly great book you read?

Katherine Boo's *Behind the Beautiful Forevers*. A book of extraordinary intelligence, humanity, and (formalistic) cunning. Boo's four years reporting on a single Mumbai slum, following a small group of garbage recyclers, have produced something beyond groundbreaking. She humanizes with all the force of literature the impossible lives of the people at the bottom of our pharaonic global order, and details with a journalist's unsparing exactitude the absolute suffering that undergirds India's economic boom. The language is extraordinary, the portraits indelible, and then there are those lines at the end that just about freeze your heart: "The gates of the rich, occasionally rattled, remained unbreached. The politicians held forth on

Junot Díaz is the author of *The Brief Wondrous Life of Oscar Wao*, *This Is How You Lose Her*, and *Drown*.

the middle class. The poor took down one another, and the world's great, unequal cities soldiered on in relative peace."

In fiction, though, the "last truly great book" I read has to be Alejandro Zambra's *Bonsai*. A subtle, eerie, ultimately wrenching account of failed young love in Chile among the kind of smartypant set who pillow-talk about the importance of Proust. You get the cold flesh of the story in that chilling first line: "In the end she dies and he remains alone, although in truth he was alone some years before her death." But only by reading to the end do you touch the story's haunted soul. A total knockout.

Among the many books on your shelves are *What It Is We Do When We Read Science Fiction*, by Paul Kincaid; *Shikasta*, by Doris Lessing; *The Legend of Sigurd and Gudrún*, by J.R.R. Tolkien; and *By Night in Chile*, by Roberto Bolaño. Can you tell us about any of those books—what you thought of them, what they meant to you?

Tolkien I grew up on, fed my insatiable Ungoliant-like hunger for other worlds; I was a young fan and yet, even as an adult, I continue to wrestle with Tolkien for reasons that have much to do with growing up in the shadow of my own Dark Lord—that's what some dictators really become in the imagination of the nations they afflict. *Shikasta* was a book I used to see at the library a lot when I was growing up but which finally came into my hands when I was in college. A strange anti-novel that purports to be the history of our world from the perspective of our sympathetic alien caretakers. *Shikasta* takes that sub-zeitgeist "theory" that God and his angels are actually alien visitors to its logical conclusion. Not the easier read, but the book had a lasting impact on me. I've always wanted to write something with *Shikasta*'s scope, with its thematic and structural bravura. Alien ethnographic reports on our Old Testament history mixed with cranky letters home by overworked alien bureaucrats and a moving realistic journal written by a young Lessing-like teenager living in Africa in the years before a worldwide youth revolt—bananas stuff. As for Bolaño, what can one say? One of our greatest writers, a straight colossus. Is there really anything in print even remotely approaching *By Night in Chile*? For anyone like me obsessed with the interplay between the personal and the historical, *By Night in Chile* is a master class in which Bolaño manages to distill the perverse brutal phantasmagorical history of an entire continent down to 150 seductive pages. A halfhearted priest secretly teaching Marxism to Pinochet so the demon general might better know his enemy? Latin American letters (wherever it may reside) has never had a greater, more disturbing avenging angel than Bolaño.

What was the last book that made you cry?

That's easy: the winner of the Yale Younger Poets prize, Eduardo Corral's collection, *Slow Lightning*. When I finished that book I bawled. Wise and immense, but peep for yourself: "Once a man offered me his heart and I said no. Not because I didn't love him. Not because he was a beast or white—I couldn't love him. Do you understand? In bed while we slept, our bodies inches apart, the dark between our flesh a wick. It was burning down. And he couldn't feel it."

The last book that made you laugh?

K.J. Bishop's *The Etched City*. I'm a sucker for lines like "He had numerous stories of recent adventure and suffering—specifically, his adventures and other people's suffering, almost invariably connected—that he told with the air of an amiable ghoul."

The last book that made you furious?

The Femicide Machine, by Sergio González Rodríguez. The notorious femicides in Juárez were not unknown to me, but González Rodríguez's grisly postmortem of the cultural, political, and economic forces behind these atrocities would infuriate anyone.

What were your most cherished books as a child? Do you have a favorite character or hero from children's literature?

I loved Encyclopedia Brown as a kid. Donald Sobol passed recently, and that really brought it all back to me, how important his books were to my little self. I didn't learn to read until I was seven, so I missed out on the early stuff, jumped right to chapter books, right to Encyclopedia Brown. What I loved about Boy Detective Leroy Brown was that (1) he was unabashedly smart (smart was not cool when and where I grew up) and (2) his best friend was a girl, tough Sally Kimball, who was both Leroy's bodyguard and his intellectual equal. Sobol did more to flip gender scripts in my head than almost anybody in my early years.

If someone really wanted to understand the Dominican Republic, and the Dominican-American experience, what books would you suggest?

That's a tough one. We need a lot more books in English about the Dominican experience. Fortunately the field is growing, and there's some good stuff out there. I recommend one start with one of the country's greatest poets, Pedro Mir, his *Countersong to Walt Whitman and Other Poems*. Pure genius. Then read Ginetta Candelario's *Black Behind the Ears* for a superbly guided journey through the complexities of Dominican racial identity. Also

Frank Moya Pons's *The Dominican Republic: A National History* is excellent, and so is Julia Alvarez's novel *In the Time of the Butterflies*.

Other great novels about the immigrant experience in America you'd recommend?

Gish Jen's *Typical American* is another one of my personal classics. A masterpiece of a novel bursting with wit, yearning, and truth, and for an immigrant kid like me looking for an idiom with which to write about an experience that we in this country don't talk about enough—absolutely indispensable. Maxine Hong Kingston's *The Woman Warrior* is not exactly a novel, but few books out there can rival its powerful vision of what it means to live simultaneously in two worlds.

You teach creative writing at MIT. What books do you find especially useful as a teacher?

All depends on the class. If I'm teaching straight creative writing I try to flood the students with great fiction, from Jamaica Kincaid to Pam Houston, and essays on craft by folks like Samuel R. Delany (his "About Writing" is spectacularly useful). I'm always trying to sneak Octavia Butler into all my syllabi. She is a master for all seasons.

Read any good graphic novels recently?

Yes, Jason Shiga's *Empire State: A Love Story (or Not)*. Oakland boy loses best female friend to New York City and takes a cross-country bus trip to try to transform friendship into love. A bicoastal heartbreaker, beautifully rendered and deeply moving.

You're organizing a dinner party of writers and can invite three authors, dead or alive. Who's coming?

José Martí, because he lived so many lives and because he was such a fantastic writer and because, damn it, he was José Martí (he also lived in the New York City area, so that will help the conversation). Octavia Butler because she's my personal hero, helped give the African diaspora a future (albeit a future nearly as dark as our past) and because I'd love to see her again. And Arundhati Roy because I'm still crushing on her mind and on *The God of Small Things*.

Who are the best short story writers?

People who like to suffer or perhaps people tempted by perfectibility. For that is the short story's great lure—that you can write a perfect one. With novels it's quite the opposite—the lure of the novel is that you can never write a perfect one. But do you mean who are the best short story writers by name? Wow. I'm certainly the worst judge of this as I've not read even one one-thousandth of what's out there in English. But if I had to cobble together a short list from what I've read, I'd have to say Roberto Bolaño is my number one; read *Last Evenings on Earth* and tremble. Mary Gaitskill as well; she makes the rest of us look like we don't know jack about the human soul. And then Sandra Cisneros and Anne Enright and Ted Chiang, who have each written as perfect a collection of stories as I've ever read. Also Michael Martone, Lorrie Moore, Edwidge Danticat, Tobias Wolff, Louise Erdrich, George Saunders, Annie Proulx, Yiyun Li, Sherman Alexie. Honestly the list is long; the form is blessed with awesome practitioners.

You can bring three books to a desert island. Which do you choose?

This is a question that always kills me. For a book lover this type of triage is never a record of what was brought along but a record of what was left behind. But if forced to choose by, say, a shipwreck or an evil *Times* editor, I'd probably grab novels that I'm still wrestling with. Like Samuel R. Delany's *Dhalgren* (which in my opinion is one of the greatest and most perplexing novels of the twentieth century) or Toni Morrison's *Beloved* (to be an American writer or to be interested in American literature and not to have read *Beloved*, in my insufferable calculus, is like calling yourself a sailor and never having bothered to touch the sea) or Cormac McCarthy's *Blood Meridian* (so horrifyingly profound and compellingly ingenious it's almost sorcery). Maybe Octavia Butler's *Dawn* (set in a future where the remnants of the human race are forced to "trade" genes—read: breed involuntarily—with our new alien overlords). Or Gilbert Hernandez's *Beyond Palomar* (if it wasn't for *Poison River* I don't think I would have become a writer). Perhaps Leslie Marmon Silko's *Ceremony* or Alan Moore's *Miracle-man* or Margaret Atwood's *The Handmaid's Tale*—books that changed everything for me. To be honest I'd probably hold a bunch of these books in hand and only decide at the last instant, as the water was flooding up around my knees, which three I'd bring. And then I'd spend the rest of that time on the desert island dreaming about the books that I left behind and also of all the books, new and old, that I wasn't getting a chance to read.

What do you plan to read next?

Our Kind of People, by Uzodinma Iweala, and *Mountains of the Moon*, by I.J. Kay. I loved Iweala's first book, so I'm eager for this nonfiction follow-up, and I've heard strong things about Kay's debut.

The J writer, or Yahwist, of the Torah. I'd want to ask him what he intended to be literal and what he intended to be figurative. And I'd point out that confusion around this question has had a toxic effect on the rest of history.
—**Andrew Solomon**

Shakespeare's wife, of course. So I could settle this whole thing once and for all.—**Malcolm Gladwell**

The *Wizard of Oz* novelist, L. Frank Baum . . . If he really was a racist as is rumored. And if so, how could he write such a heartfelt story? Were the Munchkins a metaphor? Did he have the Wicked Witch of the West killed off because he hated green people?—**Bryan Cranston**

I'd like to ask Raymond Chandler about chapter thirteen of *The Little Sister*. It describes a drive around 1940s Los Angeles, and it still holds up as a description of the city right now. Beautiful. I'd ask him how he pulled that off. And I'd tell him that that short chapter of his was what made me want to become a writer. I'd also ask him whether it takes a tortured life to produce something like that. I'd say, Ray, can a writer be happy and still be good at it?
—**Michael Connelly**

I'm fascinated by the idea of James Joyce, but I doubt we would have much to talk about. I'd like to have a lunch with Bill Clinton. Maybe a drink with Hunter Thompson. Just one—or two. Dinner with Angelina Jolie would be nice. Does she write?—**James Patterson**

Oscar Wilde. Anyone who could pen the phrase "We are all in the gutter, but some of us are looking at the stars" gets a seat at my dinner table.—**Neil deGrasse Tyson**

Claude Debussy was distant and brilliant, a compulsive smoker, a letter-writing genius. I'd like to know what his voice sounded like.—**Nicholson Baker**

Isaac Bashevis Singer said something like, "If Tolstoy lived across the street, I wouldn't go meet him." I know what he meant about Tolstoy, but I'd like to live across the street from Jane Bowles, Robert Walser, Gogol, Kafka, or Heinrich von Kleist. Or maybe at the Spanish campground where Roberto Bolaño worked as a watchman.—**Francine Prose**

Emily Dickinson. She is such a puzzle. Her startling genius seems to have come from nowhere. She lived her life as a recluse; her work remained essentially unpublished and undiscovered until well after her death. Yet she turned language and poetry on end.—**Drew Gilpin Faust**

I wish I could have been present when Kafka read *The Metamorphosis* aloud to his friends, who couldn't stop laughing. The humor is still there in the text, but I would love to know what he did with his voice.—**Jonathan Franzen**

Henry James is my idea of the perfect friend. He was a brilliant talker, journalist, traveler, gardener, decorator, correspondent, as well as my favorite writer. He is not primarily an intellectual like Proust or Tolstoy, deeply interested in abstract ideas, but he is much warmer, sensitive, and compassionate.—**Sylvia Nasar**

Gore Vidal. I admire his range, his passion, and the rate at which he cranked out work. Novels, essays, plays. My process is very, very slow, and I am in awe of writers like Vidal. I'm in awe of writers who write like it's what they, you know, actually do for a damn living.—**Dan Savage**

Joyce Carol Oates

What book is on your night stand now?

The Priceless Gift: The Love Letters of Woodrow Wilson and Ellen Axson Wilson, edited by Eleanor Wilson McAdoo, and *Woodrow Wilson: Life and Letters*, volumes one and two, by Ray Stannard Baker. (Research for my next novel.)

When and where do you like to read?

Anywhere! If my favorite, most comfortable place is by our fireplace in cold weather, expedient places are on an airplane, in a waiting room, or even waiting in line; frequently these days, while on the phone having been "put on hold." Reading material has to be at hand for such desperate emergencies.

Do you listen to audiobooks? What makes a book worth listening to?

Yes, I've listened to just a few audiobooks—but hope to listen to more. I've wanted to investigate how my own books sound in this format and find the experience of listening, and not reading, quite fascinating. Even for the author, there is the sense of not knowing what will come next, and being drawn along by the actor's captivating voice.

What's the last truly great book you read?

James Joyce's *Ulysses*. In June of this year I reread this ever-astonishing classic with my neuroscientist husband, who had not read it before, in preparation for a trip to Dublin, which overlapped, just barely, with the annual Bloomsday celebration. (And my favorite chapter? "Ithaca.")

Joyce Carol Oates is the author of more than forty novels, including *We Were the Mulvaneys*, *Blonde*, and *The Accursed*.

Are you a fiction or a nonfiction person? What's your favorite literary genre? Any guilty pleasures?

What engages me is the mysterious, indefinable music of a writer's voice. I first read Henry David Thoreau's *Walden* when I was fifteen years old, and if I'd been told that it was a young man's autobiographical novel, I would not have been surprised. Proust's great novel might well be memoir, like virtually all of the first-person fiction of my friend Edmund White, who blurs the line, as it's said, between "fiction" and "nonfiction." The sparely, scrupulously crafted early short stories of Ernest Hemingway about the young Nick Adams might well be "nonfiction"—of surpassing beauty. If the reader wants information primarily, of course nonfiction is preferred. But what is executed by way of "information" makes literature, whether fiction, nonfiction, or poetry

A typical biography relying upon individuals' notorious memories and the anecdotes they've invented contains a high degree of fiction, yet is considered "nonfiction." My favorite literary genre is, in fact, the "literary novel" (unfortunate term roughly translated as the Kiss of Death). I also enjoy anything noir (often, though not inevitably, set in Los Angeles).

What book had the greatest impact on you? What book made you want to write?

Lewis Carroll's *Alice in Wonderland* and *Through the Looking-Glass*, which my grandmother gave me when I was nine years old and very impressionable. These were surely the books that inspired me to write, and Alice is the protagonist with whom I've most identified over the years. Her motto is, like my own, "Curiouser and curiouser!"

If you could require the president to read one book, what would it be?

Our great American tragic-epic, Melville's *Moby-Dick*. This truly contains multitudes of meanings: the Pequod is the ship of state, the radiantly mad Captain Ahab a dangerous "leader," the ethnically diverse crew our American citizenry. And to balance this all-male adventure, *The Collected Poems of Emily Dickinson*.

What are your reading habits? Paper or electronic? Do you take notes?

Obviously I prefer "paper" books—they are aesthetic objects, usually quite distinct from one another with striking covers and page designs, while electronic books are more or less interchangeable, their words as alike as ants floating in water. As a frequent reviewer, I rely upon bound galleys, in which I take notes. But I do read online, constantly, and on a Kindle if I'm traveling.

Do you prefer a book that makes you laugh or makes you cry? One that teaches you something or one that distracts you?

Why either/or? Most good books evoke a variety of responses, not just one. I've tried to secret a certain slant of humor (if dark) in virtually all of my writing, but few readers notice—it's in the mode of Aubrey Beardsley "secreting the obscene" in his drawings. I love being "taught" something worthwhile—but I don't love being "distracted" to no purpose.

What were your favorite books as a child?

Since I grew up on a not-very-prosperous small farm in western New York, north of Buffalo, there were few books in our household, and those that came into my hands were precious—like the Alice books. Probably at too young an age I was reading *The Gold-Bug and Other Stories*, by Edgar Allan Poe.

Your most recent book, *Two or Three Things I Forgot to Tell You*, is for young adults. Tell us about some of your favorite young adult novels.

By today's standards, by which I mean our radically extended sense of what "young adult literature" can be, such classics as *Huckleberry Finn*, *The Call of the Wild*, *The Member of the Wedding*, *To Kill a Mockingbird*, *The Catcher in the Rye*, *Lord of the Flies* are all great YA novels.

What makes a great YA novel versus a great novel for adults?

I don't think that the two are distinct. Literary-minded young people can read virtually anything and understand it to a degree. And it's said that YA fiction today, given its mature subject matter and relatively uncomplicated language, is often read by adults.

Disappointing, overrated, just not good: What book did you feel you were supposed to like, and didn't? Do you remember the last book you put down without finishing?

I was trained to consider "disappointment" of this sort a character flaw of my own, a failure to comprehend, to appreciate what others have clearly appreciated. My first attempt at reading, for instance, D. H. Lawrence was a disappointment—I wasn't old enough, or mature enough, quite yet; now, Lawrence is one of my favorite writers, whom I've taught in my university courses many times. Another initial disappointment was Walt Whitman, whom I'd also read too young (I know, it's unbelievable, how could anyone admit to have been "disappointed" in Walt Whitman? Please don't send contemptuous e-mails).

If a book I've committed myself to review turns out to be "disappointing" I make an effort to present it objectively to the reader, including a good number of excerpts from the text, so that the reader might form his or her own opinion independent of my own. (I don't think that opinions are very important, in fact. Does it matter that a reader doesn't "like," in the trivial way in which one might not "like" Chinese food, a classic like *Beowulf*?)

What is your favorite book to use as a teacher to students of writing? What book do you think all writers should read?

No single text or anthology is a favorite. By this time—since I've been teaching at Princeton since 1978—I've assembled my favorite short stories and prose pieces into several anthologies, which I often teach in my fiction workshops. These include *The Oxford Book of American Short Stories*, *The Ecco Anthology of Contemporary American Short Fiction*, and *Telling Stories: An Anthology for Writers*.

If you could meet any writer, dead or alive, who would it be? What would you want to know? Have you ever written to an author?

We would probably all want to meet Shakespeare—or so we think. (We could ask the man if he'd really written all those plays, or if, somehow, he'd acquired them from—who?—Sir Philip Sidney's sister, perhaps? Wonder what W. S. would say to that.) Some of us have fantasized meeting Emily Dickinson. (The problem is, would either W. S. or E. D. want to meet us? Why?)

I'm afraid that I squander as much as 90 percent of my time writing letters—e-mails—to authors, my writer-friends. The problem is that they write back, and so do I. And suddenly the morning has vanished irretrievably, or ineluctably (as Stephen Dedalus would say).

And I certainly receive many letters, a goodly proportion of them beginning bluntly: "Our teacher has assigned us to write about an American writer and I have chosen you, but I can't find much information about you. Why do you write? What are your favorite books? Where do you get your ideas? I hope you can answer by Monday because my deadline is . . ."

Of the writers you've met, who most impressed you?

I've met 1,449 writers so far, and many more await meeting. I'm sure that I've been enormously impressed by all of them, especially my dazzlingly talented writer-friends, but the greatest surprises are yet to come, I believe.

Which of your own books is your favorite?

No more than we have favorite siblings, friends, or relatives, or will admit to having favorites, does a writer single out his or her "favorite" book. But I can say that the novel that exhausted me the most, wrung my emotions the most, and left me determined never again to write a thousand-page novel with a sympathetic protagonist who must die on the last page is *Blonde*, imagined as a tragic-epic of the life of Norma Jeane Baker/"Marilyn Monroe."

Do you have a least favorite? Or one you regret having written?

The novel of mine that everyone has hated, or had hated (since it has been out of print virtually since its publication), is *The Assassins* (1975), which I have not looked at since perhaps 1976. I would never dare reread it—I could accept that it is not a good novel, but I would be very upset to discover that it wasn't, or anyway, wasn't "nearly so bad" as everyone said. That would hurt.

What's the one book you wish someone else would write?

A work of such brilliant prose, such imaginative powers, such sweep, such flair, with such an irresistible story and riveting characters that simply by reading it attentively one could understand those discoveries of molecular biology, neuroscience, psycholinguistics, "philosophy of mind," and "string theory" in the way that their discoverers/creators understand them.

What do you plan to read next?

My in-box, containing sixteen very promising e-mails, most from writer-friends, that have come in since this interview began.

Every writer I'm reading and loving seems underappreciated to me—then you mention the name and people say either, "Everyone reads them!" (Charles Portis, Dawn Powell) or, "You're being willfully obscure!" (Ronald Hugh Morrieson, Anna Kavan). That said, this is a major sport for me—I bore my friends with this all the time—so let's go: Laurie Colwin. Iain Sinclair. James Tiptree Jr., Stanley Elkin, and Stanley Ellin. And . . . But I'll stop.
—**Jonathan Lethem**

At the top would have to be Paul Monette, author of *Becoming a Man*. He was a superbly gifted writer who died during the AIDS epidemic that deprived us of a generation of talent. I've often thought to myself, if they took the graphic sex scenes out of that book, it could be required reading in public schools. But maybe I'm dreaming.
—**James McBride**

I don't know if he's unheralded, but there's a writer named J. Malcolm Garcia who continually astounds me with his energy and empathy. He writes powerful and lyrical nonfiction from Afghanistan, from Buenos Aires, from Mississippi, all of it urgent and provocative. I've been following him wherever he goes.—**Dave Eggers**

For years, I have been heralding the work of Rabih Alameddine, a Lebanese-American writer. His prose is gorgeous, his approach irreverent, and the ideas in his stories are sometimes comical or fantastical, but always deadly serious—very relevant to understanding the complex history behind multiple holy wars today. In Italy and Spain, his books are best sellers. In the United States, he's hardly known. Why is there a geographic divide in literary appreciation?—**Amy Tan**

I don't know about egregious, but there's a book I loved called *When the Shooting Stops . . . the Cutting Begins*, by Ralph Rosenblum, that any fan of the early Woody Allen would like, and that nobody seems to know about.
—**Ira Glass**

Let's assume that I've overlooked most of the good ones myself, but I'm a fan of *Mrs. Bridge* and *Mr. Bridge*, by the late Evan S. Connell. It was Connell, and also Jerzy Kosinski (*Steps, The Painted Bird*) who first made me aware of the power of short, very concise and witty chapters.—**James Patterson**

Geoffrey Wolff! I asked Vintage to put *A Day at the Beach* back in print so I could take it with me on book tour in November. I'm a big fan of all of Wolff's work, but this is the best book of essays I know.—**Ann Patchett**

I am just getting into Zora Neale Hurston, who is possibly a much better writer than the critics and rivals who tried to erase her from history, resulting in a life in which she worked as a maid and died in a welfare nursing home. She's clever. She does something modern to the sentence. Her race politics (outlined in her memoir, *Dust Tracks on a Road*) are a bit over my head, a bit strange, but fascinating.—**Rachel Kushner**

All writers are underrated. They're all trying to do their best. It's hard to finish a book. But Denton Welch deserves more of a fuss. Also John McNulty and that Long-Winded Lady, Maeve Brennan. Shakespeare is probably the most overrated writer of all time, although I must say his sonnets are incredible.—**Nicholson Baker**

Nicholson Baker

What book is on your night stand now?

The floor next to the bed is my true night stand. On it is a heap of books—things like John Masters's *Bhowani Junction*, Joan Aiken's *Nightbirds on Nantucket*, Grace Paley's *Enormous Changes at the Last Minute*, Harold Robbins's *The Carpetbaggers*, and Lederer and Burdick's *The Ugly American*. Some books have been there a very long time. I reach down without looking and grab something and read a little of it, and then I put it back in the heap.

Last night my hand landed on John Toland's *Infamy*, about Pearl Harbor, and I read fifty pages—it's tremendous in a certain way. All books are incomplete. In my briefcase, which is perhaps my true, true night stand, I've been carrying around the galleys of Katie Roiphe's *In Praise of Messy Lives*. Roiphe's willing to say risky things, and she has a prosey astringency that makes me happy.

What was the last truly great book you read?

Recently I listened to Graham Greene's *The Human Factor*, read by Tim Pigott-Smith. It's a little repetitive here and there, especially at the beginning, but honestly, it's an extraordinary, careful novel that works up to something true and sad and worth spending time with. I also liked Greene's autobiography, *A Sort of Life*.

What's your favorite literary genre? Any guilty pleasures?

I keep thinking I'll enjoy suspense novels, and sometimes I do. I've read about twenty Dick Francis novels. I also sometimes like reading romance novels by people like Sylvia Day—not ones about vampires or werewolves

---

Nicholson Baker is the author of novels including *The Anthologist*, *Vox*, and *The Fermata*, and works of nonfiction including *Human Smoke* and *Double Fold*.

or shape-shifters. When I really want to be soothed and reminded of why people bother to fiddle with sentences, I often read poetry. Many good poets are really essayists who write very short essays. I go back to the poetry collections I read in my twenties—Stanley Kunitz's *Collected Poems*, Howard Moss's *Selected Poems*. Also I love reading diaries. Recently I've been reading diaries by May Sarton and Thomas Merton.

What was the last book that made you cry?

I cried reading Mary Berg's diary of hunger in the ghetto in Warsaw. More recently and trivially, I cried when I read through my own book of essays and realized: thank God, it's done.

The last book that made you laugh?

Well, I've got Mark Twain's *Innocents Abroad* on Eucalyptus, a nice simple app for the iPhone. The animated page-turns are better than the page-turns in iBooks! Twain's a genius, no question. Read his "War Prayer," too. It isn't funny—it'll make you mad.

Which novels contain the best sex?

Sometimes I think there are no good sex novels. When you're not in the mood, there's nothing worse than a sex scene. Words fail. Although I have liked listening to *Fanny Hill*. You can hear a marvelous free audio rendition of *Fanny Hill* on LibriVox.org. All the different readers, male and female, with their different accents, enhance the experience.

What's the best book about Maine?

E. B. White's essays are the best things I've read about Maine—especially the one in which he's not sure if he can go out sailing anymore in his sloop.

Which writers are egregiously overlooked or underrated?

All writers are underrated. They're all trying to do their best. It's hard to finish a book. But Denton Welch deserves more of a fuss. Also John McNulty and that Long-Winded Lady, Maeve Brennan. Shakespeare is probably the most overrated writer of all time, although I must say his sonnets are incredible.

Do you have a favorite character or hero from children's literature?

Tintin is my favorite children's book hero, or maybe it's Captain Haddock. Tintin was willing to walk around on the bottom of the sea, trusting the two detectives to crank his air pump. Nobody can draw Tibetan mountainsides like

Hergé. In the morning, in bed, I sometimes raise my fist and cry, "Action Stations!"—as Haddock did when he was startled awake from a doze.

What's your favorite library in the world? Your favorite bookstore?

I suppose my favorite library is the one I use the most—the Dimond Library of the University of New Hampshire. It's quiet, full of blond wood, full of neatly shelved books, and in the summer very few people are there in the reading room. I find a table near an electrical outlet and sit and listen to the HVAC system blow through the building—keeping all those books cool, waiting for readers who will want them.

I'm also partial to the rare books and special collections division of Duke University's library system, because they were willing to take many tons of rich and rare bound newspapers that my wife and I happened to be in a position to watch over for a while.

My favorite bookstore is RiverRun Bookstore in Portsmouth. A woman there, a poet, once suggested that I read Mary Oliver's collected poems. RiverRun is not as intimidating as a Barnes & Noble, where there are so many books that you think: No more! Stop the presses!

What's the one book you wish someone else would write?

I'd like somebody to write a book that really told the truth about life now. Leo Tolstoy but with drive-through windows.

If you could meet any writer, dead or alive, who would it be? What would you want to know?

Claude Debussy was distant and brilliant, a compulsive smoker, a letter-writing genius. I'd like to know what his voice sounded like.

And among authors you've met already, who most impressed you?

I'm impressed by all of them. They seem to be able to work hard and finish big shiny books and keep going and complain about their hotels and give bouncy interviews and readings and do all the things you're expected to do.

We're in the middle of a presidential administration in which one man in an office with velvet couches goes down a kill list. Our president has become an assassin. This sickens me and makes me want to stop writing altogether.

Who inspired you to write?

In fourth grade, I read Robert Sheckley's *Shards of Space*. I loved the title, and Sheckley made me want to write short stories about far-off vacuum-packed futures.

In seventh grade, my English teacher told me to read a poetry collection called *Reflections on a Gift of Watermelon Pickle*. There's a poem in there about a burro sent by express that ends, "Say who you are and where you're going." There's also a bit by Robert Francis that goes, "Or tell me clouds / Are doing something to the moon / They never did before." That poem really got to me.

What do you plan to read next?

Why bother to plan? I'll probably reach down tomorrow morning and haul up some old paperback from the floor.

Emma Thompson

What book is on your night stand now?

Mary Poppins, by P. L. Travers. *Dancing to the Precipice*, by Caroline Moorehead. *Bring Up the Bodies*, by Hilary Mantel. I've always got two or three on the go.

What was the last truly great book you read?

Wolf Hall, by Hilary Mantel. It was a marvel.

Any literary genre you simply can't be bothered with?

Horror. I can't manage it. I become—well—horrified. Self-help books have a similar effect.

A young, aspiring actress wants your advice on what to read. What books do you suggest?

A Strange Eventful History, by Michael Holroyd, because it's so interesting about the discipline of acting. Any biography on Marilyn Monroe, just to convey the pointless destructiveness of fame.

What's your favorite Shakespeare?

King Lear. The most humane portrait of the human condition I know.

If you could require the president to read one book, what would it be? The prime minister?

The president—any president—could usefully acquaint him/herself with Walt Kelly's cartoon strip of Pogo Possum living in the swamps of Georgia. Very perspicacious about politics. The prime minister might revisit Geoffrey Willans's *Molesworth*, which is so illuminating about the character and

---

Emma Thompson is an Oscar-winning screenwriter and actress who is also the author of two children's books.

habits of little boys. I am not being rude. Both president and prime minister have to deal with a great quantity of childish behavior.

What was the last book that made you cry?

I was on holiday years ago with *Corelli's Mandolin*. Rendered inconsolable and had to be put to bed for the afternoon.

The last book that made you laugh?

In Wells Tower's first collection of short stories, there is a description of a mouse emerging from behind a fridge eating a coupon which made me laugh for a good ten days.

The last book that made you furious?

In Michel Houellebecq's *The Elementary Particles*, there's a passage on cruelty which includes a granny, a little boy, and a pair of secateurs. I hurled the book across the room and would have hurled Michel too, had he been in reach.

Name a book you just couldn't finish.

Les Misérables. I agreed with him on all fronts and finally just became sort of exhausted.

What were your favorite books as a child? Did you have a favorite character or hero?

All of Joan Aiken, Alan Garner, Leon Garfield, and John Masefield. In particular—*The Wolves of Willoughby Chase* (Aiken), *The Weirdstone of Brisingamen* (Garner), *The Box of Delights* (Masefield), and *The Strange Affair of Adelaide Harris* (Garfield).

As far as heroes—from the age of ten, it was Sherlock Holmes. Before that, probably Asterix.

What's the best book your mother ever gave you to read?

I had my heart broken for the first time when I was sixteen. My mother gave me *War and Peace*, which, in three volumes, soaked up a lot of the tears.

If you could meet any writer, dead or alive, who would it be? What would you want to know?

I wasn't sure how to answer this one so I discussed it with my twelve-year-old daughter. She suggested Plato. I was impressed. So Plato it is. I think I'd want to ask him how he'd imagine life had changed by 2012.

Have you ever written to an author? Did he or she write back?

I wrote to René Goscinny when I was seven or eight, a fan letter about Asterix. He wrote back, saying that he was very proud to have made a little English girl laugh.

You're organizing a literary dinner party and inviting three writers. Who's on the list?

Sappho, for a bit of ancient gender politics; Aphra Behn for theater gossip; and George Eliot because everyone who knew her said she was fascinating. All women, because they know how to get talking about the nitty-gritty so quickly and are less prone to telling anecdotes. I'd have gone for Jane Austen if I weren't convinced she'd just have a soft-boiled egg and leave early.

What's the best book by an actor you've ever read?

I've never read a book by an actor. I was brought up by actors. All my family are actors. I'm an actor. Give me a break.

Of all the literary adaptations you've acted in, which is your favorite?

I love *Remains of the Day*—Ruth Prawer Jhabvala adapted Ishiguro's book so brilliantly that both film and book lose nothing and gain so much. Tony Hopkins is at his best. Selfishly though, *Sense and Sensibility* must take precedence because there's nothing to compare to the experience of acting something you've spent five years adapting whilst convinced that it will never be made.

What's the best movie based on a book you've seen recently?

The Social Network. I admired it in a kind of breathless fashion.

If you could play any character from literature, who would it be?

I've plumped for Barnaby Rudge since I've been in love with him for thirty-five years and he could just as easily be played by a girl as a boy. I'd like to explore my inner idiot.

P.S. My daughter suggested Peter Rabbit.

First, there's a primal wow to be had from seeing your characters walking and talking, larger than life, played by faces I've known for much of my life. Second, there's a slower-burning pleasure in merely thinking of your story being out in the world, trickling into minds, wherever there are cinemas. Then, inevitably, the film gets lost in the hurly-burly of life, and I don't think about it at all, at least until the next interview.

—**David Mitchell**

Who doesn't love a good movie? For this reason, I would enjoy seeing all of my books adapted to film. There are currently three or four "in production"—not sure what that means but I suspect it means little is happening. Gone are the days when I sold the film rights for a nice check, then sat back and waited eighteen months for the movie. Long gone. *Calico Joe* is being developed by Chris Columbus, who wrote a great script and plans to direct. It appears to be a fast track and should be fun to watch. My involvement is always limited, as it should be. I know nothing about making movies and have no desire to learn.

—**John Grisham**

Lasse Hallstrom's *The Cider House Rules* [is my favorite movie adaptation of my books]. I loved working with Lasse. I wrote the screenplay, but it is Lasse's film; he is why it works. I also think Tod Williams's *The Door in the Floor* is an excellent adaptation of *A Widow for One Year*; he smartly adapted just the first third of that novel, when the character of Ruth (the eponymous widow) is still a little girl. He did a great job; he was the writer and director, but I enjoyed working with him—just giving him notes on his script, and then notes on the rough cut.

—**John Irving**

In [my] TV career, as well as my day job, I was the union organizer for the last couple of years. It was a time of huge change and upheaval, and management strategy depended on what they thought I was going to think. One time I found (OK, stole) a psychological profile of me they had commissioned. It was absolutely fascinating—someone else's detailed opinion of me. The movie is like that—someone else's detailed opinion of Reacher. Someone else's view. In this case, the someone is a bunch of smart, savvy film people who are also genuine fans of the books. I'm well aware of the alchemy that has to take place, and my observation of the process was obviously intensely personal and self-interested, but also academic in a surprisingly detached way. I found myself agreeing with their choices 99 percent of the time. I would have done it no differently. Cruise instinctively understood Reacher's vibe and attitude, and his talent gets it all on the screen. When I read that psychological profile all those years ago, I found myself nodding along, ruefully. They nailed it, I thought. Same with the movie. Which is more than just a cute metaphor. There's always a little autobiography in fictional characters, and actors try to inhabit the character, so to an extent I was watching Cruise play a version of me, and yes, I recognized myself.

—**Lee Child**

Sadly, I feel my books have been better than the movies made from them. I'm a total movieholic, so that state of affairs is more depressing to me than it ought to be. My current paranoid theory is that I'm a victim of "caricature assassination" in certain Hollywood quarters—"Oh, that airport author has another best-selling page-turner." True story: When *Along Came a Spider* was in galleys, I got a large offer from a studio. All I had to do was change Alex Cross into a white man.

—**James Patterson**

Michael Chabon

What book is on your night stand now?

Moonraker, Ian Fleming, 1955.

What's the last truly great book you read?

If I might be permitted to count them as a single overarching work—a great work—the five Patrick Melrose novels by the English writer Edward St. Aubyn. But *Moonraker* is pretty awesome.

What was the last book that made you cry?

That is a very rare occurrence. I remember tearing up the first time I read Nabokov's description, in *Speak, Memory*, of his father being tossed on a blanket by cheering muzhiks, with its astonishingly subtle foreshadowing of grief and mourning.

The last book that made you laugh?

A more common occurrence, if not exactly frequent. Again, St. Aubyn takes the prize. I don't think I would be able to define a work of literature as great if it didn't make me laugh at least a little.

What were your most cherished books as a child? Do you have a favorite character or hero from children's literature?

The D'Aulaires' *Norse Gods and Giants*. *The Phantom Tollbooth*. *A Wizard of Earthsea*. *From the Mixed-Up Files of Mrs. Basil E. Frankweiler*. *Harriet the Spy*. John Christopher's Tripods trilogy. Bradbury's *R Is for Rocket*. *The Adventures of Sherlock Holmes*. I loved trickster heroes . . . and Holmes.

Michael Chabon is the author of *The Mysteries of Pittsburgh*, *Wonder Boys*, *The Amazing Adventures of Kavalier & Clay*, *The Yiddish Policemen's Union*, and *Telegraph Avenue*, among other books.

What was the last book you enjoyed reading with one of your children?

We are presently reading a collection of Holmes stories, as a matter of fact. Just finished *The Blue Carbuncle*. Before that, there was a great Kipling dog story, *Garm—A Hostage*.

Any contemporary comics you'd recommend?

I am a huge, raving fan of writer Matt Fraction. His semi-indie Casanova series is an ongoing masterpiece of twenty-first-century American comics—and his run on Immortal Iron Fist with Ed Brubaker was pure, yummy martial-arts-fantasy deliciousness.

You've worked on the screenplays for both *Spider-Man 2* and *John Carter*. Is there any comic book adaptation that you'd consider a dream project?

If Marvel Studios ever gets around to doing Jim Starlin's Warlock, the most rollicking, existential, soul-vampiric, cosmo-lysergic work of funky space opera ever created, I hope they will think of me.

Do you and your wife (the novelist Ayelet Waldman) like reading the same books? What books has she suggested you read, and vice versa?

Our reading does not often overlap, mostly because she reads everything (no, I'm serious: she reads everything) and I just keep reading the same books over and over again. But every so often she'll hand me something she knows I'm going to love. St. Aubyn happened that way. Sebald. *Cloud Atlas*. I had her reading Elmore Leonard a while back. He's somebody I keep going back to.

What are the best books about Judaism and the Jewish-American experience?

God, I just love *A Journey to the End of the Millennium*, by A. B. Yehoshua. My favorite novel by an American Jew is probably *Humboldt's Gift*.

You're organizing a dinner party of writers and can invite three authors, dead or alive. Who's coming?

Well, I eat dinner with writers a lot, and—like eating with children—the experience can really go both ways. I'd probably make it potluck, and then invite the best cooks who are (or were) also good company. If you were to assign writers an Invitability Score (prose style × kitchen chops × congeniality at the table), Ben Marcus (*The Flame Alphabet*) is always going to rate pretty high.

Do you like reading poetry?

Yes, I do, but my taste is very old-fashioned (with the exception of my beloved Frank O'Hara, unless he's now old-fashioned, too): I like Keats, Tennyson, Milton, Shakespeare, Hopkins, all those dudes.

Mythology has often played a role in your fiction. Is there any myth in particular that's especially meaningful to you? Or that you just like rereading?

Hard to pick. Tyr willingly sacrificing his arm in the jaws of Fenris the wolf. Daedalus and Icarus. Jacob wrestling with the angel.

You can suggest three books to a literary snob who believes genre fiction has no merit. What's on the list?

The Turn of the Screw. Heart of Darkness. Blood Meridian.

Is there any genre you'd be afraid of trying to tackle yourself?

SpongeBob/Patrick fanfic.

You can bring three books to a desert island. Which do you choose?

Moby-Dick, Ulysses, and *How to Build a Working Airplane Out of Coconuts.*

What do you plan to read next?

Beyond Black, by Hilary Mantel. And *Diamonds Are Forever.*

Rain creates a Pavlovian response in me to relax with a good book. I find that peace at our beach house, and created a cozy nook just for that purpose. I admit that I am driven to work and have to remind myself that reading is not an indulgence or a luxury. I have to improve that aspect of my life.—**Bryan Cranston**

I probably shouldn't admit this since I work in the tech industry, but I still prefer reading paper books. I travel with an iPad, but at home I like holding a book open and being able to leaf through it, highlight with a real yellow pen, and dog-ear important pages. After I finish a book, I'll often look to see how many page corners are turned down as one gauge of how much I liked it. I tried the Kindle app for the iPad on the elliptical, but when you get sweaty, you can't turn the pages.—**Sheryl Sandberg**

The most pleasurable reading experience I've had recently was just last week—jogging on the beach with an audiobook of Malcolm Gladwell's *What the Dog Saw*. I was so engrossed in his essay "The Ketchup Conundrum" that I ran an extra mile just to find out how it ended.—**Dan Brown**

I read on my iPad when I travel. I listen to audiobooks in the car. I read books in my bedroom, where I have a comfortable couch, a lamp, and two dogs to keep me warm. I confess that I am a messy, disorganized, and impatient reader: if the book doesn't grab me in the first forty pages, I abandon it. I have piles of half-read books waiting for me to get acute hepatitis or some other serious condition that would force me to rest so that I could read more.—**Isabel Allende**

I like to read either in motion or in water. And so I am most satisfied reading on subway cars, trains, planes, ferries, boats, or floating on some kind of air-filled device or raft in a pool, pond, or lake. But I am happiest reading in the bathtub; lying back with my head resting on the curved end of the tub, one leg bent and the other resting along the edge. Now and then I add a little hot water with a circular motion of my toe. I decided on my apartment because it had a deep tub with water jets to massage me while I read science fiction and magical realism.—**Walter Mosley**

The only two places where I can read for long stretches are in airplanes and in bed at nighttime. I read actual physical books and have thus far avoided the electronic lure.—**Khaled Hosseini**

I've often fantasized I would get a lot of writing done if I were put in prison for a minor crime. Three to six months. Incarceration would be good for reading as well. No e-mail, no useless warranties to get steamed about, no invitations to fund-raisers.—**Amy Tan**

In my ideal reading day there would be no time limit, no e-mails stacking up, and dinner would appear on a floating tablecloth, as if brought by spirit hands. In practice, this never happens. I read in snatched hours on trains, or late at night, or purposively and on a schedule, with pen in hand and a frown of concentration. But when I think harder . . . my ideal reading experience would involve time travel. I'd be fourteen, and in my hand would be the orange tickets that admitted to the adult section of the public library. Everything would be before me, and I would be ignorant of the shabby little compromises that novelists make, and I would be unaware that many nonfiction books are just rehashes of previous books by other writers. My eyes would be fresh. I would be chasing glory.—**Hilary Mantel**

Jeffrey Eugenides

What book is on your night stand now?

Right now I'm shuttling between *The Map and the Territory*, by the French novelist Michel Houellebecq, and *The Patrick Melrose Novels* by Edward St. Aubyn, which everyone I know seems to be reading.

Houellebecq's known for being a provocateur. He'll say things like "Life was expensive in the west, it was cold there; the prostitution was of poor quality." His book *Platform*, which is about sex tourism and Islamic terrorism, got him sued in France. What's less appreciated is how acute he is on the subjects of business and the macro effects of global capitalism. His books are the strangest confections: part Gallic anomie, part sociological analysis, part Harold Robbins. He says a lot of depressing, un-American things I get a big kick out of.

What's the last truly great book you read?

The Love of a Good Woman, by Alice Munro. There's not one story in there that isn't perfect. Each time I finished one, I just wanted to lie down on the floor and die. My life was complete. Munro's prose has such a surface propriety that you're never prepared for the shocking places her stories take you. She pulls off technical feats, too, like changing the point of view in each section of a single story. This is nearly impossible to do while carrying the necessary narrative freight forward, but she makes it look easy. Most readers don't notice how technically inventive Munro is because her storytelling and characterization overwhelm their attention.

And what's the best marriage plot novel ever?

The Portrait of a Lady, by Henry James. Unlike the comedies of Austen, where the heroines all get married at the end, this book presents an anti-

Jeffrey Eugenides is the author of *The Virgin Suicides*, *Middlesex*, and *The Marriage Plot*.

marriage plot. Old Mr. Touchett gives Isabel Archer a huge inheritance in order to secure her independence. The irony, however, is that the money ends up attracting the wrong suitor. James fills the book with the traditional energies of a marriage plot. You've got Caspar Goodwood and Lord Warburton courting Isabel, too, but here the heroine makes the wrong choice (the connoisseur!), and the question isn't who will she marry but how will she survive her marriage. It's much darker than anything Austen did, and it leads straight to the moral ambiguities and complexities of the modern novel.

And the most useful book you read while at Brown?

I arrived at college keen to develop a life philosophy. The idea was to begin with the Greeks and stop somewhere around Nietzsche. By reading the canonical works, I thought I could bring an order to my mind that would manifest itself in my behavior and decisions. Now, thirty years later, I look back and have to admit it didn't happen. I've forgotten a lot of what I read at college. It's all in pieces, bright patches of embroidered detail about Augustan Rome or early Islam or Renaissance Italy or the modernists, but not a complete tapestry. I've got Jacques Barzun's *From Dawn to Decadence* on my bookshelf here. That's the kind of book I'm a sucker for. I want to get it all explained in one shot. But you know what? I've tried to read that book three separate times, and I never get past page fifty.

In the end, it was the useless books I read at college that have stayed with me. I think of the last pages of *Lolita*, where Humbert Humbert hears children's voices and recognizes the harm he's brought Dolores Haze, and the sentence comes immediately back: "I stood listening to that musical vibration from my lofty slope, to those flashes of separate cries with a kind of demure murmur for background, and then I knew that the hopelessly poignant thing was not Lolita's absence from my side, but the absence of her voice from that concord." To see a writer describe the world with such specificity, and to learn that this formulation of words went beyond words—that it taught you about pity and shame, as well as beauty, liveliness, and compassion—that's what stuck with me. Not a coherent system, maybe. But a few constellations to set my course by.

Any guilty reading pleasures—book, periodical, online?

The only thing I'm high-minded about is literature. It's not an elitist stance; it's temperamental. Whenever I try to read a thriller or a detective novel I get incredibly bored, both by the language and the narrative machinery. Since I'm so naturally virtuous on the literary front, I don't see why I can't slum elsewhere, and I do, guiltlessly. I'm the guy in the waiting room flipping through *People*. Bellow said that fiction was "the higher autobiography," but really it's the higher gossip.

What was the last book that made you cry?

The South Beach Diet.

The last book that made you laugh?

The Houellebecq and St. Aubyn are both making me laugh, but the St. Aubyn is more intentionally funny. And Christopher Hitchens's memoir. There's a line in there that goes something like, "By that time, my looks had declined to such a degree that only women would go to bed with me."

The last book that made you furious?

It's a while ago now, but James Atlas's biography of Saul Bellow irked me to no end. Bellow's talent fills Atlas with envy. And so he avoids any true accounting of the work to spend his time telling the reader that Bellow wasn't so hot in the sack, etc. But readers of literary biographies don't want to sleep with their subjects; they want to read them.

You teach creative writing at Princeton. What books do you find most useful as a teacher?

I teach a writing workshop, so there's not a big reading list. It's "useful" (you like that word) to provide models of the form: Chekhov, Joyce's *Dubliners*, etc. But I teach undergraduates, and sometimes they're not ready to receive the lessons in craft that those writers exemplify. The story I assign every year that gets my students most enthralled with the idea of writing fiction is "Jon," by George Saunders.

Your first novel was made into a film by Sofia Coppola. If *The Marriage Plot* were made into a movie and you could give the director a few words of advice, what would they be?

Well, I should be able to give the director a few words of advice, because I'm cowriting the screenplay with him. In fact, we had drinks the other day, and I said: "Forget about making a faithful adaptation. What we have to do is break the book apart and find a cinematic equivalent of its literary mechanics." What you want, if your novel becomes a movie, is for the movie to be good. Of course, you want to tell the same story. But you have to find a new way of presenting it. Plus, I wrote the book already. It would be boring to replicate it scene by scene. As well as unwise.

What's the one book you wish someone else would write?

My worst book. I wish someone would write that one so I won't have to.

You're organizing a dinner party of writers and can invite three authors, dead or alive. Who's coming?

First I call Shakespeare. "Who else is coming?" Shakespeare asks. "Tolstoy," I answer. "I'm busy that night," Shakespeare says. Next I call Kafka, who agrees to come. "As long as you don't invite Tolstoy." "I already invited Tolstoy," I tell him. "But Kundera's coming. You like Milan. And you guys can speak Czech." "I speak German," Kafka corrects me.

When Tolstoy hears that Kundera's coming, he drops out. (Something about an old book review.) So finally I call Joyce, who's always available. When we get to the restaurant, Kafka wants a table in back. He's afraid of being recognized. Joyce, who's already plastered, says, "If anyone's going to be recognized, it's me." Kundera leans over and whispers in my ear, "People might recognize us too if we went around with a cane."

The waiter arrives. When he asks about food allergies, Kafka hands him a written list. Then he excuses himself to go to the bathroom. As soon as he's gone, Kundera says, "The problem with Kafka is that he never got enough tail." We all snicker. Joyce orders another bottle of wine. Finally, he turns and looks at me through his dark glasses. "I'm reading your new book," he says. "Oh?" I say. "Yes," says Joyce.

You've said your next book will be a collection of stories. Any recent short story collections you'd recommend?

How about a long story? Claire Keegan's "Foster." It's told from the point of view of an Irish girl whose parents, lacking the money to care for her, send her to live with childless relatives, whom she ends up preferring. The ending is absolutely heartbreaking, every single word in the right place and pregnant with double meanings.

You can bring three books to a desert island. Which do you choose?

The King James Bible. *Anna Karenina*. And a how-to book on raft-building.

What do you plan to read next?

T. M. Luhrmann's *When God Talks Back: Understanding the American Evangelical Relationship with God*. I'm reading this despite my aversion to books with colons in their titles. Luhrmann's an anthropologist who teaches at Stanford. I heard an interview with her on the radio and was struck by how nonjudgmental she sounded. And it's a subject that interests me for a lot of reasons, historical, political, and artistic.

J. K. Rowling

What's the best book you read this summer?

I loved *The Song of Achilles*, by Madeline Miller.

What was the last truly great book you read?

Team of Rivals, by Doris Kearns Goodwin. I lived in it the way that you do with truly great books; putting it down with glazed eyes and feeling disconcerted to find yourself in the twenty-first century. I met the author at a reception in the American Embassy in London last year, and I was so excited that I was bobbing up and down on the spot like a five-year-old.

Any literary genre you simply can't be bothered with?

"Can't be bothered with" isn't a phrase I'd use, because my reading tastes are pretty catholic. I don't read "chick lit," fantasy, or science fiction, but I'll give any book a chance if it's lying there and I've got half an hour to kill. With all of their benefits, and there are many, one of the things I regret about e-books is that they have taken away the necessity of trawling foreign bookshops or the shelves of holiday houses to find something to read. I've come across gems and stinkers that way, and both can be fun.

On the subject of literary genres, I've always felt that my response to poetry is inadequate. I'd love to be the kind of person that drifts off into the garden with a slim volume of Elizabethan verse or a sheaf of haikus, but my passion is story. Every now and then I read a poem that does touch something in me, but I never turn to poetry for solace or pleasure in the way that I throw myself into prose.

J. K. Rowling is the author of the Harry Potter series and the novels *The Casual Vacancy*, *The Cuckoo's Calling*, and *The Silkworm*, the last two under the pseudonym Robert Galbraith.

What was the last book that made you cry?

The honest answer is *The Casual Vacancy*. I bawled while writing the ending, while rereading it, and when editing it.

The last book that made you laugh?

The Diaries of Auberon Waugh. It's in my bathroom, and it's always good for a giggle.

The last book that made you furious?

As Margaret Thatcher might say, I don't wish to give it the oxygen of publicity.

If you could require the president to read one book, what would it be? The prime minister?

The president's already read *Team of Rivals*, and I can't think of anything better for him. I'd give our prime minister *Justice*, by Michael Sandel.

What were your favorite books as a child?

The Little White Horse, by Elizabeth Goudge; *Little Women*, by Louisa May Alcott; *Manxmouse*, by Paul Gallico; everything by Noel Streatfeild; everything by E. Nesbit; *Black Beauty*, by Anna Sewell (indeed, anything with a horse in it).

Did you have a favorite character or hero as a child? Do you have a literary hero as an adult?

My favorite literary heroine is Jo March. It is hard to overstate what she meant to a small, plain girl called Jo, who had a hot temper and a burning ambition to be a writer.

What's the best book your mother ever gave or read to you?

She gave me virtually all the books mentioned above. My most vivid memory of being read to is my father reading *The Wind in the Willows* when I was around four and suffering from the measles. In fact, that's all I remember about having the measles: Ratty, Mole, and Badger.

What books have your own children introduced you to recently? Or you to them?

My son introduced me to Cressida Cowell's dragon books, which are so good and funny. My younger daughter is pony mad, so we're halfway through a box set by Pippa Funnell. I recently started pressing Kurt Vonnegut Jr. on my elder daughter, who is a scientist.

If you could meet any writer, dead or alive, who would it be? What would you want to know?

I took this question so seriously I lost hours to it. I went through all of my favorite writers, discarding them for various reasons: P. G. Wodehouse, for instance, was so shy that it might be a very awkward meeting. Judging by his letters, his main interests were Pekingese dogs and writing methodology. As I don't own a Peke I've got a feeling we'd just discuss laptops rather than exploring the secrets of his genius.

I finally narrowed the field to two: Colette and Dickens. If Colette were prepared to talk freely, it would be the meeting of a lifetime because she led such an incredible life (her biography, *Secrets of the Flesh*, by Judith Thurman, is one of my all-time favorites). By the narrowest of margins, though, I think I'd meet Dickens. What would I want to know? Everything.

Do you remember the best fan letter you ever received? What made it special?

There have been so many extraordinary fan letters, but I'm going to have to say it was the first one I ever received, from a young girl called Francesca Gray. It meant the world to me.

So many children's books today try to compare themselves to Harry Potter. If your new book, *The Casual Vacancy*, were to be compared to another book, author, or series in your dream book review, what would it be?

The Casual Vacancy consciously harked back to the nineteenth-century traditions of Trollope, Dickens, and Gaskell; an analysis of a small, literally parochial society. Any review that made reference to any of those writers would delight me.

Of the books you've written, which is your favorite?

My heart is divided three ways: *Harry Potter and the Philosopher's Stone*, *Harry Potter and the Deathly Hallows*, and *The Casual Vacancy*.

There's a whole publishing subindustry of books about Harry Potter. Have you read any of them, or any of the scholarly articles devoted to the books?

No, except for two pages of a book claiming to reveal the Christian subtext. It convinced me that I ought not to read any others.

What's the one book you wish someone else would write?

The Playboy of the Western World, the second volume of Nigel Hamilton's biography of JFK and sequel to *Reckless Youth*.

If you could bring only three books to a desert island, which would you pack?

Collected works of Shakespeare (not cheating—I've got a single volume of them); collected works of P. G. Wodehouse (two volumes, but I'm sure I could find one); collected works of Colette.

If you could be any character from literature, who would it be?

Elizabeth Bennet, naturally.

What was the last book you just couldn't finish?

Armadale, by Wilkie Collins. Having loved *The Woman in White* and *The Moonstone*, I took it on tour with me to the United States in 2007 anticipating a real treat. The implausibility of the plot was so exasperating that I abandoned it midread, something I hardly ever do.

What do you plan to read next?

There are three books that I need to read for research sitting on my desk, but for pleasure, because I love a good whodunit and she's a master, I'm going to read *The Vanishing Point*, by Val McDermid.

David Mitchell

What book is on your night stand now?

Postwar, by the historian Tony Judt; David Finkel's account of US forces in Iraq, *The Good Soldiers*; and a proof of Nadeem Aslam's new book, *The Blind Man's Garden*, which I haven't started yet. Plus my notebook, in case a decent idea ambushes me after turning out the light.

What was the last truly great book you read?

The Icelander Halldor Laxness's *Independent People*, which I read last year on a trip to the country. Even in chapters where nothing happens, it happens brilliantly. I thought Kevin Powers's *The Yellow Birds* was shot through with greatness, too. If "a truly great book" implies thickness and scope, then maybe it doesn't qualify, but either way Powers has written a superlative novel.

And the worst or most disappointing thing you've read recently?

I'd rather not put the boot in publicly—it spoils my day when I'm on the receiving end.

Where do you get your books, and where do you read them?

If the book is still in print and from a mainstream publisher, I'll use my local bookshop here in Clonakilty in West Cork; I'll Amazon it if I'm after something more oddball from, say, the University of Hawaii Press; or use AbeBooks if it's out of print or print-on-demand. I like to browse the bookshelves of charity shops in university towns, in case serendipity hands me something wonderful I had no idea I wanted. Up to ten proofs a week wriggle through my letterbox from editors and publishers (even though I've stopped blurbing), and occasionally there's a well-chosen diamond.

David Mitchell is the author of *The Thousand Autumns of Jacob de Zoet*, *Black Swan Green*, *Cloud Atlas*, *Number9Dream*, and *Ghostwritten*.

What's it like to see *Cloud Atlas* turned into a movie? Any major changes in the transition that threw you off?

First, there's a primal wow to be had from seeing your characters walking and talking, larger than life, played by faces I've known for much of my life. Second, there's a slower-burning pleasure in merely thinking of your story being out in the world, trickling into minds, wherever there are cinemas. Then, inevitably, the film gets lost in the hurly-burly of life, and I don't think about it at all, at least until the next interview.

None of the major changes the film made to my novel "threw me off" in the sense of sticking in my craw. I think that the changes are licensed by the spirit of the novel, and avoid traffic congestion in the film's flow. Any adaptation is a translation, and there is such a thing as an unreadably faithful translation; and I believe a degree of reinterpretation for the new language may be not only inevitable but desirable. In the German edition of my last novel, my translator Volker Oldenburg rendered a rhyming panoramic tableau by rescripting the items in order to make it rhyme in German too. He judged that rhythm mattered more than the exact items in the tableau, and it was the right call. Similarly, when the Wachowskis and Tykwer judged that in a translation (into film) of *Cloud Atlas* Zachry and Meronym's future needs more certitude, then I trusted them to make the right call. They want to avoid melodrama and pap and cliché as much as I do, but a film's payoff works differently to a novel's payoff, and the unwritten contract between author and reader differs somewhat to the unwritten contract between filmmaker and viewer. Adaptations gloss over these differences at their peril.

There is one brief scene where the directors continue a character's story arc further than I imagined, in the case of Cavendish. This extension feels so right that I've incorporated it into the book I'm working on, making it "canonical" so to speak. Here's hoping the Wachowskis won't object. . . .

You spent many years living in Japan. Were there Japanese writers you particularly admire you discovered while there?

Haruki Murakami, probably the most famous living Japanese person, is hardly a "discovery," but it was a pleasure to read him in his natural habitat. Shusaku Endo was perhaps the closest thing to a "national conscience" writer (in the Amos Oz mold, say) to emerge in Japan. His historical novel *Silence* is wonderful. I have a soft spot for Junichiro Tanizaki, too. His earlier, Poe-drenched work is good fun, but his masterpiece, *The Makioka Sisters*, serves—Austen-like—as a sort of Lonely Planet guide to the matrix of social obligations which people in Japan still navigate. For a crash course in ultranationalism and the pathology of obsession, Yukio Mishima is the man, even if his humorlessness can wear you down. (The end of his Sea of Fertility tetralogy, however, is surely one of the best final scenes in the history of the novel.) To mention the war, Akira Yoshimura's *One Man's Justice* and Saiichi Maruya's *Grass for My Pillow* both examine Japan's bruised relationship with its recent history. Sawako Ariyoshi's *The Doctor's Wife* is an excellent historical novel on the status of women in Japan.

What was it like teaching English while you were there? Did you enjoy it?

Yes, I liked teaching very much, and I have many good memories. My students taught me more about Japan than its authors, really. By the end of my eight years there, however, I'd published two novels, had begun work on *Cloud Atlas*, and had come to see my future in fiction. I remember writing very short stories as comprehension exercises for my college students. I never kept any copies, and now I sometimes wonder if they were any good.

In 2003, you were selected by *Granta* as one of the best young British novelists, alongside Zadie Smith and Hari Kunzru, among others. If you had to name the best young British novelists of today, who would be on your list?

How middle-aged does this question make me feel?! It's tricky to answer, because I'm not very plugged in to the current scene here in the west of Ireland, and I tend to read the dead more than I do the living. But since you insist, three possible candidates for the *Granta* UK class of 2013 are Ned Beauman, Joe Dunthorne, and Simon Lelic. Lelic's three novels are breakneck, intelligent "social thrillers" that even invade my dream-life.

You've mentioned reading Ursula Le Guin and Susan Cooper as a child. What drew you to fantasy, and do you still read it?

Many children are natural fantasists, I think, perhaps because their imaginations have yet to be clobbered into submission by experience. When you're ten, there is still an outside chance that you might find Narnia behind the wardrobe, that the fur coats could turn into fir trees. The state of childhood resonates with life inside a fantasy novel. If you have no control over how you spend large chunks of your day, or are at the mercy of flawed giant beings, then the desire to bend the laws of the world by magic is strong and deep. I don't mean that kids can't distinguish fantasy from reality—the playground bully will clarify the matter gratis—but fantasy offers a logic to which kids are receptive, and escapism for which kids are hungry. As an adult, I read less fantasy (aside from bedtime-story duties), but perhaps nomenclature plays a role here, too: both fantasy and SF have made inroads into literary fiction and influence even those novels whose imprint logo is reassuringly conservative. Murakami's *Wind-Up Bird Chronicle* isn't regarded as a fantasy novel, but the plot is propelled by occult magic. Kazuo Ishiguro's masterly *Never Let Me Go* is old-money dystopian SF, as is Margaret Atwood's *The Handmaid's Tale* and Cormac McCarthy's *The Road*. Philip K. Dick would recognize both Michael Chabon's *Yiddish Policemen's Union* and Philip Roth's *Plot Against America* as alternate-history SF in the grandest, proudest tradition. We imbibe more SF and fantasy than we notice. On my last visit to New York, by the by, I had a dinner with a group of literary writers, and the whole main course was spent in earnest and learned discussion of *A Game of Thrones*.

Do you have a favorite character or hero from children's literature?

Edmund from the Narnia books is an interesting one. In *The Lion, the Witch and the Wardrobe* he commits an act of exquisite treachery by refusing to corroborate Lucy's experiences in Narnia, before selling his siblings for a box of crack-laced Turkish delight. Way to go, Ed. Yet by *The Voyage of the Dawn Treader*, Edmund has evolved the strength of character to tell Eustace calmly, "You were only an ass, but I was a traitor." Stumbling heroes linger longer.

Have you discovered any good new books for young people through your own two children?

Lots, yes. In the 1970s and 1980s there was so little decent fiction for young people, but we're now in a golden age that shows no sign of fading. Philip Pullman, J. K. Rowling, Lemony Snicket are only three of the best-known among a good number of equals. Michael Morpurgo is a great evoker of place and emotion, and a cool stylist. Neil Gaiman's *Coraline* and *The Graveyard Book* are both gorgeous pieces of work which will outlive most of us, I expect.

You have written that you see your stammering as "an informant about language." In what ways has it informed your approach to reading, and to writing?

Reading, maybe not a lot, other than to nudge me toward books and away from people, which maybe is a lot, after all. As a future writer, however, my stammer was an effective if merciless boot-camp instructor. It (or "He" as I imagined it) trained me to amass a vocabulary flexible and muscular enough to avoid words beginning with stammer-consonants, and do so on the hoof, before the other person caught on. My stammer also taught me about register—it was no good substituting "autodidact" for "I taught myself" because in a bog-standard state school in 1980s Britain using a word like "autodidact" got you convicted of talking posh, an offense punishable by being hung from iron railings by your underpants. What I didn't know at the time was how linguistic register helps a novelist flesh out character and lends authenticity to dialogue or narrated thought. So while I wouldn't say that stammering drove me to become a writer—this impulse comes from elsewhere—it did influence the type of writer I have become. What feels like a curse when you're younger can prove to be a long-term ally.

If you could match three writers, dead or alive, with three topics of your choice, who would you have write about what?

I've puzzled for days over this, but drawn a blank. In order to concoct a pleasing combo—Mark Twain on the Tea Party, for example—you must already imagine what the author would write—an all-you-can-eat of gourmet ridicule—so there's no element of surprise. There's also a "changing the eye of the beholder" problem: sending an age-of-sail novelist into space, for example, would involve so much technical bringing-up-to-speed that I'm not sure whether Conrad, say, would still be writing like Conrad by the time he was climbing into his spacesuit. My only other idea is more vengeful than illuminating: to gather up a party of the most vociferous climate change deniers and send them one hundred years into the future so they have to share the fates of their own great-grandchildren. But even then, I suspect, they would find reasons why it was someone else's fault.

If you could meet any writer, dead or alive, who would it be? What would you want to know?

Chekhov. I don't want to know anything in particular—I'd just like to carve up a pheasant with him, served with new potatoes and green beans from the garden. Then we could polish off some dodgy Crimean wine and play a few rounds of Anglo-Russian Scrabble and lose track of time and the score. If Isaac Bashevis Singer could be there, too, I think they'd get on well. And if Dorothy Parker could drop by at some point, and maybe Katherine Mansfield, and Sylvia Townsend-Warner . . . And suddenly it's a party.

And if you were forced to name your one favorite author?

I'd have to say, "I'm sorry, but books just don't work like that, and neither does music, Amen," and take the consequences.

It seems to me that Barack Obama is sufficiently well read. The president might consider E. M. Forster's *Two Cheers for Democracy* or even Tina Fey's *Bossypants*, which would have helped him surround himself with people who don't think they know everything about everything: being poor, being wealthy, getting sick, getting old, fighting a war. If it matters to anybody, I voted for Mr. Obama.—**James Patterson**

Meditations, by Marcus Aurelius—Stoicism and the limitations of power. "When you wake up in the morning, tell yourself: The people I deal with today will be meddling, ungrateful, arrogant, dishonest, jealous, and surly. They are like this because they can't tell good from evil. But I have seen the beauty of good, and the ugliness of evil, and have recognized that the wrongdoer has a nature related to my own—not of the same blood or birth, but the same mind, and possessing a share of the divine."—**Sting**

Physics for Future Presidents, by Richard A. Muller (2009) is, of course, already conceived for this purpose. The president's science adviser has traditionally been a physicist. Parting the layered curtains of science reveals that there's no understanding of biology without chemistry, and there is no understanding of chemistry without physics. Informed people in government have known this from the beginning. And all of engineering derives from the laws of physics themselves. So the physics literacy of a president is a good thing, especially since innovations in science and technology will drive the engines of twenty-first-century economies. Failure to understand or invest wisely here will doom a nation to economic irrelevance.—**Neil deGrasse Tyson**

The Torture Report: What the Documents Say About America's Post-9/11 Torture Program, by Larry Siems, head of PEN American Center's Freedom to Write Program. But since the president probably already knows what's in it, I'd suggest he read *The Complete Stories of Anton Chekhov*. Chekhov helps you imagine what it's like to be someone else, a useful skill for a political leader.—**Francine Prose**

End This Depression Now, by Paul Krugman.—**Dan Savage**

Definitely *Don't Bump the Glump!*, by Shel Silverstein. It's about how a great many creatures you encounter will try to eat you, even if you start out acting all bipartisan.—**Gary Shteyngart**

Our great American tragic-epic, Melville's *Moby-Dick*. This truly contains multitudes of meanings: the Pequod is the ship of state, the radiantly mad Captain Ahab a dangerous "leader," the ethnically diverse crew our American citizenry. And to balance this all-male adventure, *The Collected Poems of Emily Dickinson*.—**Joyce Carol Oates**

I would want him to read *Is There No Place on Earth for Me?*, Susan Sheehan's great nonfiction book about a young schizophrenic woman. It really conveys the grinding wheel of mental illness.—**David Sedaris**

It would be my late father, Kenneth Lamott's, nonfiction work, *Anti-California: Report from Our First Parafascist State*, on the years when Ronald Reagan was governor. I love the image of Barack Obama holding and reading my father's amazing book. It would mean my father was alive again—because books are living organisms, outside of the time-space continuum.—**Anne Lamott**

John Grisham

What book is on your night stand now?

There are a dozen. I'm halfway through *All the King's Men*, by Robert Penn Warren. I haven't read it since college.

When and where do you like to read?

I usually read at night, in the bed, before falling asleep. In the summertime, I love to read on the porch in a rocker under a ceiling fan.

What was the last truly great book you read?

The word "great" gets tossed around too easily. The last book that kept me completely engrossed while delivering a powerful story was *Life After Death*, by Damien Echols. He spent eighteen years on death row in Arkansas for crimes he didn't commit, and was released last year. Though he's innocent, the state refuses to exonerate him.

Are you a fiction or a nonfiction person? What's your favorite literary genre: Any guilty pleasures? Do you like to read other legal thrillers?

I read much more nonfiction, usually while researching the next novel. Books and studies on unlawful convictions, unfair trials, overcrowded prisons, prosecutorial misconduct, etc. I read most of the other legal thrillers on the bestseller lists to keep up with the competition.

Who are your favorites among the competition?

When *Presumed Innocent* was published in 1987, I was struggling to finish my first novel. Scott Turow re-energized the legal suspense genre with that book, and it inspired me to keep plugging along. Scott is still the best lawyer-novelist.

John Grisham is the author of *The Firm*, *A Time to Kill*, and *Sycamore Row*, among other novels.

What book had the greatest impact on you? What book made you want to write?

The Grapes of Wrath, by John Steinbeck. I read it when I was a senior in high school and was struck by its clarity and power. I'm not sure if it inspired me to write, but I do recall thinking, "I wish I could write as clearly as John Steinbeck."

If you could require the president to read one book, what would it be?

Fifty Shades of Grey. Why should he miss all the fun? Plus, it might loosen him up a bit.

What are your reading habits? Paper or electronic? Do you take notes?

My wife gave me a Kindle Fire for Christmas and I am having great fun with it. I'm not sure I am reading more, but I am certainly ordering more. But there is always a stack of hardbacks on the night stand waiting to be read. I'll start three a week and try to finish one. I'm too lazy to take notes.

Do you prefer a book that makes you laugh or makes you cry? One that teaches you something or one that distracts you?

I love humor and for this reason I've always enjoyed Mark Twain. He was without a doubt the funniest writer who ever picked up a pen. I'm not sure I ever cried while reading a book.

What were your favorite books as a child? Do you have a favorite character or hero from one of those books? Is there one book you wish all children would read?

As a small child I loved Dr. Seuss. Later, the Hardy Boys and Chip Hilton. Then I discovered Mark Twain with Tom Sawyer and Huck Finn. Tom Sawyer is still my all-time favorite literary hero.

Disappointing, overrated, just not good: What book did you feel as if you were supposed to like, and didn't? Do you remember the last book you put down without finishing?

I tried a couple of times to read *The Girl with the Dragon Tattoo* but never finished it.

If you could meet any writer, dead or alive, who would it be? What would you want to know? Have you ever written to an author?

Mark Twain, but when he was forty, not seventy. He was a pretty nasty old man. I'm not sure what I would ask Mark Twain, but I'm pretty sure it would not be for investment advice. I wrote him a letter when I was a kid but never heard back. What an ass.

Which of the books you've written is your favorite? Your favorite character? What's your favorite movie adaptation of a book you've written?

My first book, *A Time to Kill*, is still my favorite, and Jake Brigance is still my favorite character. The best adaptation was *The Rainmaker*, with Francis Ford Coppola.

If you could choose among your novels the next to be adapted into a movie, which would it be and why?

Who doesn't love a good movie? For this reason, I would enjoy seeing all of my books adapted to film. There are currently three or four "in production"—not sure what that means but I suspect it means little is happening. Gone are the days when I sold the film rights for a nice check, then sat back and waited eighteen months for the movie. Long gone.

Calico Joe is being developed by Chris Columbus, who wrote a great script and plans to direct. It appears to be a fast track and should be fun to watch. My involvement is always limited, as it should be. I know nothing about making movies and have no desire to learn.

What's the best book about the law ever written?

To Kill a Mockingbird.

The best book about baseball?

Bang the Drum Slowly, by Mark Harris.

What's the one book you wish someone else would write?

My next legal thriller. No—make that my next five.

You've traveled all around the country for your book tours. Do you have a particular favorite place to visit as an author? A city that's especially welcoming to writers?

I've visited several death rows doing research, and they are fascinating. Prisons in general give me inspiration for stories and characters. My next book is about a lawyer in prison, and I went to visit a couple. Rich stuff.

I don't understand how anyone can write in a city. I live in the boondocks where it's quiet and peaceful and when the words are slow I go for long walks through the hills. To my recollection, I've never written a single word of a novel in town.

What do you plan to read next?

I have a friend who is an obnoxious Yankee fan (aren't they all?) and he's hounding me to read the latest biographies of Mantle and Maris: *The Last Boy: Mickey Mantle and the End of America's Childhood* and *Roger Maris: Baseball's Reluctant Hero*. I'll give 'em a shot.

On Poetry

My taste is very old-fashioned (with the exception of my beloved Frank O'Hara, unless he's now old-fashioned, too): I like Keats, Tennyson, Milton, Shakespeare, Hopkins, all those dudes.
—**Michael Chabon**

We have many shelves of poetry at home, but still, it takes an effort to step out of the daily narrative of existence, draw that neglected cloak of stillness around you—and concentrate, if only for three or four minutes. Perhaps the greatest reading pleasure has an element of self-annihilation. To be so engrossed that you barely know you exist. I last felt that in relation to a poem while in the sitting room of Elizabeth Bishop's old home in rural Brazil. I stood in a corner, apart from the general conversation, and read "Under the Window: Ouro Preto." When I finished the poem I found that my friends and our hosts had left the room. What is it precisely, that feeling of "returning" from a poem? Something is lighter, softer, larger—then it fades, but never completely.
—**Ian McEwan**

On the subject of literary genres, I've always felt that my response to poetry is inadequate. I'd love to be the kind of person that drifts off into the garden with a slim volume of Elizabethan verse or a sheaf of haikus, but my passion is story. Every now and then I read a poem that does touch something in me, but I never turn to poetry for solace or pleasure in the way that I throw myself into prose.
—**J. K. Rowling**

I have many poetry collections—that's my version of self-help. Yeats, Robert Lowell, W. S. Merwin. Most of my books have a poem as an epigram to guide me; the most recent one starts with "Late Fragment," the poem Raymond Carver has on his headstone. Not enough people read poetry.
—**Anna Quindlen**

P. J. O'Rourke

What book is on your night stand now?

Kearny's March, by Winston Groom. The author of *Forrest Gump* has become a wonderful military historian and tells us how, as a result of the Mexican War, we acquired not just Texas but New Mexico, Arizona, Colorado, Utah, Nevada and—every silver lining has its cloud—California.

When and where do you like to read?

Every evening by my living room fireplace in a splendid Eames chair, giving thanks to my bad back for excusing this extravagant purchase.

What was the last truly great book you read? Do you remember the last time you said to someone, "You absolutely must read this book"?

Jane Eyre, last week. I hadn't read it in forty-five years. If then. (I suspect CliffsNotes were involved.) I didn't even remember who was locked in the attic. I told my wife she had to read it. She'd just done so (which I didn't remember either) and gave me a look that conveyed Charlotte Brontë's message to all men: The secret of a happy marriage is to have a burning house fall on you.

Do you consider yourself a fiction or nonfiction person? What's your favorite genre? Any guilty pleasures?

I like fiction and the kind of history that gives the grace and flavor of fiction to the past. No bloviation on current events, please. I can write that junk myself. My favorite genre is the comedy of manners, where Christopher Buckley reigns. My guilty pleasures are the usual—crime and suspense.

P. J. O'Rourke is the author of books on politics, economics, and cultural commentary, including *Parliament of Whores*, *Give War a Chance*, and *Eat the Rich*.

But my literary conscience doesn't bother me about Ruth Rendell, P. D. James, Elmore Leonard, and Alan Furst.

What book had the greatest impact on you? What book made you want to write?

Friedrich Hayek's *The Road to Serfdom* gave cogent shape to a slew of inchoate feelings. No particular book made me want to write. I like to make things but, being clumsy with my hands and glib with my tongue, words are my raw material.

If you could require the president to read one book, what would it be?

The Road to Serfdom, no matter who is president. But a president is a busy man, and Hayek's syntax is heavy going. Being a native German speaker, Hayek strings together railroad sentences ending in train wreck verbs. For an easier read about the connection between economic and personal liberty, I suggest Milton and Rose Friedman's *Free to Choose*.

What are your reading habits? Paper or electronic? Do you take notes? Do you snack while you read?

Behold the book with its brilliant, nonlinear search engine called flipping-through-the-pages. A Kindle returns us to the inconvenience of the scroll except with batteries and electronic glitches. It's as handy as bringing Homer along to recite the *Iliad* while playing a lyre. I dog-ear all my books, underline passages, and scribble "Huh?" and "How true!" in the margins. The only fit snack while reading is the olive in a martini.

Do you prefer a book that makes you laugh or makes you cry? One that teaches you something or one that distracts you?

A good book does all four. Three out of four isn't bad. Two is acceptable, except for books that make you cry and teach you something, which are to be avoided at all costs.

What were your favorite books as a child? Do you have a favorite character or hero from one of those books? Is there one book you wish all children would read?

I didn't care much for children's literature. I liked to read at random in the *World Book Encyclopedia*. My favorite character was Julius Caesar. His leadership style was refreshingly different from my grade school principal's. I wish children would read Emily Post's original *Etiquette*, in which Mrs.

Post says—in so many words—"Pull your pants up, turn your hat around, and get a job."

Disappointing, overrated, just not so good: What book did you feel as if you were supposed to like, and didn't? Do you remember the last book you put down without finishing?

Ian McEwan's *Saturday*—I quit just when the plot reached its crisis. I didn't care what happened to any of the characters. (On a related note, I was reading the Harry Potter series to my ten-year-old daughter, and she made me stop in the middle of the last volume. "Too much teenage mush," she said. I said, "Don't you want to know if Lord Voldemort wins?" And she said, "Oh, come on, all those books and you think Harry Potter is going to die at the end?")

What's the worst book about politics you've ever read?

Economics, by Paul Samuelson and William Nordhaus, the standard textbook on the subject for my generation. Although not supposedly about politics, it contains as much bad political thinking as can be packed into a decent liberal democratic framework. (I'm not counting *Das Kapital*, which I consider a comedy of manners, or *Mein Kampf*, the worst book I've ever read, period.)

Which of the books you've written is your favorite?

Parliament of Whores, published twenty years ago and subtitled *A Lone Humorist Attempts to Explain the Entire U.S. Government*. I'll never get such a large, slow-moving target in my sights again.

If somebody walked in on you writing one of your books, what would they see? What does your work space look like?

A mess—books, notes, clippings piled everywhere, an IBM Selectric for first drafts, a computer for second drafts, pencils and legal pads for really difficult passages, and me in the middle of it, doing nothing. My (very prolific) friend, the late John Hughes, said, "The hardest thing about being a writer is convincing your wife that lying on the sofa is work."

Do you remember the last book someone personally recommended you read that you enjoyed? Who recommended it and what convinced you to pick it up?

Fifty-odd years ago my Sunday school teacher said I should read the Bible. It was thirty years before I got around to it. The King James version should be read by everyone who loves language or, for that matter, God. Divine intervention aside, I don't listen to many recommendations.

Is there a book you wish you could write, but feel you can't or never will?

I have a lovely mess of an Irish/English-American family. There's a mash-up of *Studs Lonigan* and *The Old Wives' Tale* in there somewhere. But I'm a reporter, not a novelist. I'm reasonably alert to what people do. Why eludes me.

What's the book you wish someone else would write?

A definitive history of bohemianism, that ever-present undercurrent of antinomian thought and behavior wearing funny clothes. It should start with Petronius and his Satyricon hipsters. And I'll bet ancient China and Pharaonic Egypt had beatniks too.

Which do you prefer, traveling or reading travel books?

Having recently written a travel book and just returned from taking the kids to Disney World, I loathe them both.

Anne Lamott

What book is on your night stand now?

Three books: one is *Gypsy Boy*, by Mikey Walsh; a novel, *The Darlings*, by Cristina Alger; and a wonderful collection of stories by Alethea Black, *I Knew You'd Be Lovely*, which reminds me so much of the late, great Laurie Colwin.

When and where do you like to read?

I like to read away as much of the afternoon as possible, until real life rears its ugly head. During the day, I read on the couch in the living room, and tend to read nonfiction or *The New Yorker* during this time. Then I am in bed by eleven p.m. and read for an hour or so, often a novel. Sometimes I also sneak into the guest room to read in the early evenings—although since I live alone, sneaking from room to room is just a personal preference. Reading various books at once is sort of like doing an enjoyable Stations of the Cross. I read *The New York Times* and the *San Francisco Chronicle* every morning in bed, then end up at the couch, possibly the guest room, and then back to bed.

What was the last truly great book you read?

Behind the Beautiful Forevers, by Katherine Boo, about life in a Mumbai slum. It's nonfiction that is as riveting as a great novel—so absolutely exquisite that it made me sort of sick. I will never write anything nearly that good and accomplished. It's the same with Adam Hochschild's *To End All Wars*, about World War I. Just sickening. I have known him for thirty years, though, so it's not entirely objective. Junot Díaz's *The Brief Wondrous Life of Oscar Wao* is extraordinary. *After Mandela*, by Douglas Foster, is exquisite,

Anne Lamott is the author of many books, including *Operating Instructions*, *Bird by Bird*, *Traveling Mercies*, *Some Assembly Required*, and *Help, Thanks, Wow*.

an epic work of nonfiction about South Africa's struggle for freedom after apartheid. But he's one of my very best friends so I'm not sure if it's legal for me to mention it in the tiniest possible way. If I promise to get rid of him, can I include it here?

Are you a fiction or a nonfiction person? What's your favorite literary genre? Any guilty pleasures?

I read the same amount of nonfiction and fiction. I love memoirs, literary novels, and, secretly, legal thrillers, but could not finish the last John Grisham—we must have standards, no matter how low. My guiltiest secret is that every Thursday, I buy *People* magazine, *Us Weekly*, and the *National Enquirer*. If anyone asks about this, I will lie and maintain that I just said it to be funny. If people call when I am reading the *Enquirer*, I say, "Oh, lah de dah, I'm just lying here reading the new *New Yorker*."

What book changed your life?

A Wrinkle in Time saved me because it so captured the grief and sense of isolation I felt as a child. I was eight years old when it came out, in third grade, and I believed in it—in the plot, the people, and the emotional truth of their experience. This place was *never* a good match for me, but the book greatly diminished my sense of isolation as great books have done ever since. I must have read it a dozen times.

If you could require the president to read one book, what would it be?

It would be my late father, Kenneth Lamott's, nonfiction work, *Anti-California: Report from Our First Parafascist State*, on the years when Ronald Reagan was governor. I love the image of Barack Obama holding and reading my father's amazing book. It would mean my father was alive again— because books are living organisms, outside of the time-space continuum.

What is your ideal reading experience? Do you prefer a book that makes you laugh or makes you cry? One that teaches you something or one that distracts you?

I used to love to laugh out loud—I would weep with laughter at Charles Portis or Dorothy Parker. Now I love to pick up a book, read two pages, and shake my head with wonder and gratitude that I'm going to be covered for the ten or so days I've got this book to which I will keep returning. Two pages into *The Poisonwood Bible*, *Middlemarch*, and *In the Garden of Beasts*, I said, "I'm in."

What were your favorite books as a child? What book do you like to read to children?

I so loved E. B. White as a child—*Stuart Little*, *Charlotte's Web*. In the '50s when I was small, parents read their kids Robert Louis Stevenson, Rudyard Kipling, and Roald Dahl; *A Wrinkle in Time*, E. B. White, Louisa May Alcott, and having those books read to me are some of my absolutely most precious memories. My father hated Christians, so I didn't read the Narnia books until I was a grown-up. They're actually brilliant. I read my son *A Wrinkle in Time*, E. B. White, Roald Dahl, and Harry Potter.

Disappointing, overrated, just not good: Which book(s) did you feel as if you were supposed to like, and didn't?

I don't enjoy Jonathan Franzen, although I *mean* to. I couldn't finish *The Corrections* and thought *Freedom* was hilariously overrated. Maybe I am just bitter because it was such a gigantic success. I couldn't read *The Shipping News*, but I pretended to love it because we had the same agent when it came out. It drove me crazy, but I later forgave the author everything for those later great, life-changing short stories.

If you could meet any writer, dead or alive, who would it be? What would you want to know?

Rumi or Virginia Woolf—I love them both beyond all others. I would not be able to speak or communicate in any way while in their presence. I would sit before them, rocking autistically. There is nothing I would need to know beyond what they have written.

What are your reading habits? Do you read paper or electronic books? Do you take notes? Have you ever written to an author?

I've written to lots of writers. Laurie Colwin, after reading and foisting *Happy All the Time* many times. I saved her note for twenty years. Alice Adams wrote a sweet note to me after my first novel came out when I was twenty-six, and I was so blown away that I sent her a bunch of stamps by return mail. I have no idea what I was thinking. It was a star-struck impulse.

I read both paper and e-books, but please don't tell my publisher this. E-books are great for instant gratification—you see a review somewhere of a book that interests you, and you can start reading it five minutes later. At least I still know it is *wrong*. But when all is said and done, holding a printed book in my hands can be a sacred experience—the weight of the paper, the windy sound of pages turning, like a breeze. To me, a printed book is like a cathedral or a library or a beach—holy space.

What book made you want to become a writer?

You mean, besides *Pippi Longstocking*?

Nine Stories blew me away—I can still remember reading "For Esmé—With Love and Squalor" for the first time, and just weeping with the poignancy of the damaged soldier and the young girl. And "Teddy"—I still remember the moment when the little boy Teddy, who is actually a sadhu, tells the reporter on the ship that he first realized what God was all about when he saw his little sister drink a glass of milk—that it was God, pouring God, into God. Or something like that—maybe I don't remember it quite as well as I thought. But it changed me both spiritually and as a very young writer, because both the insight and the simplicity of the story were within my reach.

Oh, and "A Perfect Day for Bananafish," and "Down at the Dinghy," with the great Boo Boo Glass. And "Uncle Wiggily in Connecticut"—don't even get me started. . . .

Which of the books you've written is your favorite?

I guess I like *Operating Instructions*, *Bird by Bird*, and *Traveling Mercies* the most, because they have helped people the most.

What's the best memoir you've ever read?

I loved *The Seven Storey Mountain*, by Thomas Merton. Nabokov's *Speak, Memory* is pretty great.

What do you plan to read next?

Ann Patchett's *State of Wonder*. I am about to head out on book tour, and this book seems like an ideal blend of highly intelligent and readable. The only problem is going to be all those snakes. Maybe there is a redacted snake-free edition.

Ian McEwan

What's the best book you've read so far this year?

Stephen Sedley's *Ashes and Sparks*. Sedley was a senior judge in our court of appeal until last year and in this collection of essays he writes on a range of issues that concern the individual and the state. He belongs, as one commentator noted, to the English tradition of radical nonconformism—the title is taken from a seventeenth-century Leveller pamphlet. But you could have no interest in the law and read his book for pure intellectual delight, for the exquisite, finely balanced prose, the prickly humor, the knack of artful quotation, and an astonishing historical grasp. A novelist could be jealous.

And what was the last truly great book you read?

Epithet inflation has diminished "great" somewhat so we have to be careful. Last year I reread *Hamlet*. I believe the play really did represent a world historical moment—when there leapt into being a sustained depiction of a fully realized and doubting human being whose inner life is turned outward for our consideration. Even then, I blasphemously wondered whether the last two acts were as great as the first three. Is some vital tension lost when Hamlet returns from England? Another recent encounter has been Joyce's "The Dead," which I've read many times. It needs to be considered as a novella, the perfect novella, entirely separate from the rest of *Dubliners*. An annual winter party; afterwards, a scene of marital misunderstanding and revelation in a hotel room; a closing reflection on mortality as sleep closes in and snow begins to fall—I'd swap the last dozen pages of "The Dead" for any dozen in *Ulysses*. As a form, the novel sprawls and can never be perfect. It

---

Ian McEwan is the author of the novels *Amsterdam, Atonement, Saturday, Solar,* and *On Chesil Beach,* among other books.

doesn't need to be, it doesn't want to be. A poem can achieve perfection—not a word you'd want to change—and in rare instances a novella can too.

Do you have a favorite literary genre?

The novella. See above.

Do you read poetry?

We have many shelves of poetry at home, but still, it takes an effort to step out of the daily narrative of existence, draw that neglected cloak of stillness around you—and concentrate, if only for three or four minutes. Perhaps the greatest reading pleasure has an element of self-annihilation. To be so engrossed that you barely know you exist. I last felt that in relation to a poem while in the sitting room of Elizabeth Bishop's old home in rural Brazil. I stood in a corner, apart from the general conversation, and read "Under the Window: Ouro Preto." The street outside was once an obscure thoroughfare for donkeys and peasants. Bishop reports overheard lines as people pass by her window, including the beautifully noted "When my mother combs my hair it hurts." That same street now is filled with thunderous traffic—it fairly shakes the house. When I finished the poem I found that my friends and our hosts had left the room. What is it precisely, that feeling of "returning" from a poem? Something is lighter, softer, larger—then it fades, but never completely.

Do you remember the first book that made you cry?

It was *The Gauntlet,* by Ronald Welch. I was ten years old and in hospital, so I had time to read this wonderful historical novel for children in a day. Its hero, Peter, is transported in a dreamlike state back six hundred years to a late medieval Welsh castle. Many adventures and battles and much falconry ensue. When at last Peter returns to the present, the castle is the awesome ruin it was in the opening pages, and all the scenes and the dear friends he has made have vanished. "Their bones must have crumbled into dust in the quiet churchyard of Llanferon." It was a new idea to me then, time obliterating loved ones and turning them to dust—and I was stricken for a while. But no other novel on the children's book trolley would do. The next day I read *The Gauntlet* again.

If you could require the president to read one book, what would it be?

I wouldn't trouble the president with advice, or with one more transient treatise on America's supposed terminal decline. For the sake of the general good, I'd have him absorbed in poetry. What would suit him well, I believe, is the work of James Fenton. His *Selected* would be fine. The range of subject matter and tone is immense. The long, wise reflections on conflict ("Those whom geography condemns to war") would be instructive to a commander in chief, and the imaginative frenzy of "The Ballad of the Shrieking Man" would give him the best available measure of the irrational human heart. There are poems of mischief and wild misrule. A lovely consolatory poem about death is there, "For Andrew Wood." ("And there might be a pact between / Dead friends and living friends.") And there are the love poems—love songs really, filled with a sweet, teasing, wistful lyricism that could even (but probably won't) melt the heart of a Republican contender. "Am I embarrassing you?" one such poem asks in its penultimate line.

If you could meet any writer, dead or alive, who would it be? What would you want to know?

I apologize for being obvious, but every time I watch the curtain come down on even a halfway decent production of a Shakespeare play I feel a little sorrowful that I'll never know the man, or any man of such warm intelligence. What would I want to know? His gossip, his lovers, his religion (if any), the Silver Street days, his thoughts on England and power in the seventeenth century—as young then as the twenty-first is for us. And why he's retiring to Stratford. The biographies keep coming, and there's a great deal we know about Shakespeare's interactions with institutions of various kinds. England was already a protomodern state that kept diligent records. But the private man eludes us and always will until some rotting trunk in an ancient attic yields a Pepys-like journal. But that's historically impossible. He's gone.

Have you ever written a fan letter to an author? Did he or she write back?

In my experience an appreciative letter from a fellow writer means a lot. (More than a review. I've stopped reading reviews.) So of course I write them occasionally. I owe Zadie Smith one for *NW*. The last I wrote was to Claire Tomalin about her biography of Dickens.

Do you remember the best fan letter you ever received? What made it special?

An Italian reader wrote to describe how he met his wife. She was on a bus, reading one of my books, one that he himself had just finished. They started talking, they started meeting. They now have three children. I wonder how many people owe their existence to their parents' love of books.

Of the books you've written, which is your favorite?

At the moment I put my latest, *Sweet Tooth*, just ahead of *Atonement*.

If you could be any character from literature, who would it be?

I don't much like airports, long flights, and lines for passport control and immigration, so I'd like to take on the form of Shakespeare's Puck, who boasts of being able to "put a girdle round the earth in forty minutes." That would put London to New York at around five minutes.

What do you plan to read next?

I'm well into a book in typescript about Iran and nuclear weapons, *Mullahs Without Mercy*, by Geoffrey Robertson, a well-known human rights lawyer here in England. It gives a history of the murderous revolutionary theocracy, including an account of the rarely discussed mass execution of imprisoned communists and atheists in 1988. We do not want a country so careless of life to have the bomb, nor do we want the forty or so other countries waiting in the wings to have it.

But bombing Iran is not a solution. Robertson wants to bring international human rights law to bear on the problem. It should be a violation of rights to design or procure, let alone use, a nuclear weapon. The big five need to stand by their treaty obligations and set about the process of steady disarmament. Out of a dire situation, Robertson argues a case for optimism. If we can outlaw the dum-dum bullet, if we can put tyrants on trial for genocide, we can get serious about a nuclear weapon–free world.

Lee Child

What book is on your night stand now?

Pedantically, none, because I don't have a night stand. My décor is maximally minimalist, and my bedroom has a bed and nothing else. But even if I had a night stand, there wouldn't be a book on it, because I can't read in bed. I don't drift off. I'm too eager to follow the story or the argument. The few times I've tried it I have read all night and haven't slept a wink.

So my version of the question would be: What book is on your kitchen counter now, waiting to be picked up in the morning while the first pot of coffee brews? And today's answer is: *Live by Night*, by Dennis Lehane. I always read for an hour or two in the morning, before I do anything else. And Lehane was in my graduating class, so to speak, in that we came up together, and in some ways he's the best of us.

What was the last truly great book you read?

The words "truly great book" set a very high bar, don't they, in the context of the last couple of centuries. Therefore I'd have to pick *The Lost*, by Daniel Mendelsohn. Nonfiction, but only incidentally. It's a memoir, a Holocaust story, a detective story, both a rumination on and an analysis of narrative technique, a work of Old Testament and ancient Greek historiography, and a work of awful, heartbreaking, tragic suspense. A book of the decade, easily, and likely a book of the century.

Who are your favorite mystery writers?

I have many, many reliable favorites. But true admiration depends on them doing things not too close to what I can do myself. So, from way back, the

---

Lee Child is the author of a series of thrillers featuring the protagonist Jack Reacher, including *Killing Floor*, *The Enemy*, and *One Shot*.

Brit Dorothy L. Sayers, perhaps. From slightly more recently, and unsurprisingly, Raymond Chandler. From the middle distance, the Swedes Maj Sjowall and Per Wahloo. From the current day, Joseph Kanon.

Is there a particular author or genre you enjoy that might surprise your readers?

I read anything and everything, so there's bound to be many things. I just read a book about geometric patterns in medieval English brickwork. But, notably, I'm a sucker for long, multigenerational sagas, especially "wronged girl grows up and gets rich and gets revenge" stories, like Barbara Taylor Bradford's *A Woman of Substance*. I even enjoyed Jeffrey Archer's *Kane and Abel*.

You've lived in the United States since 1998. Any significant differences you've noticed in the way British and American readers view your books?

No real differences, and I think we can see that, with rare and random exceptions, the same books tend to do well or badly in both countries, in a kind of cultural lockstep. With my books, the difference seems to be between Britain and America on one hand, and Western Europe and Scandinavia on the other. The English Channel is the threshold, not the Atlantic. Europeans and Scandinavians seem to see my books as super-guilty pleasures, possibly because they're appalled by the kind of lawless vigilantism that we see as in some way metaphoric.

You spent many years working in TV. In what way did that experience influence the way you approach your novels?

In very few obvious ways, but in one very fundamental way. The two media are very different, and the skill set of one doesn't really translate to the other. But in television you learn very quickly that this isn't about you. It's about the audience. It's not about being a cool guy, impressing your friends, buying a black turtleneck and a black leather jacket. It's about satisfying the audience, first, second, and third. That's your only responsibility. That's the lesson I learned.

The first Jack Reacher movie is coming out this week. How does it feel to see a man you've written seventeen books about reenvisioned on film? Does Tom Cruise seem like Reacher to you?

In that aforementioned TV career, as well as my day job, I was the union organizer for the last couple of years. It was a time of huge change and upheaval, and management strategy depended on what they thought I was going to think. One time I found (OK, stole) a psychological profile of me they had commissioned. It was absolutely fascinating—someone else's detailed opinion of me. The movie is like that—someone else's detailed opinion of Reacher. Someone else's view. In this case, the someone is a bunch of smart, savvy film people who are also genuine fans of the books. I'm well aware of the alchemy that has to take place, and my observation of the process was obviously intensely personal and self-interested, but also academic in a surprisingly detached way. I found myself agreeing with their choices 99 percent of the time. I would have done it no differently. Cruise instinctively understood Reacher's vibe and attitude, and his talent gets it all on the screen. When I read that psychological profile all those years ago, I found myself nodding along, ruefully. They nailed it, I thought. Same with the movie. Which is more than just a cute metaphor. There's always a little autobiography in fictional characters, and actors try to inhabit the character, so to an extent I was watching Cruise play a version of me, and yes, I recognized myself.

Which of the books you've written is your favorite?

I think writers generally might agree that no book comes out quite as well as they hoped. So while I'm fairly satisfied with some of them, my favorite is always the next one. The potential is still there. I haven't screwed it up yet. But if forced to choose (and "you've written" is past tense, after all, not future) I might pick *Gone Tomorrow*, which starts well and then continues with the kind of audacity that presses hard against the line without, I hope, ever quite falling over the edge.

If you could require the president to read one book, what would it be?

Probably *The Gathering Storm*, the first volume in Winston Churchill's World War II memoir, for its sense of helpless spectatorhood as the world stumbled toward utter catastrophe. There were several opportunities to forestall disaster, but all of them were blocked by apparently implacable opposition. Perhaps the rise of a Nazi state won't happen again (or perhaps it will), or perhaps the potential disaster might be financial or meteorological, but I would hope the book might show a president that any and all efforts are worth it, come what may, that success is absolutely mandatory, and that prevention is always, always better than cure.

Regrets: Is there a book you wish you'd never read?

Not really. I've read plenty of subpar stuff, but bad can be as illuminating as good. What I regret is that perhaps because of the time and place I grew up, and the way I was raised and educated, I was far too deferential for far too long: if I didn't enjoy a book, I assumed it was my fault. Later I realized it could be the book's fault. I wish that had happened earlier.

What were your favorite books as a child?

Too many to list individually, but they all fell into one of two categories: either straightforward wish fulfillment, or explorations of exotic foreign places. The wish-fulfillment books were, looking back, simple psychological triggers: kids roaming free, having fun, with parents and authority figures notably absent. I remember wishing I was an orphan, which was unkind, I suppose. The Famous Five books, by Enid Blyton, would be typical examples.

The exotic foreign adventures were obvious antidotes to late-'50s, early-'60s provincial Britain, which was a pinched, narrow, dull, gray place from a child's perspective. In my mind I was always in jungles or on tropical islands. I remember very well *The White Rajah*, by Nicholas Monsarrat, which had the added advantage of being a good-brother, bad-brother story (I was the bad, obviously), and it had the first real "wow moment" I can remember in terms of plotting.

If you could meet any writer, dead or alive, who would it be? And what would you want to know?

I'll have to go with the elephant in the room—William Shakespeare. I'd ask him: Dude, did you know how great you were? Were you aware at the time of the sheer incandescent beauty of, say, *Romeo and Juliet*? Or were you just scuffling along like the rest of us, trying to make a living?

And possibly as a supplementary: Why did you make *Richard III* so damn long? Were you getting paid by the word, or what?

And if you could meet a fictional character?

Sherlock Holmes, probably. I'd say, Teach me something.

If somebody walked in on you writing one of your books, what would they see? What does your work space look like?

I live on the twenty-fifth floor of my building (without a night stand) and work in an identical apartment line on the seventh floor. So my commute to the office is seventeen floors in the elevator. (Not eighteen, because of the building's apparent triskaidekaphobia.) The office is a 950-square-foot loft-style space. I simplified the kitchen—no stove, just a sink and two coffee machines. The main room has a fifteen-foot run of desking, backed by file cabinets, with bookcases on the end walls. My productivity breakthrough was to keep my writing computer off-line. If I want to surf or check e-mail, I have to move six feet to another computer. Not far, but enough of a physical disincentive to mostly keep my nose to the grindstone. What would be the bedroom is a library, with an Eames lounge chair and ottoman, for the essential lying-down-staring-into-space component of writing, and on the shelves I try to collect my foreign editions, one of every title in every language.

If someone walked in, they'd see me at the right-hand desk, typing in an inelegant two-index-finger style, periodically sitting back, scratching my head, and looking at the view, which is of the Empire State and Chrysler Buildings, and which never fails to delight me.

What book should everyone read before dying?

My newest hardcover.

What do you plan to read next?

My to-be-read pile is enormous, but winking ominously at me is Jane Austen's *Emma*. I have never read Jane Austen—in my American wife's eyes an incredible deficiency for an Englishman, matched only by the fact that I don't really like Mozart. I hadn't read *Jane Eyre* either, until she made me, and I'm glad I did, so I'll get to *Emma* eventually—but perhaps not soon.

I would enjoy having lunch with J. K. Rowling. I'd probe her imagination and ask how she is dealing so well with her success and multimillionaire celebrity status.—**Colin Powell**

Edgar Allan Poe. I don't have a question, but dude just seems like he could use a hug.—**Ira Glass**

I took this question so seriously I lost hours to it. I went through all of my favorite writers, discarding them for various reasons: P. G. Wodehouse, for instance, was so shy that it might be a very awkward meeting. Judging by his letters, his main interests were Pekingese dogs and writing methodology. As I don't own a Peke I've got a feeling we'd just discuss laptops rather than exploring the secrets of his genius. I finally narrowed the field to two: Colette and Dickens. If Colette were prepared to talk freely, it would be the meeting of a lifetime because she led such an incredible life (her biography, *Secrets of the Flesh*, by Judith Thurman, is one of my all-time favorites). By the narrowest of margins, though, I think I'd meet Dickens. What would I want to know? Everything.—**J. K. Rowling**

Mark Twain, but when he was forty, not seventy. He was a pretty nasty old man. I'm not sure what I would ask Mark Twain, but I'm pretty sure it would not be for investment advice.—**John Grisham**

A wonderful writer has given the best of herself or himself in the work. I think many of them are frustrated by the thinness and inadequacy of ordinary spoken language, of ordinary contact even with the people they know best and love best. They turn to writing for this reason. I think many of them are magnanimous in a degree their lives cannot otherwise express. To meet Emily Dickinson or Henry James would be, from their side, to intrude on them, maybe even to make them feel inadequate to expectation. I can't imagine being a sufficient reason for the disruption. We do have their books. That said, I would like to meet William James.—**Marilynne Robinson**

George Orwell. I would start by asking about the mustache.—**Dave Eggers**

I would love to meet J. K. Rowling and tell her how much I admire her writing and am amazed by her imagination. I read every Harry Potter book as it came out and looked forward to each new one. I am rereading them now with my kids and enjoying them every bit as much. She made me look at jelly beans in a whole new way.—**Sheryl Sandberg**

I think I would like to meet Charles Dickens—I would just really want to ask him, "Really, how do you do that?"—**Caroline Kennedy**

Old Daddy Shakespeare, of course. I don't believe in asking writers questions. I'd just follow him about for a day and see what the routine was. I'd be invisible, of course. I wouldn't want to spook him.
—**Hilary Mantel**

Sorry to be boringly predictable, but Shakespeare. Who are you? And how did a humble country boy like you become the greatest genius, and part creator, of our beloved English language? Might you have been even better if you'd studied at Oxford or Cambridge?—**Richard Dawkins**

I'd like to ask Shakespeare if he composed while walking, or was he entirely sedentary?—**Sting**

Arnold Schwarzenegger

What book is on your night stand now?

Right now I'm reading a book called *Incognito*, by David Eagleman, about the human brain. I've always been interested in psychology, so learning about the things that influence our thinking is really important for me. In bodybuilding, I was known for "psyching" out my opponents with mind tricks. I wish I had this book then because the stuff I was doing was Mickey Mouse compared with what's in this book.

What was the last truly great book you read?

Walter Isaacson's biography of Steve Jobs. I absolutely love to hear stories about people who have tremendous vision; and when you talk about vision, Steve Jobs has to be in the conversation. He was such a revolutionary. It is completely inspirational to read about someone who saw the world, imagined something better, and then went out and made his vision a reality.

I got to know Steve when I was governor of California, and he wanted to help pass a law to encourage organ donation. A lot of people have the drive to be successful, but not the same drive to give back once they've found success. Steve saw what it was like to desperately need an organ, and he could have easily just paid for his operation and been done with it. Instead, he came with his big vision and wanted to rewrite the laws to make it easier. He did the necessary work, and we were able to hammer out a law and push it through. I think that his compassion should be a bigger part of his legacy. His story is the ultimate California dream.

Arnold Schwarzenegger served as governor of California from 2003 to 2011. Before that, he was an actor and a champion bodybuilder. He is the author of the memoir *Total Recall*, among other books.

What is your favorite literary genre? Any guilty pleasures?

I prefer nonfiction, especially biographies and history books. You could spend your whole life reading history and you would still have several more lifetimes' worth of learning to do. I don't have much time in my schedule to read, so when I have a chance to sit down and get into a book, I want to make sure it is a story of greatness that inspires and teaches.

Some of my favorite books about politics are Reagan's autobiography, *An American Life*, as well as Lou Cannon's incredible anthology about him, and James Wooten's *Dasher: The Roots and the Rising of Jimmy Carter*. Of course I have mentioned many times how much Milton and Rose Friedman's *Free to Choose* contributed to my economic views.

And what books would you suggest to an aspiring governor?

I think Doris Kearns Goodwin's *Team of Rivals* is incredibly important. Today's politicians can learn so much from Lincoln. I think the most important lesson is that, despite our politics, we should never treat each other as enemies. We can have disagreements about the direction of the country, but at the end of the day we all want to serve our country. Lincoln proved a powerful lesson by appointing his critics and political foes to his cabinet. He wanted the best minds around him offering advice. Not Republican or Democrat minds. Just the best minds. All of us can learn from that.

Are there any books you found to be particularly insightful about California?

I think any of Kevin Starr's books fit the bill. No one—no one—knows California like Kevin Starr. When I ran for governor, I read binder after binder of briefings, but none of it taught me as much as one lunch with Kevin. He is an incredible historian, and he writes in a way that always makes what he's saying interesting. To this day, every time I see Kevin, I learn something new.

If you could require the president to read one book, what would it be?

I could never choose one book for a president. There are so many things you need to learn. I would have to say, "Here is a book about Eisenhower building the highway system, so you can read about the vision it takes to build up our country, because we need to build again. Here is a book about how we developed our current energy policy, because we need to learn from that as we plan for our future energy needs." Then I would give them a kindergarten teacher's manual and let them know, "You're going to need this when you deal with Congress."

What were your favorite books as a child? Did you have a favorite character or hero?

When I was young, we were constantly exposed to the works of Peter Rosegger, who was a hero in Styria, my home state. He wrote incredible stories with a focus on our region, so he was one of the favorites.

We also constantly read these terribly violent stories by the Grimm Brothers. I mean, the cleaned-up versions of these are nowhere near the horror stories we used to read. It's no wonder my brother was a total scaredy-cat and afraid to walk home alone after you realize he had been exposed to the tales of the Grimm Brothers.

But I have to say that Karl May wrote my favorite stories. He was a German who had never seen a real cowboy or Indian, but somehow he wrote fantastic stories about this wise Apache chief named Winnetou and his cowboy friend Old Shatterhand. The stories taught me a powerful lesson about getting along despite differences, but more importantly, they opened up my world and gave me a window to see America. I still don't understand how Karl May was able to paint such an incredible picture of something he had never seen, but I do know that the cowboy stories immediately captured my attention and made me interested to learn everything I could about America.

If you could meet any writer, dead or alive, who would it be? What would you want to know?

Winston Churchill. He is one of my heroes, and when I look at all of the books he somehow had time to write, it just blows my mind. To be such a vital figure in modern history and at the same time write incredible history . . . I would love to talk to him about how he had time to be great as a leader and as a writer. If there is one person who shows us the power of history, it has to be him. It's an old cliché that history repeats himself, but when you read Churchill's speeches attacking the idea of appeasing Hitler or warning about the Cold War, you realize how brilliant he was. He was ahead of the game, which is a funny thing to say about someone who spent his spare time writing and researching history.

What's the best movie based on a book you've seen recently?

I love everything about the Harry Potter franchise. You have an incredible, epic journey with amazing characters that I think plays just as well on the screen as it does on the page. But I'm also a sucker for a major success story, and it is very difficult to match J. K. Rowling in that category. Talk about inspiration: to go from being a struggling single parent to where she is today, it's just incredible. I love to hear stories like that, and her personal story is as epic as the stories she wrote about Harry Potter.

If you could play any character from literature, who would it be?

One of my favorite characters in history is Cincinnatus, and I've read everything I can find about him. I would love to play him in a film about ancient Rome. He was given the keys to the kingdom—pure, absolute power!—and he did the job and then went back to his farm. He didn't get drunk on the power. He did the job he was asked to do, dealt with the invasion, and walked away. That is the purest form of public service I can imagine, and it would be fun to try to capture that character on film.

The United States was lucky to have George Washington as a founding father, because he had that same civic virtue, and of course he had read about and admired Cincinnatus.

Francine Prose

What book is on your night stand now?

A volume of Brassaï photographs. Alain-Fournier's *Le Grand Meaulnes* (the new translation calls it *The Lost Estate*). And *Hard Measures: How Aggressive CIA Actions After 9/11 Saved American Lives*, by Jose Rodriguez.

When and where do you like to read?

The passenger seat of a car on the New York State Thruway, on a sunny day without much traffic.

What was the last truly great book you read? Do you remember the last time you said to someone, "You absolutely must read this book"?

A year after reading it, I'm still urging people to read Peter Nadas's dense, filthy, brilliant 1,100-page novel, *Parallel Stories*. I've told lots of people to read Mavis Gallant's stories; Jo Ann Beard's *In Zanesville*; *A Chronology*, a collection of Diane Arbus's writings; and Mark Strand's recent book of prose poems, *Almost Invisible*.

Do you consider yourself a fiction or a nonfiction person? Any guilty pleasures?

I consider myself a sentence person. Really guilty pleasures? Skimming memoirs by writers I know for gossip about people I know.

What book had the greatest impact on you? What book made you want to write?

One Hundred Years of Solitude convinced me to drop out of Harvard graduate school. The novel reminded me of everything my PhD program was trying to make me forget. Thank you, Gabriel García Márquez.

Francine Prose is the author of many books, including *Lovers at the Chameleon Club, Paris 1932; A Changed Man; Blue Angel; Anne Frank;* and *Reading Like a Writer.*

If you could require the president to read one book, what would it be?

The Torture Report: What the Documents Say About America's Post-9/11 Torture Program, by Larry Siems, head of PEN American Center's Freedom to Write Program. But since the president probably already knows what's in it, I'd suggest he read *The Complete Stories of Anton Chekhov*. Chekhov helps you imagine what it's like to be someone else, a useful skill for a political leader.

Do you prefer a book that makes you laugh or makes you cry? One that teaches you something or one that distracts you?

Distract me. I cry enough. Though some books I love—Mrs. Gaskell's *Life of Charlotte Brontë*, Kosztolanyi's *Skylark*—are almost unbearably sad. Books make me laugh out loud so rarely I remember the ones that have: Hunter Thompson's *Fear and Loathing in Las Vegas*. Iris Owens's *After Claude*. Geoff Dyer's *Zona*. Here's a funny bit from Jess Walter's novel *Beautiful Ruins*, another book I have been telling friends to read: "The first impression one gets of Michael Deane is of a man constructed of wax, or perhaps prematurely embalmed. After all these years, it may be impossible to trace the sequence of facials, spa treatments, mud baths, cosmetic procedures, lifts and staples, collagen implants, outpatient touch-ups, tannings, Botox injections, cyst and growth removals, and stem-cell injections that have caused a seventy-two-year-old man to have the face of a nine-year-old Filipino girl."

What were your favorite books as a child? Is there one book you wish all children would read?

Mary Poppins. The Borrowers. The Martian Chronicles. Little Women. The fairy tales of Hans Christian Andersen. I was a very early reader with a child's ability to slip back and forth between fantasy and reality—and an intermittent inability to tell the difference. I lived inside those books. Their characters were my friends, especially the melancholy exile Earthlings on Mars. I was always disappointed to find myself back in my room.

I wish all children (American or not) would read large-print versions of the US Constitution and the Bill of Rights. James Marshall, William Steig, and Maurice Sendak are gods of the picture book. Parents, check out Marshall's *The Stupids* and Steig's *The Amazing Bone*.

Disappointing, overrated, just not good: What book did you feel as if you were supposed to like, and didn't? Do you remember the last book you put down without finishing?

I read ten pages of Cormac McCarthy's *The Road*, then put it down (forever) and went to see if there was anything good to eat. Whenever I admit I can't read Trollope, some helpful person suggests the one Trollope novel I should try, and I always promise to try, even if I already have.

Which of the books you've written is your favorite?

People seem to like *Blue Angel*. I can no more reread my own books than I can watch old home movies or look at snapshots of myself as a child. I wind up sitting on the floor, paralyzed by grief and nostalgia. Like most writers, I assume, my favorite is the novel I'm working on now. It's called *Lovers at the Chameleon Club, Paris 1932*. I can still get lost in it. I have to, in order to write it.

Do you remember the last book someone personally recommended that you read and enjoyed? Who recommended you read it and what convinced you to pick it up?

My husband read aloud so much of *Parallel Stories* that I figured I might as well finish the rest. It was as good as he promised, and we were both glad to have someone to talk to about this crazy book. Marriage counselors should advise client couples to read extremely long, difficult, bizarrely entertaining Hungarian novels.

What's the one book you wish someone else would write?

The poet Charles Simic says there should be a book called *The History of Stupidity*. He says it would be the world's longest book: an encyclopedia. I don't think he plans to write it, but I wish that someone would.

If you could meet any writer, dead or alive, who would it be? What would you want to know?

Isaac Bashevis Singer said something like, "If Tolstoy lived across the street, I wouldn't go meet him." I know what he meant about Tolstoy, but I'd like to live across the street from Jane Bowles, Robert Walser, Gogol, Kafka, or Heinrich von Kleist. Or maybe at the Spanish campground where Roberto Bolaño worked as a watchman.

What do you plan to read next?

Jonathan Dee's *A Thousand Pardons*, which I just received in galleys. Maybe I'll read it next, or maybe I'll save it for when I really need it: in the dentist's waiting room or on a long airplane trip.

I have never read any Tolstoy. I felt badly about this until I read a Bill Simmons column where he confessed that he'd never seen *The Big Lebowski*. Simmons, it should be pointed out, has seen everything. He said that everyone needs to have skipped at least one great cultural touchstone.

—Malcolm Gladwell

I'm looking at Shelby Foote's three-volume history of the Civil War on my shelf—somehow I've never managed to read the whole thing. And I've never read most of the novels of Thomas Hardy, although I don't feel embarrassed about it. Even though I love a lot of his poetry, his novels are just too sad for me.

—Donna Tartt

In the matter of putting things down unfinished, I'm too old now not to do it all the time, when something's not working. No harm, no foul, just mutual détente. As for the classics unread, in that too I try to leave shame out of my game. The existence of vastly more great books than I can ever hope to read is a primary locus of joy in this life, and weight on the scale in favor of human civilization.

—Jonathan Lethem

Ah yes, David Lodge's Humiliation game. I'd be champion at that. There are so many, but I'll say *War and Peace*.

—Richard Dawkins

Moby-Dick.

—Andrew Solomon

Dickens's *Bleak House*. What's wrong with me? On the other hand, I finished *Middlemarch*! So lay off me.

—Gary Shteyngart

I've never read the great Russian writers. Fact is, I just don't have any great interest in Russia or Russian culture or Russian history. None at all. Who knows why. I suppose we're all allowed to be dumb here once or twice.

—James McBride

War and Peace. My standard excuse for this appalling illiteracy is: "I'm saving it for my final illness." But when the doctors tell me I have six months to live, I wonder: Will I really reach for *War and Peace* instead of P. G. Wodehouse?

—Christopher Buckley

Jared Diamond

What book is on your night stand now?

Sabine Kuegler, *Child of the Jungle.* This unique book is the autobiography of the daughter of a German missionary linguist couple, who moved when she was a child to live with a Fayu clan in a remote area of swamp forest in Indonesian New Guinea. The Fayu experienced first contact with outsiders under terrifying conditions, while I was working in the area in 1979. In the Fayu village while Sabine was growing up there, the only non-Fayu were Sabine, her parents, and her two siblings. Sabine grew up speaking Fayu (as well as German, Indonesian, and English), with all of her playmates Fayu children, and learning to think and act like a Fayu. At the age of seventeen her parents sent her back to Europe to attend boarding school.

The result for Sabine was an extreme case of culture shock. This book approximates an account of Western society through the eyes of a New Guinean. Europe was as much of a shock to Sabine as the New Guinea jungle is to a Westerner. Through Sabine's words, we experience what it is like to encounter traffic lights, trains, and strangers for the first time. By Fayu standards, the variety of chocolates in Europe is wonderful, but the way that Europeans treat each other is not wonderful. This book gives a view of Western life from a fresh perspective shared by no Westerner.

What was the last truly great book you read?

Primo Levi, *If This Is a Man* (original, *Se Questo È un Uomo*, 1947). At one level, Levi's book is about how as a young Italian Jewish chemist joining the resistance during World War II, he was captured, sent to Auschwitz,

---

Jared Diamond is a professor of geography at UCLA and the author of *Guns, Germs, and Steel; Collapse;* and *The World Until Yesterday;* among other books.

and survived. At another level, the book is about our everyday life issues, magnified: the life-and-death consequences of chance, the problem of evil, the impossibility of separating one's moral code from surrounding circumstances, and the difficulties of maintaining one's sanity and humanness in the presence of injustice and bad people. Levi dealt with these issues and was lucky, with the result that he survived Auschwitz and went on to become one of the greatest authors (both of nonfiction and fiction) of postwar Italy. But he survived at a price. One of the prices, the loss of his religious beliefs, he summarized as follows: "I must say that the experience of Auschwitz for me was such as to sweep away any remnants of the religious education that I had had. . . . Auschwitz existed, therefore God cannot exist. I find no solution to that dilemma. I seek a solution, but I don't find it."

If you had to come up with your own Best of 2012 list, what book would be at the top?

There were so many good books in 2012 that rather than attempt to identify the best of them, I'll mention here one that is among the best and that deserves more attention than it has received. It's Howard Steven Friedman, *The Measure of a Nation: How to Regain America's Competitive Edge and Boost Our Global Standing*. Despite the subtitle, this book is not just another one of hundreds of books making recommendations about what the United States should be doing. Instead, Friedman compares the United States with thirteen other rich countries in five vital measures of individual and national security: health, safety, education, democracy, and equality. Friedman explains clearly and convincingly, writes engagingly, and laces his text with personal examples. Contrary to what many Americans think, the United States does not lead the world by these measures. Friedman's recommendations are specific and feasible. I'm glad that I resisted my instinct of dismissing the book when I first saw its cover: it's thought-provoking, and good reading.

What's your favorite genre? Any guilty pleasures?

The genre in which I do most of my leisure reading (i.e., reading not targeted for researching my own next book) is Italian literature. My original motive was to practice my grasp on the Italian language, which I took up at age sixty-one. But it turns out that Italy has been blessed with some of the world's great writers, from Dante, Boccaccio, and Machiavelli in the past to several modern authors whom I mention here in answers to other questions.

If you could require the president to read one book, what would it be?

It would be Niccolò Machiavelli, *The Prince*. Machiavelli is frequently dismissed today as an amoral cynic who supposedly considered the end to justify the means. In fact, Machiavelli is a crystal clear realist who understands the limits and uses of power. Fundamental to his thinking is the distinction he draws between the concepts expressed in Italian as *virtù* and *fortuna*. These don't mean "virtue" and "fortune." Instead, *virtù* refers to the sphere in which a statesman can influence his world by his own actions, contrasted with *fortuna*, meaning the role of chance beyond a statesman's control. But Machiavelli makes clear, in a wonderful metaphor contrasting an uncontrollable flood with protective measures that can be taken in anticipation of a flood, that we are not helpless at the hands of bad luck. Among a statesman's tasks is to anticipate what might go wrong, and to plan for it. Every president (and all of us nonpoliticians as well) should read Machiavelli and incorporate his thinking.

What were your favorite books as a child? Did you have a favorite character or hero?

Two books stand out. One is *The Complete Sherlock Holmes*: all 1,122 pages, containing four novels and fifty-six short stories. I read them first as a child and have reread them about every ten years since then, including reading them to my own sons when they were children. The other book is Thoreau's *Walden*, which I read once when I was young, and which was the single book that has most influenced me. Thoreau's message that I took away was: Be honest with yourself, think clearly, decide what is most important, and do it regardless of what other people think. Reading Thoreau felt like standing in dazzlingly bright light.

What's the best book for a parent to buy for a child interested in learning more about geography and the relationship between geography and society?

I believe that I'm being realistic, not egotistical or self-promoting, when I answer: my own book *Guns, Germs, and Steel: The Fates of Human Societies*. The book explains the long-term effects of geography—especially continental differences in wild plant and animal species available for domestication, and in shapes, areas, and isolations—in molding the different histories of the peoples native to the different continents. While I wrote the book for adults, to my surprise it has been frequently adopted in schools. I discovered this when one day my twin sons, then in seventh grade, came home from school angry at me. They explained, "Daddy, our class has been assigned a chapter of your book to read, and the teacher will invite you in to discuss your book, and we haven't read your book yet, but we are sure that it is a bad book." When I did receive the teacher's invitation and arrived at the class, my sons were seated in the back row, with their gazes averted in embarrassment and disgust. But my sons warmed up when they saw that their classmates hadn't hated but had enjoyed my book. By the end of the class, my sons were smiling. Since then, they have been among my most devoted defenders, and they erupt in indignation if they hear any of my books criticized. Since that visit to my sons' school, I've had many school visits and invitations, and letters daily from schoolchildren of all ages who have been stimulated by my books.

What was the last book that made you cry? The last book that made you laugh?

The answers to both of those questions are: the same book or series of books. It's the series of Don Camillo stories, by the modern Italian author Giovanni Guareschi, collected in three volumes. The stories are set in a small Italian town and involve three protagonists: the local priest Don Camillo; the mayor Peppone; and the church's Christ statue, which Don Camillo consults regularly for advice and which answers. Don Camillo and Peppone clash constantly in words and occasionally with their fists. But the two of them are joined by a common sense of humanity. The Don Camillo stories range from gut-wrenchingly tragic to hilarious. Whenever I start the next story in Guareschi's collection, I never know in advance whether it will make me cry or laugh.

What's the best love story you've ever read?

Tolstoy's *Anna Karenina*—even though the love goes sour and the book has a sad ending.

Name a book you just couldn't finish.

Modern Italy's leading woman author is Dacia Maraini. She has written many wonderful, realistic, emotionally rich novels and short stories, all of which I have enjoyed—with one exception. Her book *Woman at War* (*Donna in Guerra*) describes unpleasant protagonists experiencing unpleasant events and relationships. Precisely because Dacia Maraini's writing is so convincing, by page ninety-seven I couldn't stand to submerge myself any longer in that unpleasantness, and I stopped reading.

If you could meet any writer, dead or alive, who would it be? What would you want to know?

My choice would be the classical Greek historian Thucydides, who devoted the latter part of his life to a book detailing the history of the long series of wars between Athens and Sparta in the fifth century BC. His book is considered to have laid the foundations of the discipline of history. I read Thucydides every decade or so, about as often as I read Sherlock Holmes. The reasons why Thucydides is still widely read today, over 2,400 years after he lived, are that his insights into politics and war are universal and still relevant; his moral and psychological reflections on war and history are profound; and his accounts of debates and battles are thrilling. If I met him, I would be curious to discover whether he was really as devoid of humor as is his book. In his entire book there is not a single sentence that could be considered remotely humorous, no less a joke. Second, I would want to ask him how he managed to write such a calm and dispassionate account of a passionate and vicious war, when he himself served as an Athenian general but was fired and exiled after a defeat, and when he loved and admired one of the two sides (the Athenians). Finally, I would ask him the same question that all subsequent historians have wondered: How close to the original does he think are his verbatim accounts of lengthy speeches at whose delivery he was not present?

What are you planning to read next?

I am going to reread Thucydides.

I'm a self-help queen, dedicated to continuous improvement. I read books about problems I don't have, just in case I develop obsessive-compulsive disorder or crippling phobias. Of course there's nothing I recommend. If I ever found anything useful, I'd keep it to myself, to steal a mean advantage.

—Hilary Mantel

I guess we shouldn't count Freud, although I have felt helped by him. I also remember feeling helped, at least momentarily, by Harriet Lerner's *Dance of Anger* at a dark moment in my early thirties. It's the rare self-help book that acknowledges the true difficulty of helping the self.

—Jonathan Franzen

The best self-help books, in my opinion, are memoirs. If people are honest about what happened to them, those stories are astonishing gifts to those of us grappling with—or just trying to understand—similar situations. I give away my memoirs like aspirins to friends who are going through tough times. Sometimes, it's easier to have perspective on someone else's life than your own.

—Jeannette Walls

I don't read self-help, although I recently found myself helped inadvertently by reading *Moonwalking with Einstein*, which centers on the science of remembering. I picked up the book because I've always been interested in why some people have great memories and others (like myself) do not. Strangely, I discovered that simply reading about the methods used by memory champions helped me improve my own memory. Now at least I can remember where I left my glasses.

—Dan Brown

As a kid I used to compulsively reread Alan Watts's *Wisdom of Insecurity*. I didn't think of that as self-help at the time, but I think of it that way now. It's still the help I need.

—Jonathan Lethem

I was a great fan of the now defunct Loompanics press, which published such self-help classics as *The Complete Guide to Lock Picking* and *How to Disappear Completely and Never Be Found*.

—Donna Tartt

I loved my mother very much, but she kind of ruined the self-help genre for me. She was big into self-help books—and religion—when I was a tween and a teen. Leo Buscaglia was right up there with Matthew, Mark, Luke, and John as far as my mom was concerned. Her collection of self-help books got her through some tough years (the end of her marriage, having four children between the ages of thirteen and sixteen at once), and she thought they could help me. I was her sensitive kid, I was a loner, and she sensed that I was unhappy. But I wasn't unhappy. I was closeted. The stress of keeping my sexuality secret from my siblings and parents was making me nuts. Once I came out, I was fine. But self-help titles drag me back to those unhappy days—my parents' divorce, my time in the closet—and leave me feeling more anxious, not less.

—Dan Savage

Literature has always been and will forever be my only form of self-help.

—Jhumpa Lahiri

Alain de Botton

What book is on your night stand now?

I'm reading *Zona*, the latest book by one of my favorite contemporary writers, Geoff Dyer. The premise of the book sounds immensely boring—an essay on Andrei Tarkovsky's film *Stalker*—but fortunately, like most of Dyer's works, it isn't about anything other than the author: his obsessions, his fears, his encroaching (and always endearing) feelings of insanity. The book is held together by the sheer quality of the author's voice, a feat in itself.

What was the last truly great book you read?

I remain predictably in thrall to Marcel Proust's *In Search of Lost Time*. There is so much in the novel, it's possible for two committed Proustians to love it for entirely different reasons. Some like the dinner parties, some the art history, some the jealousy, some the young girls in bloom. The Proust I respond to is the psychological essayist who observes the motives and emotions of his characters with some of the forensic acuity (and dry deadly wit) of the great French moralists like Pascal, La Rochefoucauld, and Stendhal; the Proust who writes things like: "There is no doubt that a person's charms are less frequently a cause of love than a remark such as: 'No, this evening I shan't be free.'"

What is your favorite literary genre? Any guilty pleasures?

I'm devoted to the essay. This is a much less defined genre than, say, the history book or the novel. The kind of essays I have in mind come down in a line from Montaigne, and tackle large quasi-philosophical themes in a tone that is warm, human, digressive, and touching. You feel like you have come to know a friend,

---

Alain de Botton is the author of *How Proust Can Change Your Life*, *The Art of Travel*, and *The Consolations of Philosophy*, among other books.

not just a theme. I have loved essays by, among others, Emerson, Thoreau, Virginia Woolf, Donald Winnicott, Cyril Connolly, Joseph Brodsky, Lawrence Weschler, Milan Kundera, Julian Barnes, Adam Gopnik, and Nicholson Baker.

Have you read any good books on philosophy lately?

I have been consoled by Arthur Schopenhauer's delightfully morbid pessimism in *The Wisdom of Life*. "We can regard our life as a uselessly disturbing episode in the blissful repose of nothingness," he tells us. "It may be said of it: 'It is bad today and every day it will get worse, until the worst of all happens.'" It's a mistaken prejudice of our times to think that the only way to cheer someone up is to tell them something cheerful. Exaggerated tragic pronouncements work far better.

If you could require the president to read one book, what would it be? The prime minister?

Your president is a complex case, a man of passion, courage, and oratory. And also, a diligent, prickly, practical law professor. I've got a weakness for the former side, so would want to put books in front of him that could bolster what I think of as his best impulses. I'd particularly keep him close to Whitman and Thoreau, those great American voices of openhearted humanity, daring, and liberty. As for the British prime minister, he urgently needs to read John Locke and Thomas Hobbes, and read up on constitutional matters from a historical perspective.

What were your favorite books as a child? Did you have a favorite character or hero?

I was a very unliterary child, which might reassure parents with kids who don't read. Lego was my thing, as well as practical books like *See Inside a Nuclear Power Station*. It wasn't till early adolescence that I saw the point of books and then it was the old stalwart, *The Catcher in the Rye*, that got me going. By sixteen, I was lost—often in the philosophy aisles, in a moody and melodramatic state. I was impressed by Kierkegaard's claim that he was going to read only "writings by men who have been executed."

What books had the greatest influence on you when you were a student?

The French essayist Roland Barthes was, and in many ways continues to be, my greatest influence. I responded to his way of approaching very large topics (love, the meaning of literature, photography) in oblique ways, with great formal innovation and originality. His essay on photography, *Camera Lucida*, is a model of what a highly rigorous but personal essay should be like. I couldn't have written my first book, *On Love*, without reading his *A Lover's Discourse*. Barthes taught me courage and innovation at the level of form.

What was the last book that made you cry?

I'm always close to tears reading Judith Kerr's delightful children's story, *The Tiger Who Came to Tea*. It tells of a tiger who turns up, quite unexpectedly, at teatime at the house of a girl called Sophie and her mother. You'd expect them to panic, but they take the appearance of this visitor entirely in their stride—and their reaction is a subtle invitation for us to approach life's unexpected challenges with resilience and good humor.

The last book that made you laugh?

I've been reading a nonfiction cartoon called *Couch Fiction*, by a British psychoanalyst, Philippa Perry. The book is simply the best single volume on analysis I've ever read, and takes us through one man's analysis and his attempts to resolve a range of problems with his mother and his girlfriend. It's done with images and speech bubbles by Junko Graat; it's constantly charming and always deeply accurate and thought provoking.

The last book that made you furious?

I got very angry about the food industry reading Jonathan Safran Foer's excellent *Eating Animals*. Now, a few years later, I'm bewildered and deeply worried by the way one can be impressed and moved by a book and yet do absolutely nothing about one's indignation and simply put all the good arguments to one's side—frightening evidence of the impotence of books in the hands of fickle readers.

What's the best love story you've ever read?

Goethe's *The Sorrows of Young Werther* is like a distillation of all the themes of the Western approach to love. It's also a study in immaturity. Werther's love for Charlotte depends on not being reciprocated. Had she said yes, his love might have foundered in the routines of child care. In other words, it's a love story that subtly points out how much the standard love story doesn't prepare us for what mature relationships are like. It's a book that should be given to the young, with warning.

Are there any architects that you think are also particularly good writers? What are your favorite books on architecture?

Le Corbusier is an outstanding writer. His ideas achieved their impact in large measure because he could write so convincingly. His style is utterly clear, brusque, funny, and polemical in the best way. His books are beautifully laid out with captions and images. I recommend *Towards a New Architecture*. It's a deep pity that while Le Corbusier's style has been much copied by architects, very few have drawn the right lessons from him about literature and prose style.

If you could meet any writer, dead or alive, who would it be? What would you want to know?

I would have liked to meet John Ruskin, who has been a big influence on me, and whose eccentric visions of the ideal society (at the level of architecture and morality) I am constantly inspired by. He felt sad, persecuted, lonely, and misunderstood. I would have wanted to try to be his friend.

And if you could meet a character from literature, who would it be?

Proust's Albertine sounds high maintenance but rewarding—and, in my eyes, a proper woman, a tomboy, rather than a hermaphrodite.

Who are your favorite writers of all time? And among your contemporaries?

My life has been variously overtaken (and ruined by) Montaigne, Stendhal, Freud, and W. H. Auden. I think a lot about W. G. Sebald and Ryszard Kapuscinski. A contemporary of sorts, albeit in a different generation, was Norman Mailer. His largely forgotten book *Of a Fire on the Moon* fascinates me: a big sprawling essay on technology and America that deserves a wider audience. Among the living, I deeply love: Milan Kundera, Michel Houellebecq, Philip Roth, and Nicholson Baker.

And if you had to give a young person a list of books to be read above all others to prepare for adulthood, what would you include?

I'd give them Theodore Zeldin's *Intimate History of Humanity*, a beautiful attempt to connect up the large themes of history with the needs of the individual soul. I'd point them to Ernst Gombrich's *Art and Illusion*, which opens up the visual arts and psychology. There's a lot of despair in adolescence, so I'd recommend comfort from pessimists like Pascal and Cioran. I'd especially give them a sad, poignant, questing little book called *The Unquiet Grave*, by Cyril Connolly (written under the alias Palinurus).

What are you planning to read next?

I'd love to read Chris Ware's new book, *Building Stories*, which was unfortunately out of stock (an extraordinary oversight) and has just become available again. In the meantime, I feel I'm going to have a great time with Douglas Coupland's new little book about Marshall McLuhan.

Dave Barry

What was the best book you read last year?

Doris Kearns Goodwin's *Team of Rivals*. I'm probably the last person on the planet to read it; I loved the movie *Lincoln* and wanted more. I am awed by the amount of research that went into that book. Most of my research consists of brief Google forays in search of factoids that I can distort beyond recognition.

When and where do you like to read?

I like to read at the beach, but the beach always turns out to be too relaxing, and I fall asleep after two pages. So I wind up doing most of my actual reading at night in bed, where I sometimes get through as many as three pages before I fall asleep.

Who are your favorite authors?

Robert Benchley and P. G. Wodehouse. Also (it goes without saying) Proust.

What's your preferred literary genre? Any guilty pleasures?

I like nonfiction, mostly history. My guilty pleasure is tough-guy-loner action novels, like the Jack Reacher series, where the protagonist is an outwardly rugged but inwardly sensitive and thoughtful guy who, through no fault of his own, keeps having to beat the crap out of people.

If you could require the president to read one book, what would it be?

The Brothers Karamazov, by Dostoyevsky. I was required to read this book in English class during my freshman year at Haverford College, but I never

---

Dave Barry is the author, most recently, of *Insane City*, *I'll Mature When I'm Dead*, and *Dave Barry's History of the Millennium (So Far)*.

finished it. I seriously doubt that Dostoyevsky ever finished it. So I figure if the president read it, he could tell me what happens.

Paper or electronic?

Definitely paper. I say this because we authors get smaller royalties on e-book sales. So I'd like to start a rumor that electronic books cause fatal diseases and sometimes explode. This must be true, because it's printed right here in *The New York Times*.

Who are the funniest writers alive?

Roy Blount Jr., Carl Hiaasen, Steve Martin, Andy Borowitz, Alan Zweibel, Gene Weingarten, and Nora Ephron (she's alive in my heart). Also the *Onion* guys, and the folks who write *South Park*, *Modern Family*, *The Office*, *Parks and Recreation*, and *Portlandia*. Also a surprising number of Internet commenters.

What's the funniest book you've ever read?

I'm not sure I could pick just one. *The Code of the Woosters* is up there. And *A Confederacy of Dunces* almost made me wet my pants on an airplane.

What makes a good humor book?

The most critical element in any work of humor—this is something Plato talked about—is that at least one of the major characters should be an orangutan.

What were your favorite books as a child? Do you have a favorite character or hero from one of those books? Is there one book you wish all children would read?

I read a lot of comics when I was a kid—Batman, Archie, Richie Rich, pretty much anything unlikely to inspire intellectual development. I bought comics for a dime each at the Armonk Stationery Store and read them walking home. I also bought a lot of mail-order products advertised in the back of the comics, such as the X-ray vision glasses. It turned out that these glasses did not actually give you X-ray vision. But the Joy Buzzer, used properly, was an effective prank device.

Later on I became a big fan of *Mad* magazine. I also read (it goes without saying) a lot of Proust. But the books I read most as a child were the Hardy Boys and Tom Swift series. I wish that children would read Tom Swift books today, so they would learn that electricity is a powerful force to be used against evil—as in *Tom Swift and His Photo Telephone*—and not just to download Justin Bieber songs.

You have a twelve-year-old daughter. Do you recommend books to her or vice versa? Any recent crossover successes?

I think the last book I recommended that she liked was *The Very Hungry Caterpillar*. She reads a lot, but she prefers *The Hunger Games* and other works belonging to a genre I would describe as "books that do not generate royalties for her father."

What book had the greatest impact on you? What book made you want to write?

The first time I read a Robert Benchley collection (I don't remember which one it was; my father had a bunch) I thought, "This is what I want to do."

Disappointing, overrated, just not good: What was the last book you hated? Do you remember the last book you put down without finishing?

I'm not a big fan of the Twilight series. I can't get past the premise, which is that a group of wealthy, sophisticated, educated, highly intelligent, centuries-old vampires, who can do pretty much whatever they want, have chosen to be . . . high school students. I simply cannot picture such beings sitting in a classroom listening to a geometry teacher drone on about the cosine. I have more respect for vampires than that.

Which of the books you've written is your favorite?

This may seem self-serving and promotional, but it's true: I really like the way *Insane City* came out. It has heart, and—more important—an orangutan.

Are you a rereader? What books in particular do you find yourself returning to, and why?

Maybe someday I'll go back and tackle *The Brothers Karamazov* again, if the president drops the ball.

What's the one book you wish someone else would write?

Dave Barry: The Greatest Human Ever.

We would probably all want to meet Shakespeare—or so we think. (We could ask the man if he'd really written all those plays, or if, somehow, he'd acquired them from—who?—Sir Philip Sidney's sister, perhaps? Wonder what W. S. would say to that.) Some of us have fantasized meeting Emily Dickinson. (The problem is, would either W. S. or E. D. want to meet us? Why?)

—**Joyce Carol Oates**

I wasn't sure how to answer this one so I discussed it with my twelve-year-old daughter. She suggested Plato. I was impressed. So Plato it is. I think I'd want to ask him how he'd imagine life had changed by 2012.

—**Emma Thompson**

I apologize for being obvious, but every time I watch the curtain come down on even a halfway decent production of a Shakespeare play I feel a little sorrowful that I'll never know the man, or any man of such warm intelligence. What would I want to know? His gossip, his lovers, his religion (if any), the Silver Street days, his thoughts on England and power in the seventeenth century—as young then as the twenty-first is for us. And why he's retiring to Stratford. The biographies keep coming, and there's a great deal we know about Shakespeare's interactions with institutions of various kinds. England was already a protomodern state that kept diligent records. But the private man eludes us and always will until some rotting trunk in an ancient attic yields a Pepys-like journal. But that's historically impossible. He's gone.

—**Ian McEwan**

I would have liked to meet John Ruskin, who has been a big influence on me, and whose eccentric visions of the ideal society (at the level of architecture and morality) I am constantly inspired by. He felt sad, persecuted, lonely and misunderstood. I would have wanted to try to be his friend.

—**Alain de Botton**

Homer. The Bard, being blind and the speaker of an ancient language, would pose a delicious challenge. This is the kind of challenge that any good novel would present. I'd love, after traversing the gulf of communication, to find out what he believed he was doing. I say this because writers, after a while, become fictions themselves. They are, at once, influential and lost to us.

—**Walter Mosley**

Shakespeare, whoever he really was. My dad was among the conspiracy theorists who think that the guy from Stratford-on-Avon wasn't really the Bard. I've got a lot I'd like to ask this fellow.

—**Jeannette Walls**

Joseph Campbell. His writings on semiotics, comparative religion, and mythology (in particular *The Power of Myth* and *The Hero with a Thousand Faces*) helped inspire the framework on which I built my character Robert Langdon. The PBS interview series with Joseph Campbell and Bill Moyers was hands down the most thought-provoking conversation I've ever witnessed.

—**Dan Brown**

I already met my hero: Kurt Vonnegut. I wanted to know if he liked Louis Armstrong better than Richard Wagner. I can't remember the answer. He poured me a drink, and we sat up listening to music. I left his house walking on air, soused, having drunk his liquor and smoked his filterless cigarettes. I asked him why he smoked filterless cigarettes, which are stronger and worse for you. He said, "More value."

—**James McBride**

Katherine Boo

What book is on your night stand now?

I'm currently reading *Ways of Going Home*, by the Chilean novelist and poet Alejandro Zambra. If it's only half as good as his novella, *Bonsai*, it'll still be a fine way to lose a weekend.

What was the last truly great book you read?

George Saunders's *Tenth of December*, as much as I hate to say so given that recent obnoxious headline in *The New York Times Magazine* ["George Saunders Has Written the Best Book You'll Read This Year"]. Saunders's earlier books had left me faintly less amazed than I felt I'd ought to be, but *Tenth*, in addition to being funny and stylistically cunning, contains some of the best writing about the psychological toll of inequality that I've read in years. Plus, like Alice Munro, Saunders knows when to end his stories—the moment when the best choice a writer can make is to slip away and leave the reader to assemble the last parts on her own.

What is your favorite literary genre? Any guilty pleasures?

When your work is nonfiction about low-income communities, pretty much anything that's not nonfiction about low-income communities feels like a guilty pleasure. Among recent happy diversions were Ben Fountain's *Billy Lynn's Long Halftime Walk*, Junot Díaz's *This Is How You Lose Her*, Cheryl Strayed's *Wild*, and the poet Jeet Thayil's first novel, *Narcopolis*, about the drug-hazed Bombay of the 1980s. Fountain, Díaz, Strayed, and Thayil have nothing in common except the most important thing, a total lack of pretension. They don't beat you down with their self-seriousness,

---

Katherine Boo is a staff writer at *The New Yorker* and the author of *Behind the Beautiful Forevers*.

and it's only when you're done that you realize how much wiser you are for their books.

Were there any novels that helped prepare you to enter the world of the slums?

What helped me prepare for the slum reporting was the immersion work I'd done in the United States. Though every community is different, my personal rule is pretty much the same: It's OK to feel like an idiot going in as long as you don't sound like an idiot coming out.

Where novels come in, for me, is when the reporting stops and the writing begins, because fiction writers seem to know more than nonfiction writers about distillation—conveying their analytical or psychological insights with economy. Being intent on conveying the diversity of experiences in a single slum (and equally intent on not writing a thousand-page tome), I paid particular attention to novels where points of view shifted quickly, among them *The Yacoubian Building*, by Alaa Al Aswany. I'm also obsessed with the documentary films of Frederick Wiseman, who stays out of the picture and allows the so-called subjects of his work to emerge gradually.

Are there any Indian writers with recent or forthcoming books you're especially excited about?

Aman Sethi's *A Free Man*, about an itinerant laborer in a Delhi slum, is one of my recent favorites—an original sensibility joined to a passion for reported fact. I'm also eagerly awaiting Naresh Fernandes's *The Re-Islanding of Mumbai*, which should be out by the end of the year. When deep in my work at Annawadi I found it difficult to meet people from more affluent parts of Mumbai because the disconnects were too great. But talking to Naresh was different. He's a genuine humanist in an age of very few, and understands the conflicts inherent in a city like Mumbai better than anyone I know.

Do you ever hear from Corean and Kim, the two women you wrote about in your National Magazine Award–winning *New Yorker* piece, "The Marriage Cure"?

Kim's not been in touch recently, but Corean is doing well, and still fighting like mad on behalf of her children and grandchildren. She's one of several women I've come to know in the course of my work whose example and insight have helped me conduct my own life less ridiculously. In fact I hold her personally responsible for my marriage.

What were your favorite books as a child? Did you have a favorite character or hero?

My sister and I loved Encyclopedia Brown, the fifth-grade nerd/observer who seldom took more than a day to unravel the nefarious conspiracies of childhood. Every child detective requires a sidekick, obviously, and I thought Encyclopedia's sidekick, Sally Kimball, was way cooler than any of Nancy Drew's. In addition to being smart, Sally was the only kid in town who could beat up Bugs Meany. About the particular criminals Encyclopedia and Sally outwitted, the only one I remember is a cheater in a disgusting-sneakers competition. But as a child I treasured the idea of this infinitely just place called Idaville. In Idaville the weak were rarely bullied for long, and the bad guys didn't get away.

What was the last book that made you cry?

I'm not usually one for leaving tear stains in the margins, but in recent weeks I caught myself sobbing twice—while reading a Saunders story and a forthcoming book by my friend David Finkel. Finkel's first book, *The Good Soldiers*, followed a battalion charged with carrying out George W. Bush's "surge." The new book follows some of those veterans as they struggle to reintegrate themselves into American life, and it's devastating.

The last book that made you laugh?

Spilt Milk, by the Brazilian novelist Chico Buarque. A deathbed monologue about class, race, love, and political history has no right to be this funny.

What's the best love story you've ever read?

Shakespeare's underrated *Troilus and Cressida*, a story of flawed people in a transactional historical context that renders notions of pure love absurd. It's a love story for our time that just happened to be written at the turn of the seventeenth century.

If you could meet any writer, dead or alive, who would it be? What would you want to know?

I'm useless when I meet writers I love—I go slack-jawed and stupid with awe. So I'm happy, even in my fantasy life, to give the Great Ones their space. It's enough to know them from what they put on the page.

Who are your favorite writers of all time? And among your contemporaries?

My top-ten list is an unstable thing, with new favorites regularly charging in and threatening to unseat the venerables, but Joseph Roth, Herman Melville, and George Eliot and Orwell are always on it. First among my contemporaries would have to be the late Roberto Bolaño. *The Savage Detectives* and *By Night in Chile* double-handedly yanked me out of a depression several years back, and reading *2666* while reporting in the slums was like a little miracle.

I was working my butt off trying to investigate the violent deaths of some homeless children, under circumstances that had been covered up by the police, when I reached the section of *2666* entitled "The Part About the Crimes." It begins with a relentless, near-forensic account of corpses and injustices (closely based on the murders of poor women in Juarez) that opens out into this fevered exploration of both the psychological cost of paying attention to the tragedies of others and the social cost of looking away. That section of the book undid me so thoroughly that I'll probably never reread it, even though I surely grasped only a sliver of what Bolaño was trying to say. And I suppose that's the built-in sorrow of my life's most profound encounters with books, beginning with *A Wrinkle in Time* in third grade. To reread what you loved most at a particular moment is to risk the possibility that you might love it less, and I want to keep my memories undegraded.

If you had to give reading assignments to an aspiring journalist, what books would make the top of your list?

Rebecca West's *Black Lamb and Grey Falcon*; Anna Funder's *Stasiland*; Barbara Demick's *Nothing to Envy: Ordinary Lives in North Korea*; Adrian Nicole LeBlanc's *Random Family*; Philip Gourevitch's account of the Rwandan genocide; Joe Sacco's graphic reportage; *The Corner*, by David Simon and Ed Burns; and Denis Johnson's nonfiction collection *Seek*, mainly for the piece about trying to meet Charles Taylor during the Liberian civil war. I could go on and on, but I'd probably end the list with Kathryn Schulz's *Being Wrong: Adventures in the Margin of Error*. It's about the animating power of doubt and correction, and a lack of self-certainty is something my favorite nonfiction writers seem to have in common.

Marilynne Robinson

When and where do you like to read?

I like to read in my own house, in any of the rooms I always mean to paint or otherwise improve and never do. Every detail is so familiar to me that it makes almost no claim on my attention. I read whenever I can, when I am not preparing to teach, or writing.

What is your favorite book (or story) in the Bible, and why?

The Bible is a very great literature, profoundly self-referential. My favorite book or story tends to be the one I've read or thought about most recently. For the moment, that is the Gospel of John and the Gospels generally. But the Old Testament is full of splendid things, too. Joseph and his brothers, David and Absalom—narratives that are as fine as any to be found anywhere.

Are you a rereader? What books do you find yourself returning to again and again?

I do reread. I tend to think of the reading of any book as preparation for the next reading of it. There are always intervening books or facts or realizations that put a book in another light and make it different and richer the second or the third time.

What's your favorite literary genre? Any guilty pleasures?

Oddly enough, my favorite genre is not fiction. I'm attracted by primary sources that are relevant to historical questions of interest to me, by famous

Marilynne Robinson is the author of *Housekeeping*, *Gilead*, *Home*, and *Mother Country*, among other books.

old books on philosophy or theology that I want to see with my own eyes, by essays on contemporary science, by the literatures of antiquity. Every period is trapped in its own assumptions, ours, too, so I am always trying, without much optimism, to put together a sort of composite of the record we have made that gives a larger sense of the constant at work in it all, that is, ourselves. The project is doomed from the outset, I know. Still.

What books might we be surprised to find on your shelves?

If you are surprised by arcana, the list would be very long. I should mention that Lombard's *Sentences* is now in English translation.

What book had the greatest impact on you? What book made you want to write?

I remember reading books that overpowered me, when I was still young enough to be an ideal reader. Dreiser's *An American Tragedy*, Maugham's *Of Human Bondage*, Garland's *Main-Travelled Roads*. These are books I have never reread because I am afraid I would dispel the fascination they had for me, a state of mind I hope to recover when I suspend my own disbelief and write fiction. Poe and Dickens were important to me, and before them *The Yearling* and *The Secret Garden*.

What does your personal book collection look like? Do you organize your books in any particular way?

Reference books in the dining room, older books needing and deserving protection in bookcases in the living room, theology and philosophy on shelves in the bedroom, classical and ancient Near Eastern literature in the study, modern history and Americana in the room that has only bookshelves in it, unclassifiable books in stacks on the stairs.

During the long years between *Housekeeping* and *Gilead*, did you ever despair of being an author of more than one novel?

My greatest fear was that I would write a fraudulent book simply to escape the embarrassments of having written only one novel. If there is nothing fictional on my mind I do best to concern myself with other things. I wrote a fair amount of nonfiction during those years and was absorbed by that work. Writing nonfiction has been my most serious education, and for all those years it kept me from even glancing in the direction of despair.

In *Home*, you quickly revisited the characters from *Gilead*. Do you foresee ever returning to Ruth and Sylvie and the rest of the *Housekeeping* crew?

I actually waited for Ruth and Sylvie to stop haunting my imagination. Finally they did stop. After *Gilead* I realized I was being haunted again, and I decided to let these souls have more life, since they seemed to want it. If there was a time when I could have done the same for Ruth and Sylvie, that time passed.

If you could meet any writer, dead or alive, who would it be? What would you want to know?

A wonderful writer has given the best of herself or himself in the work. I think many of them are frustrated by the thinness and inadequacy of ordinary spoken language, of ordinary contact even with the people they know best and love best. They turn to writing for this reason. I think many of them are magnanimous in a degree their lives cannot otherwise express. To meet Emily Dickinson or Henry James would be, from their side, to intrude on them, maybe even to make them feel inadequate to expectation. I can't imagine being a sufficient reason for the disruption. We do have their books. That said, I would like to meet William James.

If you could meet any character from literature, who would it be?

Ishmael.

What do you plan to read next?

The Cotton Kingdom, by Frederick Law Olmsted.

My favorite literary heroine is Jo March. It is hard to overstate what she meant to a small, plain girl called Jo, who had a hot temper and a burning ambition to be a writer.—**J. K. Rowling**

Edmund from the Narnia books is an interesting one. In *The Lion, the Witch and the Wardrobe* he commits an act of exquisite treachery by refusing to corroborate Lucy's experiences in Narnia, before selling his siblings for a box of crack-laced Turkish delight. Way to go, Ed. Yet by *The Voyage of the Dawn Treader*, Edmund has evolved the strength of character to tell Eustace calmly, "You were only an ass, but I was a traitor." Stumbling heroes linger longer.—**David Mitchell**

Hermione. Harry Potter to me is a bore. His talent arrives as a gift; he's chosen. Who can identify with that? But Hermione—she's working harder than anyone, she's half outsider, right? Half Muggle. She shouldn't be there at all. It's so unfair that Harry's the star of the books, given how hard she worked to get her powers.—**Ira Glass**

My favorite character was Julius Caesar. His leadership style was refreshingly different from my grade school principal's.—**P. J. O'Rourke**

Jo March in *Little Women*. She wanted to be a writer, she became a writer. She stopped caring that she wasn't pretty. She sold her hair to send her mother to visit their father during the Civil War. I even forgave her for not marrying Laurie.—**Anna Quindlen**

As with a lot of writers of my generation, it's Harriet the Spy. My recollection is that her creator, Louise Fitzhugh, died in her forties. Did she have any idea how many young people decided to be writers after reading her two books about Harriet? I hope she had at least an inkling.—**Jonathan Franzen**

I identified with orphans, like Anne of Green Gables, or pioneers, like the characters of Laura Ingalls Wilder, or children who slipped in and out of different worlds and dimensions, like the siblings in *The Lion, the Witch and the Wardrobe*. And of course there was the writer, Jo, in *Little Women*. I loved the brother and sister in *From the Mixed-Up Files of Mrs. Basil E. Frankweiler*, who run away from home and survive among works of beauty. I never go to the Metropolitan Museum of Art without thinking of them.   **Jhumpa Lahiri**

I didn't know children were expected to have literary heroes, but I certainly had one, and I even identified with him at one time: Doctor Dolittle, whom I now half identify with the Charles Darwin of *Beagle* days. —**Richard Dawkins**

After I read *Charlotte's Web*, I became so obsessed with pigs that my stepfather got me one for my ninth birthday. It was because of that pig that I became a vegetarian. That's impact.—**Ann Patchett**

As someone who was sent off to boarding school, I'd have to cop to cliché and say Holden Caulfield. But it would have been a heckuva lot more fun to be Hawkeye, of *The Last of the Mohicans*.—**Christopher Buckley**

Sheryl Sandberg

What was the best book you read last year?

I absolutely loved Tina Fey's *Bossypants* and didn't want it to end. It's hilarious as well as important. Not only did I laugh on every page, but I was nodding along, highlighting and dog-earing like crazy. On page three, she offers amazing advice to women in the workplace: "No pigtails, no tube tops. Cry sparingly. (Some people say, 'Never let them see you cry.' I say, if you're so mad you could just cry, then cry. It terrifies everyone.)" It is so, so good. As a young girl, I was labeled bossy, too, so as a former—OK, current—bossypants, I am grateful to Tina for being outspoken, unapologetic, and hysterically funny.

When and where do you like to read? Paper or electronic?

I probably shouldn't admit this since I work in the tech industry, but I still prefer reading paper books. (In *Lean In*, I also admit that I carry a notebook and pen around to keep track of my to-do list, which, at Facebook, is like carrying around a stone tablet and chisel.) I travel with an iPad, but at home I like holding a book open and being able to leaf through it, highlight with a real yellow pen, and dog-ear important pages. After I finish a book, I'll often look to see how many page corners are turned down as one gauge of how much I liked it. I also still read newspapers and magazines the old-fashioned way; I tried the Kindle app for the iPad on the elliptical, but when you get sweaty, you can't turn the pages.

Sheryl Sandberg is the chief operating officer at Facebook and the author of *Lean In*.

Are you a fast or slow reader? How many books would you say you read in a year?

I am painfully slow and don't get through nearly as many books as I want to. I pile them up on my night stand, and when the piles start tipping over, I force myself to speed up or to give up on the ones that, realistically, I am never going to get to.

Recommend the best business book you've read in recent years.

Now, Discover Your Strengths, by Marcus Buckingham and Donald O. Clifton. This book has been instrumental in how we think about developing talent at Facebook. Like all organizations, we have a system for giving feedback to our employees. A few years ago, Lori Goler, Facebook's head of human resources, brought Marcus to meet with our leadership team to help us improve this system. Marcus and his colleagues surveyed employees for twenty-five years to figure out what factors predict extraordinary performance. They found that the most important predictor of the success of a company or division was how many people answered yes to the question "Do you have the opportunity to do what you do best every day?" And this makes sense. Most performance reviews focus more on "development areas" (a.k.a. weaknesses) than strengths. People are told to work harder and get better at those areas, but people don't have to be good at everything. At Facebook, we try to be a strengths-based organization, which means we try to make jobs fit around people rather than make people fit around jobs. We focus on what people's natural strengths are and spend our management time trying to find ways for them to use those strengths every day.

And what's the best book about technology? Is there a book that really gets Silicon Valley right?

The Lean Startup: How Today's Entrepreneurs Use Continuous Innovation to Create Radically Successful Businesses, by Eric Ries, provides a great inside look at how the tech industry approaches building products and businesses. Traditionally, companies have depended on elaborate business plans and in-depth tests to put out a "perfect" product. Ries advocates that for tech, a better way to perfect a product is to introduce it to the market and get customers using it and giving feedback, so you can learn and then iterate. (Facebook figured out this approach long ago. We even have posters all over our buildings that remind people, "Stay Focused & Keep Shipping.")

Who are your favorite authors?

Michael Lewis's ability to boil down the most complicated subjects is like a magic trick. You can't believe your eyes. He takes on important issues—from the 2008 Wall Street crash in *The Big Short* to parenting in *Home Game*—and breaks them down to their deepest truths. His combination of an extraordinary analytical mind and a deep understanding of human nature allows him to weave together data and events to offer a fresh and insightful narrative. Whatever the topic, the result is always compelling and even thrilling. I am in awe of him.

Somewhere in that pile of books on my night stand sits a well-worn copy of Anna Quindlen's *A Short Guide to a Happy Life*. I've read it before—and I will read it again—and just knowing it's at my bedside gives me comfort. Her wisdom resonates for me on the deepest level: "But you are the only person alive who has sole custody of your life. Your particular life. Your entire life. Not just your life at a desk, or your life on the bus, or in the car, or at the computer. Not just the life of your mind, but the life of your heart." Perfect.

I can't list my favorite authors without including my college roommate Caroline Weber. I love her books because I hear about them from start to finish—with the many ups and downs that go into publishing. Much of what she writes is for the comp lit crowd—not tech execs—but she is always willing to explain passages to me. In 2007, she published the brilliant and fun *Queen of Fashion: What Marie Antoinette Wore to the Revolution*. There are few books that I have enjoyed as much. And while I admit I'm biased, it's not just me—*The Washington Post Book World* named it one of the best books of the year.

How do you organize your personal library? Do you hold on to all books or do you like to streamline?

My husband is a streamliner; I am a pack rat. I've even hung on to all my textbooks from college—you know, just in case I have the sudden urge to read Schopenhauer's *The World as Will and Representation*.

What are your most cherished books, and where do you keep them?

I keep my books from Helen Vendler's college class on American poets in my night stand (inside the drawer, not to be confused with the stack piled up on top). Professor Vendler says that you don't own a poem until you memorize it, and I agree. Every year my New Year's resolution is to meditate for just five minutes a day. I never do it, but when I recite one of the poems I memorized, I think it comes close to having the same effect.

What book should every business executive read?

Conscious Business: How to Build Value Through Values, by Fred Kofman, had a profound effect on my career and life. I think about his lessons almost every day—the importance of authentic communication, impeccable commitments, being a player not a victim, and taking responsibility. I have given this book to so many team members at work, and I've seen it inspire people overnight to be more aware of their actions and impact on others.

What were your favorite books as a child? Do you have a favorite character or hero from one of those books? Is there one book you wish all children would read?

I wanted to be Meg Murry, the admittedly geeky heroine of *A Wrinkle in Time,* by Madeleine L'Engle. I loved how she worked with others to fight against an unjust system and how she fought to save her family against very long odds. I was also captivated by the concept of time travel. I keep asking Facebook's engineers to build me a tesseract so I, too, could fold the fabric of time and space. But so far no one has even tried.

Choosing one book (and album) for all children to read is easy: Marlo Thomas's *Free to Be You and Me.* Its messages are—sadly—still relevant today, but its stories are beautifully written.

What books have you enjoyed reading with your own children? Is there a book you particularly love to read to them?

I cherish the day my daughter learned to recite "Ickle Me, Pickle Me, Tickle Me Too" from Shel Silverstein's *Where the Sidewalk Ends.* Just thinking about it makes me smile. And both my kids first learned to understand numbers from Silverstein's poem "Smart."

If you could meet any writer, dead or alive, who would it be? What would you want to know?

I would love to meet J. K. Rowling and tell her how much I admire her writing and am amazed by her imagination. I read every Harry Potter book as it came out and looked forward to each new one. I am rereading them now with my kids and enjoying them every bit as much. She made me look at jelly beans in a whole new way.

Caroline Kennedy

What was the best book you read last year?

The most shocking book I read last year was *Slavery by Another Name: The Re-Enslavement of Black Americans from the Civil War to World War II*, by Douglas Blackmon. I hadn't heard of it when I picked it up even though it won the Pulitzer Prize a couple of years ago, so I was doubly shocked by the story it tells. The detailed chronicle of the institutional scale of horrific oppression and criminal behavior by local government and corporate interests was truly jaw-dropping, although it probably shouldn't have been.

The best fiction book I read was *The Yellow Birds*, by the Iraq war veteran Kevin Powers, which is about to get the PEN/Hemingway Award. That's especially nice as the award will be presented at the JFK Library by Patrick Hemingway (Ernest Hemingway's son), because Hemingway's papers are located there.

Your favorite book of all time?

An impossible question. Two books that made me cry real tears were *Jude the Obscure*, by Thomas Hardy, and *A Death in the Family*, by James Agee. Two books that made me laugh out loud were *A Confederacy of Dunces*, by John Kennedy Toole, and *Lucky Jim*, by Kingsley Amis.

When and where do you like to read?

I am not picky—if possible I would like to read in Rome or Paris, but since that's usually not an option, I like to read in bed.

Caroline Kennedy is the U.S. ambassador to Japan and the editor of books on American history, politics, constitutional law, and poetry, including *She Walks in Beauty* and *A Family of Poems*.

Paper or electronic?

I tried electronic, but I couldn't remember anything—maybe that's because it was *The Gnostic Gospels*, by Elaine Pagels—but probably it's because I am getting old—so I am now mostly going back to paper. I like to dog-ear important pages, and I don't know how to do that on my iPad.

Who are your favorite poets? Was there a particular poet you encountered early on who inspired your love of poetry?

One of the best things about creating poetry anthologies is that I have gotten to know some incredible poets whose work I admire. Sharon Olds, Elizabeth Alexander, and Naomi Shihab Nye write about contemporary life and relationships. They have introduced me to poems I would not otherwise have read and deepened my understanding of poets like Lucille Clifton and Gwendolyn Brooks.

What's your favorite literary genre? Any guilty pleasures?

Books about the Inquisition and the Crusades are a guilty pleasure because I feel guilty reading bad things about the Catholic Church—though it's hard to avoid these days. Biographies of famous horses and lives of the saints are among my favorite literary genres.

What books might we be surprised to find on your shelves?

Power, Sex, Suicide: Mitochondria and the Meaning of Life, by Nick Lane, and lots of books about networks, physics, and neurobiology—they belong to my husband.

What's the best book you've ever received as a gift?

Gender Outlaw, by Kate Bornstein. I got it for my birthday last year from my daughter after a family discussion on the merits of transgender surgery. It's a fascinating and illuminating memoir by a transgender playwright.

Do you ever read self-help? Anything you recommend?

I don't read much self-help—that comes from talking to people or taking a hot bath. I do read historically oriented books about religion and faith like Edith Hamilton's *Witness to the Truth*, which I found in our apartment and had belonged to my mother; or Garry Wills's *What the Gospels Meant*, which I bought in an airport. I really enjoyed *God's Secretaries: The Making of the King James Bible*, by Adam Nicolson, and *The Cistercian World: Monastic Writings of the Twelfth Century*, which my daughter brought home from college.

Where do you get your books? Do you have a favorite bookstore or library?

I love independent bookstores and always get great recommendations from the staff there. I have gotten to visit amazing ones on my book tours—like Parnassus in Nashville, Anderson's near Chicago, Elliott Bay in Seattle. At home, a lot of the small bookstores have disappeared in my neighborhood, but Crawford Doyle is great. I also love going into a huge Barnes & Noble just to wander around and find things I wasn't looking for.

What's the best book you've read about the law? Was there a particular book that influenced you as an attorney?

In law school and for the research on my two books on constitutional law, I really enjoyed reading cases and found some of them to be beautifully written. First Amendment writings by Oliver Wendell Holmes Jr. (dissent in *Abrams v. U.S.*), Louis Brandeis (concurrence in *Whitney v. California*), and Robert Jackson (*West Virginia v. Barnette*) are ones that all Americans can understand and be inspired by. I haven't read many books about the law—but two interesting ones are *Arc of Justice: A Saga of Race, Civil Rights, and Murder in the Jazz Age*, by Kevin Boyle, the story of the highly publicized trial of a black doctor who tried to move into a white neighborhood and was defended by Clarence Darrow; and *The Tyrannicide Brief: The Story of the Man Who Sent Charles I to the Scaffold*, by Geoffrey Robertson. That was the first trial of a head of state for waging war against his own people, and all the prominent lawyers left town rather than be chosen to prosecute the king. A little-known attorney, John Cooke, who eventually brought the case, showed tremendous courage and was himself beheaded by Charles II. It's also interesting because it was written by a British human rights attorney who is defending Julian Assange.

If you could require the president to read one book, what would it be?

Whatever it is, I am sure he has read it. Maybe something like *Middlemarch*, just to take his mind off things and remind him that "the growing good of the world is partly dependent on unhistoric acts; and that things are not so ill with you and me as they might have been, is half owing to the number who lived faithfully a hidden life, and rest in unvisited tombs."

Did you grow up with a lot of books? What are your memories of being read to as a child?

Both my parents loved to read. My father read lots of history, and his books are among my most treasured possessions. There are a lot on the American Civil War—both sides. I especially like the ones where he wrote in the margins, like the Federalist Papers, because it's fascinating to see which parts he thought important. My mother read all the time, and there were piles of literature, poetry, and art books around her room and down the hall. When my brother and I had dinner alone as children, we used to play a guessing game based on the titles in the bookshelves in the dining room. That's how we learned the names of Winston Churchill's forty books without actually reading them.

My father used to make up elaborate bedtime stories in which I was the central character, and my mother used to read to me at bedtime. She also taught me to recite Edna St. Vincent Millay's "First Fig" and "Second Fig" for my father when I was very little. I felt a tremendous sense of pride and accomplishment, so I had a positive experience with words and ideas when I was very young.

What were your favorite childhood books? Do you have a favorite character or hero?

My favorite childhood books were about horses and adventurous tomboys, like *Caddie Woodlawn*, by Carol Ryrie Brink. She was badder than the characters in Laura Ingalls Wilder's books, and I liked her much better. My all-time favorite character is probably the Country Bunny, from *The Country Bunny and the Little Gold Shoes*, by DuBose Heyward. I see her now as a woman who reenters the workforce after raising a family—"leans in," and does it all—much better than the big Jack Rabbits.

What does your personal book collection look like? Do you organize your books in any particular way?

We had it organized by topic for nonfiction and alphabetically by author for fiction and poetry—but then the ceiling leaked and we had to paint the rooms and now it's every book for itself.

Disappointing, overrated, just not good: What book did you feel as if you were supposed to like, and didn't? Do you remember the last book you put down without finishing?

The last book I put down without finishing was *Independent People*, by Halldor Laxness—the Icelandic winner of the Nobel Prize for literature. It was recommended by Ann Patchett when I visited her store on a recent book tour, but she said if I wasn't gripped by page fifty, I should put it down. It didn't go with anything else I was doing/reading/wearing at the time, but I have a feeling I will give it another try sometime.

If you could meet any writer, dead or alive, who would it be? What would you want to know?

I think I would like to meet Charles Dickens—I would just really want to ask him, "Really, how do you do that?"

If you could meet any character from literature, who would it be?

I was in love with the Scarlet Pimpernel for a pretty long time, but I don't know if I would want to meet him now. The moment may have passed for us.

What do you plan to read next?

I just finished a book, so I am looking for suggestions.

I love histories, biographies, and memoirs. I'm also drawn to realistic fiction. I'm not a huge fan of experimental fiction, fantasy, or so-called escapist literature. Reality is just so interesting, why would you want to escape it?
—**Jeannette Walls**

I read nonfiction almost exclusively—both for research and also for pleasure. When I read fiction, it's almost always in the thriller genre, and it needs to rivet me in the opening few chapters. I don't read horror, ever. When I was fifteen, I made the mistake of reading part of *The Exorcist*. It was the first and last horror book I've ever opened.—**Dan Brown**

Ironically enough, given the topic of my first novel, I'm wary of books about boarding school. If the author gets the details wrong and caricaturizes the milieu ("My daddy says any family without a Rolls-Royce is living in poverty!") it's tedious. But if the author gets the details right, it's uncomfortably evocative and makes me squirm. All that said, I loved Tobias Wolff's *Old School*; I loved *Oh the Glory of It All*, by Sean Wilsey (in which Wilsey gets kicked out of one boarding school after another); and I can't wait to read *& Sons*, a forthcoming novel by David Gilbert about an author like J. D. Salinger who writes a book like *The Catcher in the Rye*.—**Curtis Sittenfeld**

I like personal dramas set within the sweep of historical events: Colum McCann's *TransAtlantic* and *Let the Great World Spin*, or Ian McEwan's *Sweet Tooth*.—**Sting**

Like most people, I'm fascinated by characters who are completely flawed personalities, riven by anguish and doubt, and are psychologically suspect. Wait a minute—basically that's everybody, isn't it, in life and on the page? As a writer, I'm drawn to characters who, for one reason or another, seem to find themselves desperately out of joint, alienated but not wanting to be, and ever yearning to understand the rules of the game.
—**Chang-rae Lee**

I read little nonfiction, but I have no boundaries about the fiction I relish. The only unfailing criterion is that I can hitch my heart to the imagined world and read on. Yes, I enjoy the novels written by lawyer friends, but regard that as a busman's holiday.—**Scott Turow**

I'm not very interested in contemporary American realism, or books about marriage, parenting, suburbia, divorce. Even as a child browsing at the library I distinctly remember avoiding books that had the big silver Caldecott award sticker on the front, because I loved fairy tales, ghost stories, adventures, whereas the Caldecott prize stories often had a dutiful tone that tended more toward social issues. To paraphrase Nabokov: all I want from a book is the tingle down the spine, for my hairs to stand on end.—**Donna Tartt**

I'm open to reading almost anything—fiction, nonfiction—as long as I know from the first sentence or two that this is a voice I want to listen to for a good long while. It has much to do with imagery and language, a particular perspective, the assured knowledge of the particular universe the writer has created.—**Amy Tan**

I am drawn to any story that makes me want to read from one sentence to the next. I have no other criterion.
—**Jhumpa Lahiri**

Isabel Allende

What's the last good book you read?

The Death of Bees, by Lisa O'Donnell, the kind of edgy, crazy and horrible story that may well happen anywhere.

When and where do you like to read?

I read on my iPad when I travel. I listen to audiobooks in the car. I read books in my bedroom, where I have a comfortable couch, a lamp, and two dogs to keep me warm. I have written several historical novels that required a lot of research, and in that case I did most of the reading in my "casita," where I write. I confess that I am a messy, disorganized, and impatient reader: if the book doesn't grab me in the first forty pages, I abandon it. I have piles of half-read books waiting for me to get acute hepatitis or some other serious condition that would force me to rest so that I could read more.

Are you a rereader? What books do you find yourself returning to again and again?

There is so much to read, and time is so short! I am seventy, but I have not yet reached the age when rereading gives more pleasure than the surprise of a new story or a new writer.

What is your favorite literary genre? Any guilty pleasures?

I like literary fiction. A good novel or short story is like making love between clean ironed sheets: total pleasure. When I was a teenager my

---

Isabel Allende is the author of *The House of the Spirits*, *Eva Luna*, and *The Island Beneath the Sea*, among other works.

guilty reading was, of course, erotic stuff. At fourteen, living in Lebanon, I discovered the irresistible mixture of eroticism and fantasy reading *One Thousand and One Nights* inside a closet with a flashlight. Nothing can be compared to the excitement of a forbidden book. Today nothing is forbidden to me, so there is no guilt. Too bad! (My grandchildren would have fits of boredom with the erotic scenes that turned me on in Lebanon.)

Which books might we be surprised to find on your shelves?

You will find too many dictionaries. I write in Spanish, but I have been living in English for twenty-five years with Willie, my gringo husband, who thinks that he speaks Spanish. I end up writing like Willie talks: in Spanglish. I go back and forth between both languages, and sometimes I only remember the word in French. I have dictionaries of synonyms, of colloquialisms, of mythology, even of magical terms.

What do you think of the contemporary state of magic realism? Do you have favorite magic realist novels?

Full-blown magic realism, like in the Latin American boom of literature of the '70s and '80s, is not fashionable anymore, but elements of it are still present in novels all over the world, even in English; think Salman Rushdie and Toni Morrison, for example. Magic realism is not a literary trick for me. I accept that the world is a very mysterious place.

What's the best book you've read about Chile?

This question is almost impossible to answer. I have written about Chile extensively, and therefore I have read many books on the subject, mostly for research.

Which novels have had the most impact on you as a writer? Is there a particular book that made you want to write?

In my teens I read Russian, French, and English novelists that taught me about good storytelling. In my twenties I started reading the great writers of the Latin American boom (all of them male, unfortunately). They were a choir of different and harmonious voices narrating our crazy continent to the world and to us, Latin Americans. *One Hundred Years of Solitude* made me want to become a writer. García Márquez characters resembled my own family; his voice seemed easy. I thought, "If this guy can do it, so can I."

If you could require the president to read one book, what would it be?

Does it have to be just one book? I would send him all my books for free!

You edited a children's magazine early in your career and wrote books for children. What makes for good children's literature? Do you have favorite books for children?

First of all, books for kids need to be very entertaining. No preaching, no hidden messages, no condescending tone, no didactic stuff. Kids are smart: don't underestimate their bull detector. Contemporary kids have access to a lot of information, so don't even try to fool them. I have never been more nervous about my research than when writing for young adults because they pick up every single error. Kids like fantasy, imagination, humor, adventure, villains, and suspense.

What does your personal book collection look like? Do you organize your books in any particular way?

At home we have floor-to-ceiling bookshelves of beautiful leather-bound editions of classic literature that my husband has bought for years. They are mostly decoration: they look smart. Personally, I have my own bookshelves for books in Spanish that I keep because they are hard to get in the United States. All the rest comes and goes. I don't collect anything, not even good novels. Once a year I gather all the books I have read already or will not read ever (several boxes) and give them away. I don't miss them, because if needed I can buy them again.

Do you have a standby cookbook? What books do you keep in the kitchen?

I cook by memory and instinct, like I do most things in my life. I can't follow instructions. (I don't read a manual even when everything else fails.) My husband has a series of cookbooks, and I assume that his favorite one is *The Doubleday Cookbook*, by Jean Anderson and Elaine Hanna, because it smells like garlic and is filthy with food stains.

In the bathroom?

I don't need to read in the bathroom; it takes me less than a minute.

And on your coffee tables?

Art and photography books, illustrated poems by Pablo Neruda, fancy editions of *The Divine Comedy* and of Pedro de Valdivia's letters to the king of Spain (he conquered Chile in 1542), etc. All for show. No one reads that stuff.

Disappointing, overrated, just not good: What book did you feel you were supposed to like, and didn't? Do you remember the last book you put down without finishing?

Yes, I remember perfectly, but I won't tell because I don't want to offend the author. I would hate it if someone did that to me.

If you could meet any writer, dead or alive, who would it be? What would you want to know?

I would love to meet Mark Twain. What a character! I imagine him larger than life, sexy, handsome, full of energy, a grandiose storyteller, a fantastic liar, and a man of heart and principles. I would not ask him anything in particular; I would try to get him a little drunk (it should be easy) and then sit at his feet to listen to his stories.

If you could meet any character from literature, who would it be?

Zorro, of course. If possible, at night and in bed, with the mask but not the whip.

What do you plan to read next?

I just started *The Patrick Melrose Novels*, by Edward St. Aubyn, because everyone is talking about it. (However, that was not the case with *Fifty Shades of Grey*; I am too old for bondage.) This book has 680 pages. It will take me a while to start another one . . . unless I get acute hepatitis. But on my night table is *Tenth of December*, by George Saunders, waiting its turn.

Anna Quindlen

What's your favorite book of all time?

That is so exactly like being asked which is your favorite child. *Middlemarch*, because I think of it as perfection, although I am not as enamored of Eliot's other work? *Bleak House*, because I've learned so much from all of Dickens? *Pride and Prejudice*, because I'm thoroughly satisfied every time I finish? Too tough to declare a winner.

Describe your ideal reading experience (when, where, what, how).

I can read almost anywhere: subway, plane, car (although not while I myself am driving). But I have a big chair with an ottoman in a corner off the living room, and that's probably where I like to read best, usually in the evenings, sometimes on paper, sometimes on iPad. I acquired that chair specifically for purposes of reading and the little table next to it specifically for the putting down of a book.

Who are your favorite novelists?

Dickens, Austen, Wharton, Faulkner. Among living people, Alice McDermott, Don DeLillo, Russell Banks. I also really like Theodore Dreiser and Ford Madox Ford and John Galsworthy. It's sad, the excellent people who have fallen out of fashion. You always hope they'll fall back in again.

What are the best books you've read by women journalists?

It would be impossible to answer that question at this moment without starting with Kate Boo's *Behind the Beautiful Forevers*, which is flawless.

Anna Quindlen is the author of novels and nonfiction works including *A Short Guide to a Happy Life*, *Object Lessons*, *Still Life with Breadcrumbs*, and *One True Thing*.

When I was on book tour last year I talked about it more than my own book. Adrian Nicole LeBlanc's *Random Family* is one of the best books I've ever read about what it's like to be poor in America. I never miss Laura Lippman's novels. She was a reporter at *The Baltimore Sun*. She still has a reporter's eye. Last year Julia Keller, who was at the *Chicago Tribune*, published a mystery set in West Virginia called *A Killing in the Hills*. It made me want to read her next one.

Who are your favorite women writing today?

There are some women writing terrific novels that pass as crime fiction but transcend the genre. I buy a new Denise Mina, Tana French, or Kate Atkinson the moment it appears. Hilary Mantel is finally getting the genuflection she deserves. But there are some women whose backlists should be read by everyone. Mary Wesley should be much better known in the United States than she is.

What kinds of stories are you drawn to? Any you steer clear of?

I think "experimental fiction" is a synonym for "Give me a break," and I've never been able to warm to sci-fi. Other than that, I'm an omnivore.

What books might we be surprised to find on your shelves?

A pretty full set of Georgette Heyer. Which, by the way, no one should find surprising. Literary snobbery has it that Heyer wrote standard-issue bodice rippers, but the truth is, her Regency novels are well-crafted escapism, potato chips for the soul. If you liked *Downton Abbey*, you will love Georgette Heyer.

Do you ever read self-help? Anything you recommend?

I have many poetry collections—that's my version of self-help. Yeats, Robert Lowell, W. S. Merwin. Most of my books have a poem as an epigram to guide me; the most recent one starts with "Late Fragment," the poem Raymond Carver has on his headstone. Not enough people read poetry.

What's the best book you've ever received as a gift?

One of the first copies of *Heavy Metal and You*, by Christopher Krovatin.

What book has had the greatest impact on you?

Oh, such a Miss America answer: the Bible. I grew up Catholic, and it's hard to separate the New Testament from all my aspirations, inspiration, and political positions. I'm a liberal because of the Sermon on the Mount.

If you could require the president to read one book, what would it be?

The Best and the Brightest, by David Halberstam. Smart people make bad decisions about policy and then compound them by refusing to admit they were wrong. I wish George W. Bush had read it before invading Iraq.

Did you grow up with a lot of books? What are your memories of being read to as a child?

We had a family friend who owned hundreds of books and had them set up on shelves, library style, in her basement. She is the person who introduced me to *A Girl of the Limberlost*, *Anne of Green Gables*, and the Betsy-Tacy series. I used to go down those steps as though I was entering the US Mint.

Do you have a favorite childhood literary character or hero?

Jo March in *Little Women*. She wanted to be a writer, she became a writer. She stopped caring that she wasn't pretty. She sold her hair to send her mother to visit their father during the Civil War. I even forgave her for not marrying Laurie.

What books are on your coffee table?

Stephen Sondheim's two-volume memoir/writing primer/musical theater guide, *Finishing the Hat* and *Look, I Made a Hat*. I listen to Sondheim all the time while I'm writing.

Disappointing, overrated, just not good: What book did you feel you were supposed to like, and didn't? Do you remember the last book you put down without finishing?

There are books you outgrow and shouldn't revisit. Let them remain frozen in the amber of adolescence. *The Catcher in the Rye* seems genius when you're fifteen, and when you're thirty-five—not so much. I thought Ayn Rand was amazing when I was in high school, and now the only thing I find amazing is that I ever felt that way. As for the putting down part, I think I will pass. No less an eminence than Philip Roth has told us that writing is frustrating and humiliating. No one needs to be humiliated further by reading in the *Times* that someone chucked her book after three chapters.

If you could meet any writer, dead or alive, who would it be? What would you want to know?

That way lies disaster. Books are writers' way of becoming something else, something more, something greater. It might be that dinner with Dickens would be a disappointment. I've met some living writers who were just like their books, wonderfully, and others who ruined their books for me by being pompous and self-obsessed.

If you could meet any character from literature, who would it be?

Elizabeth Bennet. We would be buds for sure, power-walking the grounds of Pemberley. And I would get to hang out with Darcy.

What do you plan to read next?

There's a new Kate Atkinson!

Jonathan Franzen

What's the best book you read in the last year?

I loved Rachel Kushner's *Flamethrowers*. I also have to mention Mario Vargas Llosa's *War of the End of the World* and Milan Kundera's *Unbearable Lightness of Being*.

Describe your ideal reading experience (when, where, what, how).

The book creates the experience. If I'm loving something, I suddenly discover large chunks of reading time that I wasn't aware of having. But I will say there's nothing like being stuck in a middle seat on a long flight that begins with a two-hour delay. In a situation like that, a few years ago, I'd brought along a new novel that critics were wild about and that I was certain I would enjoy. It was so boring and dead that after fifty pages I just closed it and stared at the seat-back tray and suffered, resenting the author and psychoanalyzing the critics. Conversely, on an even worse pair of flights, from Zagreb to New York by way of two London airports, I'd carefully saved *The Custom of the Country*, and it kept me engrossed the entire way. I finished it in the taxi line at JFK, feeling bottomlessly grateful to Edith Wharton.

What German authors are you currently reading?

I'm reading the extremely funny Thomas Brussig, who unfortunately isn't translated into English. Last year I was reading Karl Kraus for the translations of his work that I'm publishing in the fall. Kraus was Viennese, but his language, of course, was German.

Jonathan Franzen is the author of *Freedom* and *The Corrections*, among other books.

Are there particular kinds of stories you're drawn to? Any you steer clear of?

I like fiction by writers engaged in trying to make sense of their lives and of the world in which they find themselves, writers who palpably have skin in the game, and this makes me particularly resistant to historical fiction. And yet some of my all-time favorite novels are historical—*The Greenlanders* (Jane Smiley), *The Blue Flower* (Penelope Fitzgerald), and *War and Peace*. It took some perseverance to get into *The War of the End of the World*, which is about the brutal suppression of a rebellion in late-nineteenth-century Brazil, but once I was into it I was harrowed as I've been by few other novels. The suffering and violence and death in it became, in a sense, my own. I thought it was magnificent.

Do you ever read self-help? Anything you recommend?

I guess we shouldn't count Freud, although I have felt helped by him. I also remember feeling helped, at least momentarily, by Harriet Lerner's *Dance of Anger* at a dark moment in my early thirties. It's the rare self-help book that acknowledges the true difficulty of helping the self.

What's the best book you've ever received as a gift?

A copy of *Libra*, with a nice inscription, that Don DeLillo sent me in 1989. I must have asked my publisher to send him a finished copy of my first novel; there's no way to explain the gift otherwise. But after spending my twenties working in near-total isolation and revering DeLillo from afar, I couldn't believe that I had something signed to me in his own human hand. At some level, I still can't believe it.

What's the best thing about writing a book?

The meaning it temporarily lends to my existence.

The hardest or least enjoyable part?

The years of doubting whether I actually have another story to tell.

If you could require the president to read one book, what would it be?

I wouldn't presume to require our current president to read anything, but the Vargas Llosa novel wouldn't have been a bad choice for our previous president, who I suspect could have used some help in imagining the human costs of righteous wars. Nor would *The Flamethrowers*—which, among other things, gives a subtly damning view of a powerful man through the eyes of the ambitious but pliable young woman he sleeps with—have been a bad choice for the president before that.

Did you grow up with a lot of books? What are your memories of being read to as a child?

I grew up going to the public library every week and coming home with stacks of books—my parents weren't readers, didn't have time to be. But my father read books to me every weeknight evening he was home. My mother never read to me, even when he was away on business. I wonder if she recognized that reading was the primary private thing that he and I had together.

Do you have a favorite childhood literary character or hero?

As with a lot of writers of my generation, it's Harriet the Spy. My recollection is that her creator, Louise Fitzhugh, died in her forties. Did she have any idea how many young people decided to be writers after reading her two books about Harriet? I hope she had at least an inkling.

What books are on your coffee table?

I admit that I have a coffee table and that there are books on the lower tier of it. Books of bird photographs, catalogs of painters I like (Anne Neely, Lisa Sanditz), a book of photographs of exurban sprawl. I wish I could say that I'd ever seen a guest reach down and pick one up.

Disappointing, overrated, just not good: What book did you feel as if you were supposed to like, and didn't? Do you remember the last book you put down without finishing?

Most books I pick up I put down without finishing, either because the writing is weak or feels false, or because I sense an absence of skin in the game. I picked up *The Unbearable Lightness of Being* more or less to make sure that it was as overrated as I suspected. I'd always hated the title, and I was sore with Kundera for his public rejection of Dostoyevsky, many years ago. Kundera is a committed rationalist, which is generally a big handicap for a novelist, and it's true that even the dreams in *Unbearable* are given rational readings. But they're still great dreams, and the character who has them, Tereza, is rendered with gorgeous sympathy. I wouldn't have guessed that a love story so well analyzed philosophically could be so moving in the end.

If you could meet any writer, dead or alive, who would it be? What would you want to know?

I wish I could have been present when Kafka read *The Metamorphosis* aloud to his friends, who couldn't stop laughing. The humor is still there in the text, but I would love to know what he did with his voice.

If you could meet any character from literature, who would it be?

One of Shakespeare's comic heroines, probably Rosalind, although trying to talk to her in iambic pentameter would be a strain.

What are you planning to read next?

For the past twenty years or so I've been planning to read the final four volumes of *In Search of Lost Time* next.

Hilary Mantel

What's the best book you read in the last year?

The term "best" would have to stretch. There's reading that's important to me, in a personal way: I've been working my way through the books of the psychologist Alice Miller, which are short and very easy to read but disturbing in implication: so, two hours reading, a lifetime of thinking over the content. "Best" as simply enjoyable would be Kate Atkinson's new novel, *Life After Life*, ingenious and furiously energetic: it's exhilarating to see a novelist at the top of her game. There's rereading, very important to me now. Last year I was commissioned to write an introduction to Keith Thomas's *Religion and the Decline of Magic*, and it gave me a reason to sit down with it again. It's a monumental book, yet with a living treasure on every page, and probably the book that, in my whole life, I've pressed on other people most energetically. (Selected people, of course. They have to care for history, and they need a sense of wonder and a sense of fun.)

Describe your ideal reading experience (when, where, what, how).

I'd like to be at home, in my apartment by the sea in Devon, just a few yards from the waves, sitting in the sunshine by a window, smiling, and picking up some vast immersive novel, like Sarah Waters's *Fingersmith*: a book which, when it was new, I read as if I were a child, utterly thrilled and beguiled by it. In my ideal reading day there would be no time limit, no

---

Hilary Mantel is the author of twelve books, including the novels *Wolf Hall* and *Bring Up the Bodies* and the short story collection *The Assassination of Margaret Thatcher*.

e-mails stacking up, and dinner would appear on a floating tablecloth, as if brought by spirit hands. In practice, this never happens. I read in snatched hours on trains, or late at night, or purposively and on a schedule, with pen in hand and a frown of concentration. But when I think harder . . . my ideal reading experience would involve time travel. I'd be fourteen, and in my hand would be the orange tickets that admitted to the adult section of the public library. Everything would be before me, and I would be ignorant of the shabby little compromises that novelists make, and I would be unaware that many nonfiction books are just rehashes of previous books by other writers. My eyes would be fresh. I would be chasing glory.

In addition to your novels, you've also written a memoir. What makes a good memoir? Any recent memoirs you would recommend?

It's not recent, but I would recommend *Bad Blood*, by Lorna Sage. It's a memoir of childhood and private life that has an almost eerie immediacy. When I was reading it, I felt as if the author were talking to me: and I talked back (at least, in my head). Memoir's not an easy form. It's not for beginners, which is unfortunate, as it is where many people do begin. It's hard for beginners to accept that unmediated truth often sounds unlikely and unconvincing. If other people are to care about your life, art must intervene. The writer has to negotiate with her memories, and with her reader, and find a way, without interrupting the flow, to caution that this cannot be a true record: this is a version, seen from a single viewpoint. But she has to make it as true as she can. Writing a memoir is a process of facing yourself, so you must do it when you are ready.

Are there particular kinds of stories you're drawn to? Any you steer clear of?

Sad to say, I do like a bit of action. I get impatient with love; I want fighting. I don't like overrefinement, or to dwell in the heads of vaporous ladies with fine sensibilities. (Though I love Jane Austen because she's so shrewdly practical: you can hear the chink of cash in every paragraph.) I can take the marginally magical, but I find realism more fascinating and challenging; it is a challenge for me to pay attention to surfaces, not depths. I like novels about the past, not about the future. For light reading I like novels about the present, but consider them to be an extension of newspapers.

What books might we be surprised to find on your shelves?

Stacks of books on cricket. I am fascinated by its history. It's a story told in match statistics, but it's also bred some stylish prose. My head is full of the ghosts of men in white playing games that were over before the Great War.

Do you ever read self-help? Anything you recommend?

I'm a self-help queen, dedicated to continuous improvement. I read books about problems I don't have, just in case I develop obsessive-compulsive disorder or crippling phobias. Of course there's nothing I recommend. If I ever found anything useful, I'd keep it to myself, to steal a mean advantage.

What's the best book you've ever received as a gift?

When I was nine, I was given a set of slightly abridged classics for Christmas, and the same again when I was ten. My mother got them from a mail-order catalog. We weren't a household that owned many books so it was a novelty to fill a whole shelf. There were plain cloth bindings and no pictures. (That's just the way I like it; I make my own pictures, thanks.) That's when I became enthralled by Robert Louis Stevenson, and failed to like Dickens, and met the Brontës. They were clever abridgments, too, as I came to realize when I read the full texts later. (Imagine, *Jane Eyre* without the embarrassing bits.)

What book has had the greatest impact on you?

I'm sorry if it sounds pious, unoriginal, and smug, but no book has mattered to me as much as the dirt-cheap *Complete Works of Shakespeare* I laid my hands on when I was ten. Previously I'd only read one scene from *Julius Caesar* that I found in an ancient schoolbook. It definitely qualified as the best thing I'd ever read, and I almost exploded with joy when I found there was a whole fat book of plays. I was a strange child.

What's the best thing about writing a book?

The moment, at about the three-quarter point, where you see your way right through to the end: as if lights had flooded an unlit road. But the pleasure is double-edged, because from this point you're going to work inhuman hours, not caring about your health or your human relationships; you're just going to head down that road like a charging bull.

The hardest or least enjoyable part?

I have to take a deep breath before I start the first full revision. I used to hate myself for procrastinating, but now I see it might be wise. You need to pause in holy fear at what you've done, and make sure you don't wreck it in panic.

What are your memories of being read to as a child?

My family had scant formal education, but I was lucky enough to be the only child in a three-generation household, with aunts and grown-up cousins next door. So lots of people were willing to read to me. I had the capacity to remember by heart what I heard, as if I were a throwback to a preliterate age, and so I was lazy about learning for myself because I had slaves to read for me, and I could say the passages over when I pleased. They had to read me tales of King Arthur and the Knights of the Round Table. I didn't really like anything else. It meant that by the time I went to school I had a bizarre vocabulary and a limited but martial outlook.

Do you have a favorite childhood literary character or hero?

Once I'd banished King Arthur, and I was nine or ten, the characters I lived through were the two leading men in *Kidnapped*, the strait-laced young David Balfour and the weathered desperado Alan Breck. The lessons I learned through David were that you had to leave home, go out into the world, and become your own man; and you must not despise any unlikely role models you might meet. I didn't find any similar story to teach me about being a woman.

What books are on your coffee table?

There's never anything on my table except the newspapers. I am addicted to them and read the fat Sunday supplements all through the week. I just like the stories, I don't mind if they're stale. I admire the indefatigable columnists, and yet I take a malicious pleasure in watching them struggle to get eight hundred words out of two bald facts and one unoriginal opinion.

Disappointing, overrated, just not good: What book did you feel you were supposed to like, and didn't? Do you remember the last book you put down without finishing?

I have a block about Dickens. I know I'm missing something great; everybody says so. But I didn't take to him as a child, and I can't stand his moralizing and his crass sentimentality, and the galumping humor that's sentimental too. I'm not so fond of George Eliot as I might be, perhaps because in Africa I had to teach *Silas Marner* to a class of teenagers with basic English; I kept wanting to apologize for it. And I'm still working on Henry James; at the moment I prefer William and Alice, but I think I'll like Henry by and by. I believe it's fine to give up books even after a page; there's so much to read in the world that will delight you, so why should you work against the grain? With a widely admired author you should persist, and you should always return to authors who puzzle you; maybe time needs to pass. I tried Ivy Compton-Burnett when I was twenty, and it didn't take. I thought, "She can't actually write." I came back six years later, and couldn't stop reading her; no twentieth-century novelist is closer to my heart.

If you could meet any writer, dead or alive, who would it be? What would you want to know?

Old Daddy Shakespeare, of course. I don't believe in asking writers questions. I'd just follow him about for a day and see what the routine was. I'd be invisible, of course. I wouldn't want to spook him.

What are you planning to read next?

As I have reached the stage in life where I assume the role of parent to my aged parent, I've been thinking a lot about families and have just started reading Andrew Solomon's *Far from the Tree*. Next I'm going to read Francis Spufford's *Unapologetic: Why, Despite Everything, Christianity Can Still Make Surprising Emotional Sense.*

The *Guide to Getting It On!* seems like it would have something to offer anyone, although if Obama's singing is any indication he's got it covered.—**Lena Dunham**

One of mine. Preferably on a day when he gets asked a really awkward question at a press conference he'd rather not answer. So he'd distract them by going, "The economy? Bombing Iran? Wall Street? You know . . . I read this really great book the other day by Neil Gaiman. Has anyone here read it? *American Gods*? I mean, that scene at the end of chapter one . . . What the heck was going on there?"—**Neil Gaiman**

A book of mine. What else? What am I, an altruist? He can choose which one.—**Richard Ford**

The Monkey Wrench Gang, by Edward Abbey. It would definitely transport Obama out of the Beltway. —**Carl Hiaasen**

I'm sure the president has read James Baldwin, but he may have missed *Giovanni's Room*—a short novel of immeasurable sadness. That is the novel he should read—or reread, as the case may be—because it will strengthen his resolve to do everything in his power for gay rights, and to assert that gay rights are a civil rights issue.—**John Irving**

For the sake of the general good, I'd have him absorbed in poetry. What would suit him well, I believe, is the work of James Fenton.—**Ian McEwan**

I would give them a kindergarten teacher's manual and let them know, "You're going to need this when you deal with Congress."—**Arnold Schwarzenegger**

It would be Niccolò Machiavelli, *The Prince*. Machiavelli is frequently dismissed today as an amoral cynic who supposedly considered the end to justify the means. In fact, Machiavelli is a crystal clear realist who understands the limits and uses of power. Every president (and all of us nonpoliticians as well) should read Machiavelli and incorporate his thinking.—**Jared Diamond**

Whatever it is, I am sure he has read it. Maybe something like *Middlemarch*, just to take his mind off things and remind him that "the growing good of the world is partly dependent on unhistoric acts; and that things are not so ill with you and me as they might have been, is half owing to the number who lived faithfully a hidden life, and rest in unvisited tombs."—**Caroline Kennedy**

It would behoove the president to read *Random Family*, Adrian Nicole LeBlanc's searing masterpiece of relentless close-up journalism. No other book I've read charts so clearly the trajectory of poverty and its corrosive compulsions. It's impossible to read it and not become a more empathetic person. The president could use its lessons on the quadrant of society that we've largely abandoned.—**Andrew Solomon**

The new Lee Child, of course! It might be nice for him to escape for a few hours to a world where one man can solve every one of the world's problems with nothing but his wits and his fists.—**Malcolm Gladwell**

Walter Mosley

When and where do you like to read?

I like to read either in motion or in water. And so I am most satisfied reading on subway cars, trains, planes, ferries, boats, or floating on some kind of air-filled device or raft in a pool, pond, or lake. But I am happiest reading in the bathtub; lying back with my head resting on the curved end of the tub, one leg bent and the other resting along the edge. Now and then I add a little hot water with a circular motion of my toe. I decided on my apartment because it had a deep tub with water jets to massage me while I read science fiction and magical realism.

Are you a rereader?

Reading is rereading just as writing is rewriting. Any worthwhile book took many, many drafts to reach completion, and so it would make sense that the first time the reader works her way through the volume it's more like a first date than a one-time encounter. If the person was uninteresting (not worthwhile) there's no need for a repeat performance, but if they have promise, good humor, hope, or just good manners, you might want to have a second sit-down, a third. There might be something irksome about that rendezvous that makes you feel that you have something to work out. There might be a hint of eroticism suggesting the possibility of a tryst or even marriage.

The joy of reading is in the rereading; this is where you get to know the world and characters in deep and rewarding fashion.

Walter Mosley is the author of many books, including the Easy Rawlins mysteries series, which started with *Devil in a Blue Dress*.

What makes a good mystery novel?

This question deserves examination. I could answer by saying that in a good mystery there's a crime and a cast of characters, any of whom may or may not have committed that crime. Readers have their suspicions, but most often they are wrong—if not about the perpetrator then about the underlying reason(s) for the commission of said crime. In a very good mystery, the detective comes into question and the investigator is forced to face his, or her, own prejudices, expectations, and limitations. In a great mystery, we find that the crime being investigated reveals a deeper rot.

But this answer only addresses, finally, the technical execution of the mystery. A good mystery has to be a good novel, and any good novel takes us on a journey where we discover, on many levels, truths about ourselves and our world in ways that are, at the same time, unexpected and familiar. If the mystery writer gives us a good mystery without a good novel to back it up, then she, or he, has failed.

It once seemed the Easy Rawlins mysteries might be a thing of the past, but you decided to revisit?

This month, I have a new Easy Rawlins mystery out; the title is *Little Green*. It's the first one since *Blonde Faith* (2007). I had to take some years away from the series because my writing about Easy was becoming, well . . . too easy. I needed to rebuild the fires under that continuing story about the black Southern migrant who re-created himself in the California sun.

There is now, I believe, something new about Easy in a world that is both familiar and transformational.

Do you plan to write more nonfiction?

Yes. The change of century is a challenging moment for the world. We have to face our deepest fears and prejudices in order to save the human race and the planet we inhabit. We have to encourage strange bedfellows and forgive many trespasses.

Science and religion, capitalism and socialism, caste and character are all on the auction block. The waters are rising while we are dreaming of dancing with the stars. We call ourselves social creatures when indeed we are pack animals. We, many of us, say that we are middle class when in reality we are salt-of-the-earth working-class drones existing at the whim of systems that distribute our life's blood as so much spare change.

These subjects can be addressed in fiction or plays, even in poetry, but now and again the plain talk of nonfiction is preferred.

Which books might we be surprised to find on your shelves?

Because I don't know who's reading these words or who has asked the question, I cannot say with any accuracy what you might find surprising, but I just went to my shelf and jotted down a few titles.

There's *The Third Policeman*, by Flann O'Brien. This writer, I believe, is one of the great twentieth-century wordsmiths. He is filled with humor and insight without the slightest hint of arrogance or elevation.

The Popular Educator Library is a series of hundreds of essays in ten volumes designed to provide the essence of a college education for those who were not able to attend college. Published in the late 1930s, this book covers everything from accounting to the principles of aviation. Cool.

Collingwood's *Principles of History* is the quintessential book on history and perception; of how we might imagine that which is impossible to know. *The City in History*, by Lewis Mumford, shows us how human organization, technology, and technique form us in ways that we are completely unaware of. *Bitch Reloaded*, by Deja King, is a perfect example of what they call street lit. I like it because it allows me to understand all the ways that people, all kinds of people, come to reading. It's not just college professors, librarians, and convicts. People on the street are reading, looking for themselves in books that want to tell the stories that history will inevitably wash over and forget.

Where do you get your books?

I find books in used-book stores, chain and independent stores, on friends' shelves, and being read by some woman sitting opposite me on the subway. I find books the way a cow finds a new pasture, by looking to see where the other cows are headed.

I find books on the Internet and in overheard conversations at restaurants. And, more and more, I find books in my memory; an author's name that some professor (whose name I have now forgotten) mentioned in a seminar, the topic of which I no longer remember. I remember the writer's name, and sometime later a title comes to mind. After a few days I connect the author's name and the title. It's a small step from there to reading happily on the Staten Island Ferry.

What were your favorite books as a child?

I know that as a working writer I should answer this question in such a way as to make me seem intelligent; maybe Twain or Dickens, even Hesse or Conrad. I should say that I read intelligent books far beyond my years. This

I believe would give intelligent readers the confidence to go out and lay down hard cash for my newest, and the one after that.

But the truth is that the most beloved and the most formative books of my childhood were comic books, specifically Marvel Comics. Fantastic Four and Spider-Man, The Mighty Thor and The Invincible Iron Man; later came Daredevil and many others. These combinations of art and writing presented to me the complexities of character and the pure joy of imagining adventure. They taught me about writing dialect and how a monster can also be a hero. They lauded science and fostered the understanding that the world was more complex than any one mind, or indeed the history of all human minds, could comprehend.

Which novels had the most impact on you as a writer?

I am one of those rare writers (at least I believe this to be true) who do not equate reading and writing in any kind of direct way. I know for a fact that the father of the Western tradition of the novel, Homer, was illiterate. Many of the storytellers and poets of the West were not schooled in letters. The founder of one of the world's great religions, Siddhartha Gautama Buddha, created a religion in an environment where no one wrote. The scriptures had to be submitted to memory only to be written down long after.

I'm not sure that any novels (or comic books) had an impact on me as far as me becoming a writer. I love many novels. *One Hundred Years of Solitude* is beautiful, as is *L'Assommoir*, by Émile Zola. *Cotton Comes to Harlem* is a dazzling book, and when I was very young *Winnie-the-Pooh* enchanted me.

My father once told me, when I was a child, that he had written, when he was young, a cowboy story. He sent this story to a Chicago publisher, who never responded. But a year later he saw that story, attributed to a different author, in a magazine that the same company published. He told me that he learned from this experience that he could never be a writer, at least not a published one. This was a tragic story that burrowed down into my subconscious mind. If anything, it is this story that most influenced me becoming a writer.

What does your personal book collection look like?

I am proud to say that I give away or sell at little to no profit almost all of my books. I have mentioned a few favorites earlier, but as a rule I don't believe in keeping books. After I have read, reread, and reread a book it seems sinful to keep such a reservoir of fun and knowledge fallow on a shelf. Books are meant to be read, and if I'm not reading them then someone else should get the opportunity.

What writer would you like to meet?

I mentioned him earlier—Homer. The Bard, being blind and the speaker of an ancient language, would pose a delicious challenge. This is the kind of challenge that any good novel would present. I'd love, after traversing the gulf of communication, to find out what he believed he was doing. I say this because writers, after a while, become fictions themselves. They are, at once, influential and lost to us. Meeting Homer on some Attic beach, next to an open fire, accompanied by whatever servant or wife helped him move from town to town, sounds like the ideal novelist's vacation.

What do you plan to read next?

I've been thinking that it's time to reread *The Autumn of the Patriarch*.

When my brother and I had dinner alone as children, we used to play a guessing game based on the titles in the bookshelves in the dining room. That's how we learned the names of Winston Churchill's forty books without actually reading them. My father used to make up elaborate bedtime stories in which I was the central character, and my mother used to read to me at bedtime.—**Caroline Kennedy**

I remember once going to a neighbor's house and they had a TV tuned to a show called *Lost in Space*. I watched it and then ran home as fast as I could to tell my mother all about it, but she stopped me soon after I started, saying that the show was simple-minded claptrap. If I was really interested in science fiction, she said, she had a treat for me. Then she pulled out a collection of Ray Bradbury short stories and started reading them. Even then, I had to admit that the writing was actually superior to the *Lost in Space* episode I'd just seen, but at the time I didn't realize how lucky I was.—**Jeannette Walls**

My sister and I made weekly trips to the Exeter Public Library and returned carrying armloads of our favorites— Dr. Seuss, Richard Scarry, Curious George, Madeline, and Babar. As we got older, I remember my parents reading to us every night—*Make Way for Ducklings*, *The Velveteen Rabbit*, and Maurice Sendak's *Chicken Soup with Rice*, which I preferred to his entirely terrifying *Where the Wild Things Are* (the notion of a child's bedroom transforming into a monster-infested jungle made it impossible to sleep).—**Dan Brown**

Black Beauty, by Anna Sewell, remains a star-dusted memory, because my mom read it aloud to my sister and me at night for months. I was no more than seven.—**Scott Turow**

Grimms' fairy tales. My favorite was "The Bremen Town Musicians," about a dog, cat, donkey, and rooster, all over the hill, who learn that they are about to be discarded or worse. They decide to take matters into their own hands. I made my mother and grandmother read it to me so often that I could recite the whole story word for word.—**Sylvia Nasar**

I didn't read the canon of classic children's books, at least not until I became a father and read to my own children. No doubt this was because my parents were new to the country and not comfortable speaking English and didn't read to me at night. I didn't speak English myself until the first grade. I read lots of books in elementary school—I remember winning a prize for reading the most books one year— but I can't recall a single title.—**Chang-rae Lee**

When I was five, I read *The Wonderful Adventures of Nils and the Wild Geese*, by Selma Lagerlof. It was so inspiring I wrote my own version called *Lenin and His Magical Goose*, a hundred-page tome about Lenin encountering a socialist goose and conquering Finland together. It was commissioned by my grandmother, who paid for each page with a block of Soviet cheese. Even today, Random House pays me in cheese.
—**Gary Shteyngart**

Supposedly I went into my room with *Alice in Wonderland*, which was given to me when I was five, and didn't come out until I was done. I was an early reader but I don't think that says much. Having a child and being around them, it's apparent to me that there's some kind of clock that goes off at different times for different kids. Mine went off early, and I didn't like to sleep. So my mother let me stay up as late as I wanted looking at books, and she says I stayed up all night doing that starting at age three. My best years are way behind me.
—**Rachel Kushner**

Khaled Hosseini

What's your favorite book of all time?

The collected *Poems of Hafez*, also called *Divan-e-Hafez*. Revered in the Persian-speaking world, Hafez is, for me, the supreme Persian poet. His verses of philosophy, mystical love, and bold anti-establishment statements are filled with luxuriant images and magical rhythms that always enchant me. His heartfelt *ghazals* have never failed to move me, and still do today as they did when I read them as a schoolboy.

Describe your ideal reading experience.

The only two places where I can read for long stretches are in airplanes and in bed at nighttime. I read actual physical books and have thus far avoided the electronic lure.

Who are your favorite novelists?

J. M. Coetzee, Jennifer Egan, Hemingway, Elizabeth Strout, Jhumpa Lahiri, Dave Eggers, Ian McEwan, David Foster Wallace, Junot Díaz, Kurt Vonnegut, Alice Munro (I know, she writes short stories, but many of them have the arc of condensed novels).

What books would you recommend about Afghanistan?

West of Kabul, East of New York, by Tamim Ansary; *Opium Nation*, by Fariba Nawa; *The Punishment of Virtue*, by Sarah Chayes; *The Sewing Circles of Herat*, by Christina Lamb; *The Patience Stone*, by Atiq Rahimi; *The Places in Between*, by Rory Stewart; *An Unexpected Light*, by Jason Elliot.

Khaled Hosseini is the author of *The Kite Runner, A Thousand Splendid Suns*, and *And the Mountains Echoed*.

You practiced medicine for more than ten years. What has your training and experience as a doctor brought to your work as a writer?

Qualities you need to get through medical school and residency: Discipline. Patience. Perseverance. A willingness to forgo sleep. A penchant for sado-masochism. Ability to weather crises of faith and self-confidence. Accept exhaustion as fact of life. Addiction to caffeine a definite plus. Unfailing optimism that the end is in sight.

Qualities you need to be a novelist: Ditto.

Who is your favorite overlooked or underappreciated writer?

I don't think she is underappreciated, certainly not among writers, but Alice Munro is the classic underappreciated writer among readers. It is almost a cliché now to wonder why this living legend is not more widely read.

What kinds of stories are you drawn to? Any you steer clear of?

I love just about any kind of story as long as it is well told, makes an emotional impact, and holds an elusive sense of mystery. That said, it has been many years since I've read fantasy or science fiction.

What books might we be surprised to find on your shelves?

A collection of Tintin comics. *Why Do Men Have Nipples? World War Z. I'm a Lebowski, You're a Lebowski: Life, The Big Lebowski, and What Have You.* This last book comes, needless to say, with a recipe for a White Russian and is indispensable for fans of the cult classic. But that's just like my opinion, man.

What's the best book you've ever received as a gift?

My father gave me a Farsi translation of *White Fang* when I was a boy in Kabul circa mid-1970s.

What book has had the greatest impact on you?

It has been years since I last read it, but the first time I did, in high school, *The Grapes of Wrath* really registered with me. Something about the struggles of the desperate migrant workers reminded me of the struggling people in my homeland of Afghanistan. When I visit Afghanistan now and meet displaced families moving from region to region on foot, trying to find work, home, a place to settle, I still think of Steinbeck's masterpiece. And the final scene, Rose of Sharon breast-feeding the stranger, is one that still moves me deeply.

If you could require the president to read one book, what would it be?

I think this particular president is already a well-read man, thank God, and needs no reading recs from me.

Did you grow up with a lot of books? What are your memories of being read to as a child?

I grew up around a lot of Rumi, Hafez, and Omar Khayyám books. My parents in Kabul had all the volumes around the house. No one ever really read to me as a child. I was told bedtime stories by my father or my grandmother. Books, I mostly read on my own in bed.

Do you have a favorite childhood literary character or hero?

The tragic Sohrab, the great warrior from Ferdowsi's eleventh-century *Shahnameh* (*The Book of Kings*), one of the crown jewels of classic Persian poetry. Sohrab is the son of the great warrior Rostam, though the two have never met. Sohrab sets out with an army to bring glory to his father and win him the crown, only to come face-to-face with him in battle. The last scene of that particular story, Rostam holding Sohrab's dying body, moments after he has learned the true identity of the man he has mortally wounded with his own sword, is unparalleled in the emotional wallop it packs.

Disappointing, overrated, just not good: What book did you feel you were supposed to like, and didn't? Do you remember the last book you put down without finishing?

A number of them, of course. But I am a nice guy. Ah, let's call it what it is: I'm a coward. OK, I'll say it: *The Catcher in the Rye.* There.

If you could meet any writer, dead or alive, who would it be?

I would download a video of a typical debate of creationism versus evolution in public education, and then I would time-travel to the nineteenth century and play the clip for Charles Darwin. Show him what he started. And then I would watch for his reaction.

If you could meet any character from literature, who would it be?

Dr. Manhattan from Watchmen.

What do you plan to read next?

Maya's Notebook, by Isabel Allende.

Favorite Characters and Literary Heroes

Toni Morrison (*The Bluest Eye*) got me out of bed, Richard Wright (*Black Boy*) got me to school on the bus, but Harper Lee (*To Kill a Mockingbird*) helped me sleep at night.
—**James McBride**

Jane Eyre remains a favorite. Her truthfulness sometimes made me laugh. And her loneliness and need to make her own way mirrored my feelings.
—**Amy Tan**

Prince Andrei Bolkonsky, of course. Sebastian Flyte. I suffered under the misapprehension that I was an Old World aristocrat manqué, rather than a middle-class, striving, and slightly affected New Yorker descended from peasants.
—**Andrew Solomon**

For years I admired Morris West from afar. Then I met him briefly at a cocktail party. His agent, a personal friend of mine, called the next morning: "Mary, where did you go? After the cocktails, Morris said, 'Let's collect Mary Clark and go to dinner.'" I wanted to kill myself. I had slipped away to a teacher's retirement dinner.
—**Mary Higgins Clark**

John Updike's Harry Angstrom, a.k.a. Rabbit, who gropes toward personal grace through four novels only to whiff in the end. After I finished *Rabbit at Rest*, I wrote Updike a fan letter telling him that I didn't understand how he found the strength to get up every day to write a book so sad, especially about a character whom Updike knew and revealed with such amazing intimacy. It was like sending a dear friend to the gallows. But Updike's intricate rendering of Rabbit over the course of thirty years is a profound achievement.
—**Scott Turow**

I tend to like the complicated antihero. Charlus, from Proust. Balzac's Vautrin. Bolaño's Hans Reiter/Archimboldi, in *2666*. Shrike, from *Miss Lonelyhearts*. The Judge from *Blood Meridian*. Recktall Brown from *The Recognitions*. If I could write a character like one of those? Well. I should be so lucky.
—**Rachel Kushner**

Jeannette Walls

What's your favorite book of all time?

The End of the Affair, by Graham Greene. It's such a beautiful story of the triumph of compassion over cynicism.

Describe your ideal reading experience (when, where, what, how).

I travel a lot, and having a good book on airplanes and in airports transforms tedium into treasured time. The other day, I was stuck at O'Hare for eight hours, but I had a pre-publication copy of a riveting memoir, *A House in the Sky*, by Amanda Lindhout, about being kidnapped in Somalia. A few of the other travelers were having loud hissy fits, complaining that we were being treated horribly, and I had to bite my tongue to keep from shouting out: "We got food and clean water! You all don't know how good we have it!"

Who are your favorite novelists?

Updike, Steinbeck, Balzac, and Mona Simpson.

Who is your favorite overlooked or underappreciated writer?

I feel a little uncomfortable answering this, because the author I'd choose is quite happy with his level of recognition. Who am I to say he should be more famous?

What kinds of stories are you drawn to? Any you steer clear of?

I love histories, biographies, and memoirs. I'm also drawn to realistic fiction. I'm not a huge fan of experimental fiction, fantasy, or so-called

---

Jeannette Walls is the author of books including *The Glass Castle*, *The Silver Star*, and *Half Broke Horses*.

escapist literature. Reality is just so interesting, why would you want to escape it?

Do you read a lot of memoirs? Any good ones recently, aside from Lindhout's?

I love memoirs. I devour them. *In the Sanctuary of Outcasts*, by Neil White; *The Memory Palace*, by Mira Bartok; *Denial*, by Jessica Stern; *A Long Way Gone*, by Ishmael Beah; *An Unquiet Mind*, by Kay Redfield Jamison; *Chanel Bonfire*, by Wendy Lawless; *The Center Cannot Hold*, by Elyn Saks; *After Visiting Friends*, by Michael Hainey; *The Kiss*, by Kathryn Harrison; *My Stroke of Insight*, by Jill Bolte Taylor; *Couldn't Keep It to Myself: Wally Lamb and the Women of York Correctional Institution*, edited by Wally Lamb. That's just a few. There are so many more.

What books might we be surprised to find on your shelves?

My vast collection of books on raising chickens. There's more to it than you'd think.

Do you ever read self-help? Anything you recommend?

The best self-help books, in my opinion, are memoirs. If people are honest about what happened to them, those stories are astonishing gifts to those of us grappling with—or just trying to understand—similar situations. I give away my memoirs like aspirins to friends who are going through tough times. Sometimes, it's easier to have perspective on someone else's life than your own.

What's the best book you've ever received as a gift?

Peter the Great, by Robert Massie. It kicked off my obsession with Russian history.

What book has had the greatest impact on you?

A Tree Grows in Brooklyn. I read it when I was ten years old and an outcast. Finding a "friend" like little Francie Nolan, who also was not very popular but also loved reading and her no-'count drunken dad, was a real revelation. I think it was the first time I experienced the incredible power of books.

If you could require the president to read one book, what would it be?

President Obama is a lot smarter than I am. I'm trying to keep up with his reading list.

Did you grow up with a lot of books? What are your memories of being read to as a child?

I was surrounded by books. There were times when art supplies and books were practically the only things in our house! We almost never had a television, but we always made regular pilgrimages to the library and came home with pillowcases filled with books. Sometimes, we even returned those books. I remember once going to a neighbor's house and they had a TV tuned to a show called *Lost in Space*. I thought it was wondrous. I watched it and then ran home as fast as I could to tell my mother all about it, but she stopped me soon after I started, saying that the show was simpleminded claptrap. If I was really interested in science fiction, she said, she had a treat for me. Then she pulled out a collection of Ray Bradbury short stories and started reading them. Even then, I had to admit that the writing was actually superior to the *Lost in Space* episode I'd just seen, but at the time I didn't realize how lucky I was.

Do you have a favorite childhood literary character or hero?

Horton. He's the one who heard a Who and hatched an egg. I was a big Dr. Seuss fan when I was very young—I had *The Sneetches* and *Horton Hatches the Egg* memorized before I started kindergarten, and much to the dismay of my friends, I can still recite big chunks of them.

What books are on your coffee table?

Remarkable Trees of Virginia, *The Smithsonian Book of Books*, and *Stanford White's New York*.

Disappointing, overrated, just not good: What book did you feel you were supposed to like, and didn't? Do you remember the last book you put down without finishing?

Finnegans Wake. Can't finish it. Just can't. It was required reading in one of my college classes, and I'm a pretty good crammer, so I'd planned on pulling an all-nighter, but I couldn't get past page twenty. I attributed it to lack of sleep and have tried several times since then—but fully awake, I couldn't get past page ten. If that makes me lowbrow, so be it.

If you could meet any writer, dead or alive, who would it be? What would you want to know?

Shakespeare, whoever he really was. My dad was among the conspiracy theorists who think that the guy from Stratford-on-Avon wasn't really the Bard. I've got a lot I'd like to ask this fellow.

If you could meet any character from literature, who would it be?

Tom Joad. I've had a schoolgirl crush on him since I read *The Grapes of Wrath* when I was eleven. (In my mind, he doesn't look a thing like Henry Fonda.)

What do you plan to read next?

Her, by Christa Parravani, and *Wave*, by Sonali Deraniyagala.

On Self-Help (Continued)

I don't read much self-help—that comes from talking to people or taking a hot bath. I do read historically oriented books about religion and faith like Edith Hamilton's *Witness to the Truth*, which I found in our apartment and had belonged to my mother; or Garry Wills's *What the Gospels Meant*, which I bought in an airport. I really enjoyed *God's Secretaries: The Making of the King James Bible*, by Adam Nicolson, and *The Cistercian World: Monastic Writings of the Twelfth Century*, which my daughter brought home from college.—**Caroline Kennedy**

I'm fascinated by books about time management and decluttering, which is akin to a person who weighs seven hundred pounds being fascinated by diet books. But the book I've truly been helped the most by is actually a parenting book called *Sleeping Through the Night: How Infants, Toddlers, and Their Parents Can Get a Good Night's Sleep*. It's by Jodi Mindell, a sleep researcher and psychology professor who's also a mom, and I swear by this book. It's clear, realistic, and neither excessively harsh nor ineffectively gentle. —**Curtis Sittenfeld**

My self-help books are generally restricted to cars. I started with John Muir's *How to Keep Your Volkswagen Alive* and now have the service manuals to most of the cars I've owned: 240 Volvo, Honda, Ford, etc. Jane Bryant Quinn's *Making the Most of Your Money* works for me, though she's not fond of cars. Several books on jazz arranging and technique, most notably Oliver Nelson's *Patterns for Improvisation*.—**James McBride**

I'm never clear on how "self-help" differs from "help." Books help; they've helped me to understand love, taught me empathy, and given me courage. Even when they merely entertain, they help. For a delicious analysis of the extremely unhelpful self-help industry, see Jessica Lamb-Shapiro's forthcoming *Promise Land*.—**Andrew Solomon**

A self-help book? Isn't that an oxymoron?—**Sting**

Dan Brown

What's your favorite book of all time?

We did not have a television while I was growing up, and so I read voraciously. My earliest memory of being utterly transfixed by a book was Madeleine L'Engle's *A Wrinkle in Time*. Halfway through the book, I remember my mom telling me it was time for bed and not being able to sleep because I was so deeply concerned for the safety of the characters. The next day, when I finished the book, I remember crying with relief that everything had worked out. The emotion startled me—in particular the depth of connection I felt toward these imaginary characters. It was in that moment that I became aware of the magic of storytelling and the power of the printed word.

Describe your ideal reading experience (when, where, what, how).

The most pleasurable reading experience I've had recently was just last week—jogging on the beach with an audiobook of Malcolm Gladwell's *What the Dog Saw*. I was so engrossed in his essay "The Ketchup Conundrum" that I ran an extra mile just to find out how it ended.

Who are your favorite novelists?

John Steinbeck for his vivid sense of place. Robert Ludlum for the complexity of his plotting. And J. K. Rowling for inspiring so many young people to be passionate about reading.

What kinds of stories are you drawn to? Any you steer clear of?

I read nonfiction almost exclusively—both for research and also for pleasure. When I read fiction, it's almost always in the thriller genre, and it

Dan Brown is the author of *The Da Vinci Code, Inferno, The Lost Symbol, Angels & Demons, Deception Point,* and *Digital Fortress*.

needs to rivet me in the opening few chapters. I don't read horror, ever. When I was fifteen, I made the mistake of reading part of *The Exorcist*. It was the first and last horror book I've ever opened.

What makes for a good thriller?

For me, a good thriller must teach me something about the real world. Thrillers like *Coma*, *The Hunt for Red October*, and *The Firm* all captivated me by providing glimpses into realms about which I knew very little—medical science, submarine technology, and the law. To my taste, a great thriller must also contain at its core a thought-provoking ethical debate or moral dilemma. Some of my favorites through the years have been *Memoirs of an Invisible Man*, by H. F. Saint; *Contact*, by Carl Sagan; and also the classic *Dracula*, by Bram Stoker, which, while skirting the edges of horror, was such a lesson in creating suspense that I couldn't put it down.

What books might we be surprised to find on your shelves?

I usually write about historical figures and classical art, so you might be surprised to find a host of modern biographies (Steve Jobs, Andre Agassi, Clive Davis), as well as a dozen books on modern art, especially the works of M. C. Escher.

Do you ever read self-help? Anything you recommend?

I don't read self-help, although I recently found myself helped inadvertently by reading *Moonwalking with Einstein*, which centers on the science of remembering. I picked up the book because I've always been interested in why some people have great memories and others (like myself) do not. Strangely, I discovered that simply reading about the methods used by memory champions helped me improve my own memory. Now at least I can remember where I left my glasses.

What's the best book you've ever received as a gift?

Not long ago, I had an amusing experience meeting the author of a book I received as a gift nearly two decades ago—a book that in many ways changed my life. Almost twenty years ago, I was halfway through writing my first novel, *Digital Fortress*, when I was given a copy of *Writing the Blockbuster Novel*, by the legendary agent Albert Zuckerman. His book helped me complete my manuscript and get it published. Two months ago, by chance, I met Mr. Zuckerman for the first time. I gratefully told him that he had helped me write *Digital Fortress*. He jokingly replied that he planned to tell everyone that he had helped me write *The Da Vinci Code*.

Did you grow up with a lot of books? What are your memories of being read to as a child?

I grew up surrounded by books. My sister and I made weekly trips to the Exeter Public Library and returned carrying armloads of our favorites—Dr. Seuss, Richard Scarry, Curious George, Madeline, and Babar. As we got older, I remember my parents reading to us every night—*Make Way for Ducklings*, *The Velveteen Rabbit*, and Maurice Sendak's *Chicken Soup with Rice*, which I preferred to his entirely terrifying *Where the Wild Things Are* (the notion of a child's bedroom transforming into a monster-infested jungle made it impossible to sleep). The poetry of Ogden Nash was another staple in our household, which I believe contributed to my early love of wordplay and humor in writing. On the more serious side, our bookshelves contained illustrated editions of Grimms' fairy tales and Aesop's fables, which instilled in me at a very young age a clear sense of good and evil as well as the archetypal roles of heroes and villains.

Do you have a favorite childhood literary character or hero?

Frank and Joe Hardy were responsible for my first experience in "binge reading." I remember devouring the entire Hardy Boys series over one summer, enthralled by their bravery and cleverness. I also remember feeling enormous affection for the St. Bernard Buck in Jack London's *Call of the Wild* and, in later years, Ralph in *Lord of the Flies*.

What books are on your coffee table?

It appears our coffee table is currently featuring a rather unlikely quartet—an antique edition of *The Divine Comedy* illustrated by William Blake; a copy of Stephen Hawking's *The Universe in a Nutshell*; a homemade photo journal of New England foliage; and a copy of *Mortality*, by Christopher Hitchens.

If you could meet any writer, dead or alive, who would it be?

Joseph Campbell. His writings on semiotics, comparative religion, and mythology (in particular *The Power of Myth* and *The Hero with a Thousand Faces*) helped inspire the framework on which I built my character Robert Langdon. The PBS interview series with Joseph Campbell and Bill Moyers was hands down the most thought-provoking conversation I've ever witnessed. Campbell's breadth of knowledge about the origins of religious belief enabled him to respond with clarity and logic to some very challenging questions about contradictions inherent in faith, religion, and scripture.

I remember admiring Campbell's matter-of-fact responses and wanting my own character Langdon to project that same respectful understanding when faced with complex spiritual issues.

What book did you feel you were supposed to like, and didn't?

The Sound and the Fury, by William Faulkner. I tried. I really did.

What do you plan to read next?

David and Goliath, by Malcolm Gladwell.

Dan Savage

If you had to name a favorite novelist, who would it be?

This question is unfair—to novelists, not to me. I mostly read nonfiction, typically history and biographies (I have dozens of books about the Second World War and dozens about the English Revolution, the Stuarts, James I and II, Charles I and II), so the size of my "favorite novelist" sample is tragically small. Gore Vidal's *Julian*, his historical novel about the last pagan emperor of Rome, and Mary Renault's *Persian Boy*, another historical novel, this one about a eunuch slave boy who falls in love with Alexander the Great after he conquers the Persian Empire, may be my two favorite novels. I've read them both at least four times each. But the last novels I read were Hilary Mantel's *Wolf Hall* and *Bring Up the Bodies*, both of which I enjoyed tremendously. So, let's just say that Mantel is my favorite living novelist?

Do you enjoy reading gay fiction? Any authors you'd especially recommend?

Again, I'm not really into fiction. But my husband is a huge Steven Saylor fan—a fan of the murder mysteries Saylor sets in ancient Rome and a fan of the racier/pornier stuff Saylor writes under the pen name Aaron Travis. There's a stack of Saylor's books on my night stand. Terry is insisting that I read some Saylor/Travis on vacation this year and not the book I had been planning to read—another book about Charles I (*The King's Peace: 1637–1641*, by C. V. Wedgwood). I "rescued" *The King's Peace* from the lobby of a hotel in Kansas City earlier this year. There was a wall of books with beige bindings, and it was right at eye level, calling out to me, begging to be read. I don't consider swiping a book that is being used as a decorative object to be

---

Dan Savage is the author of *It Gets Better, American Savage, Skipping Towards Gomorrah,* and *The Kid,* among other books.

theft. It's a rescue. The last really good piece of gay fiction that I read was Mark Merlis's *American Studies*.

What books might we be surprised to find on your shelves?

I have so many books about queens. Tragic queens (*Queen of Scots: The True Life of Mary Stuart*, by John Guy), murderous queens (*Queen Isabella: Treachery, Adultery, and Murder in Medieval England*, by Alison Weir), adulterous queens (*A Royal Affair: George III and His Scandalous Siblings*, by Stella Tillyard), beheaded queens (*The Wives of Henry VIII*, by Antonia Fraser), queens with poor personal hygiene (*The Trial of Queen Caroline: The Scandalous Affair That Nearly Ended a Monarchy*, by Jane Robins), and truly crazy queens (*The Mad King: A Biography of Ludwig II of Bavaria*, by Greg King). They're my beach reading. But there are no books by or about drag queens on my shelves—which is odd, since I was a drag queen in my formative years. People might also be surprised to find *Bless This Food: The Anita Bryant Family Cookbook* and *Aflame for God*, a biography of Jerry Falwell.

Do you ever read self-help? Anything you recommend?

I loved my mother very much, but she kind of ruined the self-help genre for me. She was big into self-help books—and religion—when I was a tween and a teen. Leo Buscaglia was right up there with Matthew, Mark, Luke, and John as far as my mom was concerned. Her collection of self-help books got her through some tough years (the end of her marriage, having four children between the ages of thirteen and sixteen at once), and she thought they could help me. I was her sensitive kid, I was a loner, and she sensed that I was unhappy. But I wasn't unhappy. I was closeted. The stress of keeping my sexuality secret from my siblings and parents was making me nuts. Once I came out, I was fine. But self-help titles drag me back to those unhappy days—my parents' divorce, my time in the closet—and leave me feeling more anxious, not less.

What book has had the greatest impact on you?

Strange as it sounds, the paperback edition of Mart Crowley's 1968 play *The Boys in the Band*. I shoplifted a copy—this was a petty theft, not a high-minded rescue—from Unabridged Bookstore in Chicago, where I grew up. Unabridged is a terrific independent bookstore in Chicago's gay neighborhood, and I was a closeted teenager who was too afraid to buy the book because what if the clerk knew someone who knew someone who knew my parents and it got back to my mom and dad that I bought a book about gay people? It's crazy, of course, but the closet makes you crazy. Gay people have all sorts of different feelings about that play. Yes, the guys are vicious, and there's a lot of drama and self-hatred on display. But *The Boys in the Band* gave me hope. These guys had friends, they had relationships, they had jobs and apartments. OK, some of them were vicious jerks—but lots of people are, right? I read that play and figured: "OK, one day I'll come out and I'll have lovers and friends. I'll just try to find better ones."

If you could require the president to read one book, what would it be?

End This Depression Now, by Paul Krugman.

If you could require all high school teachers to read one book, what would it be?

It seems self-serving, but all high-school and middle-school teachers should be required to read *It Gets Better: Coming Out, Overcoming Bullying, and Creating a Life Worth Living.* It's a collection of essays by contributors to the It Gets Better Project. Not all LGBT kids are miserable or being bullied, but for the ones who are—particularly the queer kids who are being bullied by homophobic or transphobic parents (and those kids are at the greatest risk)—school can either be a place of refuge or a place of additional torment. There are stories in the book by kids who were saved by something as seemingly trivial as a kind word or gesture from a single teacher.

If you could require all high school students to read one book, what would it be?

The same.

What books are in your kitchen?

Terry cooks, I clean, so the books in the kitchen are all Terry's. He was a first-wave Martha Stewart fan/acolyte, so we have a worn, greasy, battered and batter-splattered first edition of *The Martha Stewart Living Cookbook.* He also relies on Mark Bittman's *How to Cook Everything* and *Tom Douglas' Seattle Kitchen.* Terry grew up in Spokane, Washington, and his family went camping a lot when he was a child. When he's feeling nostalgic, he cooks in the yard using a scary-looking cast-iron Dutch oven. It looks like a witches' cauldron. He has a couple of cookbooks about Dutch ovens, but I've never seen him open one. When he wants to cook in his Dutch oven, he digs a pit, builds a fire, tosses some meat and vegetables in, and a couple of hours later we're eating like cavemen. He also makes the most spectacular pineapple upside-down cake in that thing. I don't know how he does it.

What books are on your coffee table?

We have no coffee tables, so no coffee-table books. On the side table next to my chair in the living room is Jon M. Sweeney's *The Pope Who Quit: A True Medieval Tale of Mystery, Death, and Salvation*. It was published in 2012 and it's already out of date. There was just one quitter pope in history back in 2012. Now there are two. Also, Aaron Hartzler's *Rapture Practice*, a terrific new memoir about growing up gay in a fundamentalist Christian home and community. Hartzler was a guest on my podcast, and I just finished his book—it's terrific. What's most interesting about it is that Hartzler hasn't come out to his parents by the end of the book. It's a coming-out story without a big coming-out scene.

If you could meet any writer, dead or alive, who would it be? What would you want to know?

Gore Vidal. I admire his range, his passion, and the rate at which he cranked out work. Novels, essays, plays. My process is very, very slow, and I am in awe of writers like Vidal. I'm in awe of writers who write like it's what they, you know, actually do for a damn living. I don't think writing comes easy to anyone. Writing is a painful process. But some writers have a higher tolerance for pain. It makes me jealous. Also, *United States*, a collection of Vidal's essays (including "The Birds and the Bees," which I consider one of the best essays ever written about sex), was the first gift I gave to Terry after we started dating.

What do you plan to read next?

My bossy husband insists that I start in on the stack of Steven Saylor/Aaron Travis books on my night stand. But last week I found a book about the writing of the King James Bible at the Fremont Sunday Market here in Seattle (*Majestie: The King Behind the King James Bible*, by David Teems). I may sneak that in first.

Christopher Buckley

What are you reading at the moment? Are you a one-book-at-a-time person?

According to the increasingly hazardous-looking ziggurat on my bedside table: Paul Scott's *The Raj Quartet*; David Nasaw's biography of William Randolph Hearst, *The Chief*; Christopher Hitchens's *Thomas Paine's Rights of Man*; Eric Jaffe's *The King's Best Highway*; Frank Langella's memoir, *Dropped Names*; the *Collected Stories* of Roald Dahl; Ellin Stein's history of the National Lampoon, *That's Not Funny, That's Sick*; Hiram Maxim's autobiography, *My Life* (he invented the Maxim gun in the 1880s, providing Hilaire Belloc with the couplet "Whatever happens, we have got / The Maxim Gun, and they have not"); Edna O'Brien's memoir, *Country Girl*; John Keegan's biography of Churchill, titled, oddly, *Winston Churchill*; Bill Bryson's biography of Shakespeare, also oddly titled *Shakespeare*; and George H. W. Bush's collection of letters, *All the Best*.

Whether this reflects catholicity or ADD, I can't say. Probably ADD. What was your question? I can say for certain that since there are 1,926 pages in *The Raj Quartet*, I will still be reading it in the year 2039.

What's the best book you've read so far this year?

I'm a Libra, so I claim astrological right of indecision as between Edmund Morris's *This Living Hand* and Alexandra Fuller's *Cocktail Hour Under the Tree of Forgetfulness*. Both are exquisitely written. Edmund Morris is of

---

Christopher Buckley is the author of *Thank You for Smoking*, *Losing Mum and Pup*, and *But Enough About You*, among other books.

course chiefly known for his Theodore Roosevelt trilogy biography; its first volume won the Pulitzer Prize. This collection of essays and articles is a calliope of talent and range. Alexandra Fuller's memoir of her mother's growing up in Kenya is breathtakingly tragic, triumphant, and lyrical. It only just occurred to me now that both authors grew up in Africa.

If you had to name a favorite novelist, who would it be?

Evelyn Waugh, hands down, even though he so despised Americans that, if he were alive to hear this compliment, he would swat it back across the net with serene contempt.

Runner-up favorite: God, assuming he actually did channel that greatest of all novels, branded under the title the Bible.

What kinds of stories are you drawn to? Any you steer clear of?

Drawn to: stories that begin with lines like, "Late in October 1914 three brothers rode from Choteau, Montana, to Calgary in Alberta to enlist in the Great War." (Jim Harrison's novella, *Legends of the Fall*.)

Steer clear of: stories that begin with "riverrun, past Eve and Adam's, from swerve of shore to bend of bay, brings us by a commodius vicus of recirculation back to Howth Castle and Environs." (Joyce's *Finnegans Wake*. I know, I know. My bad.)

Which book has had the greatest impact on you? What book made you want to write?

H. L. Mencken's *Prejudices*. He wrote these six volumes in the 1920s, but their zest, sinew, and cut and thrust are undated, fresh, and vital nearly a century after their ink dried. No American writer—except perhaps Twain and Bierce—could be so withering and gleeful at the same time. But see Favorite Book on Politics, below.

What's the best book on politics you've ever read? The worst?

Filial duty—and genuine admiration—incline me to say *The Unmaking of a Mayor*, by William F. Buckley Jr., his account of running for mayor of New York City in 1965. (Spoiler alert: He didn't win.) Joe Klein, who wrote, among other marvelous books, *Primary Colors*, told *Unmaking*'s author that it was his favorite book on politics. Coming from Klein, this is high praise.

But to answer your question: *Parliament of Whores*, by P. J. O'Rourke, his definitive and herniatingly funny account of that menagerie known as the United States Congress and zoo known as Washington, DC. It makes you thank God that the founding fathers are no longer around to see what we've done with the gift they bequeathed us.

If you could require the president to read one book, what would it be?

Title 26 of the United States Code, otherwise known as the Internal Revenue Code. No one seems to know exactly how long it is, which says something in itself. I like President Obama, but if he actually sat down and read this cetacean abomination, he might think twice before adding more pages to it.

Did you identify with any literary characters growing up? Who were your literary heroes?

As someone who was sent off to boarding school, I'd have to cop to cliché and say Holden Caulfield. But it would have been a heckuva lot more fun to be Hawkeye, of *The Last of the Mohicans*.

Disappointing, overrated, just not good: What book did you feel as if you were supposed to like, and didn't?

I should come clean and say *Remembrance of Things Past*, but that would brand me as a philistine, and we don't want that. So instead: much as it pains me to say it, *The Autobiography of Mark Twain*. I continue to revere him, but this omnium-gatherum is truly and monumentally dull and dare I say, pointless. As Garrison Keillor remarked in these pages in his review: it's the ultimate argument for burning your leftovers before you die.

If you could meet any writer, dead or alive, who would it be? What would you want to know?

Meeting one's heroes in the flesh can be very depressing and disillusioning, but to divide candidates into categories:

Party Animals: François Villon, Rabelais, Byron, Kenneth Tynan, Casanova, James Dickey. (I met Dickey, but that's another story.)

Wow Factor: Shakespeare, but only if he was really as cool as Joseph Fiennes in *Shakespeare in Love*.

Wrestler with God: Melville, but sooo gloomy.

Wit on Loan from God: Oscar Wilde and Dorothy Parker.

If you could be any character from literature, who would you be?

Ian Fleming's masterpiece creation, so that when asked my name, I could respond with a reasonably straight face: "Bond. James Bond." I say it all the time, but women do not swoon and men just laugh.

Of the books you've written, which is your favorite?

The correct answer is "The next one." But in fact, *Steaming to Bamboola: The World of a Tramp Freighter*. That was fifteen books ago now; there's something about your firstborn.

What book have you always meant to read and haven't gotten around to? Anything you feel embarrassed never to have read?

War and Peace. My standard excuse for this appalling illiteracy is: "I'm saving it for my final illness." But when the doctors tell me I have six months to live, I wonder: Will I really reach for *War and Peace* instead of P. G. Wodehouse? Fortunately, it's irrelevant, because even if I'm ninety-four, I'll still be plowing my way through *The Raj Quartet*.

What will you read next?

Marie Arana's biography *Bolívar*. She is an enchanting and fascinating writer and will make me feel better about not having read *War and Peace*.

Curtis Sittenfeld

What kinds of books do you like to read during the summer? Any favorite summer-time recommendations?

A couple summers ago, I read *Father of the Rain*, by Lily King, a novel that starts out during the summer of Nixon's resignation. This isn't exactly a romp in the sand—it's about a daughter and her cruel, charismatic alcoholic father—but it's very well written and absorbing.

Who is your favorite overlooked or under-appreciated writer?

I started graduate school at Iowa in the fall of 1999, on my twenty-fourth birthday, and in my first workshop there was only one other woman. Her name was Susanna Daniel, and we quickly became close friends—she was fun to gossip with, and she could write amazing sentences. Susanna's second novel, *Sea Creatures*, is out this month, and it's an intelligent page-turner (that is, the dream combination) about, among other things, South Florida, art, insomnia, and marriage.

What kinds of stories are you drawn to? Any you steer clear of?

Ironically enough, given the topic of my first novel, I'm wary of books about boarding school. If the author gets the details wrong and carica-turizes the milieu ("My daddy says any family without a Rolls-Royce is living in poverty!") it's tedious. But if the author gets the details right, it's uncomfortably evocative and makes me squirm. All that said, I loved Tobias Wolff's *Old School*; I loved *Oh the Glory of It All*, by Sean Wilsey (in

---

Curtis Sittenfeld is the author of the novels *Prep*, *The Man of My Dreams*, *Sisterland*, and *American Wife*.

which Wilsey gets kicked out of one boarding school after another); and I can't wait to read *& Sons*, a forthcoming novel by David Gilbert about an author like J. D. Salinger who writes a book like *The Catcher in the Rye*. (I also am wary of fiction about writers, but again I guess more in theory than in practice.)

Do you like to read memoirs?

I'm currently in the middle of *Are You My Mother?* by the cartoonist Alison Bechdel. It's much more meta and nonlinear than I had expected, and totally engrossing. I want to discuss it with someone who knows more about psychology than I do.

Do you ever read self-help? Anything you recommend?

I'm fascinated by books about time management and decluttering, which is akin to a person who weighs seven hundred pounds being fascinated by diet books. But the book I've truly been helped the most by is actually a parenting book called *Sleeping Through the Night: How Infants, Toddlers, and Their Parents Can Get a Good Night's Sleep*. It's by Jodi Mindell, a sleep researcher and psychology professor who's also a mom, and I swear by this book. It's clear, realistic, and neither excessively harsh nor ineffectively gentle.

What's the best book you've ever received as a gift?

I'm not currently teaching, but it's a wonderful feeling when a former student gets a book published and sends me a copy. This happened last year with a woman named Bianca Zander, whose terrific first novel is called *The Girl Below*. It's about a young woman who returns to London after a decade in New Zealand and confronts strange events from her past.

What book has had the greatest impact on you?

Far from the Tree, which I finished recently, is the most amazing book I've ever read—in fact, I continue to talk about it so much that my husband suggested I get a *Far from the Tree* tattoo. The book is about children whose identities greatly differ from those of their parents for various reasons— deafness, autism, transgenderism—and it's also about how we as a society define disability and react to differences. Andrew Solomon is very compassionate but also very honest; for some families, their challenges cause them to tap reservoirs of strength and patience they didn't know they had, and for others, the challenges ruin their lives. I came away with huge admiration for many of the parents and kids and for Solomon himself; he's so smart and sympathetic, and he left no stone unturned in terms of reporting and researching. The book is definitely not just for parents, by the way, and it's not a how-to on child-rearing; some of the "children" featured are now adults looking back. It's really a book for everyone.

I will, however, offer a word of warning: It's seven hundred pages not counting footnotes, and it took me months to finish (I don't have an e-reader, and the print version is too big to comfortably carry on planes or even read in bed). My sister once texted me asking, "How far from the tree are you?" This would be a great book club pick and lead to really interesting conversations, but I'd recommend breaking it into three chunks to discuss at three meetings. Because of how the chapters are divided, this would be easy to do.

Any idea whether Laura Bush read your first-lady fictionalization, *American Wife*?

When asked in an interview, she said she hadn't, and I trust that this is true. People have said to me, "Of course she read it—she's an avid reader, and it's about her!" But I suspect that having been in the public eye for so long, and being part of a family that has received so much exposure, she's developed mechanisms for ignoring certain kinds of attention. If I were her, I definitely wouldn't read it, and if I did read it, I wouldn't like it, even though the character based on her is positive. I believe I had legitimate reasons for writing the book, but I understand why novels based on real people, especially living people, make some readers queasy.

Do you have a favorite childhood literary character or hero?

I've always strongly identified with Toad from *Frog and Toad*. Especially in the story in which he won't get out of the river because he doesn't want anyone to see him looking funny in his bathing suit—and thereby attracts the attention of the nearby lizards, dragonflies, field mouse, etc.—he's so completely the ridiculous instigator of his own problems.

Disappointing, overrated, just not good: What book did you feel you were supposed to like, and didn't? Do you remember the last book you put down without finishing?

I find *The Little Engine That Could* almost unreadable—repetitive, wordy, heavy-handed—though I live with two children who don't share my opinion.

What do you plan to read next?

Months ago, I heard a writer named Attica Locke interviewed on NPR about her novel *The Cutting Season*—a murder mystery set on a former slave plantation turned tourist attraction. I was very intrigued.

Without Feathers, by Woody Allen, makes me giggle like a baby. *Holidays on Ice*, by David Sedaris. *How to Have a Life-Style*, by Quentin Crisp.—**Lena Dunham**

In Wells Tower's first collection of short stories, there is a description of a mouse emerging from behind a fridge eating a coupon which made me laugh for a good ten days.—**Emma Thompson**

The last book that made me laugh? K. J. Bishop's *The Etched City*. I'm a sucker for lines like "He had numerous stories of recent adventure and suffering—specifically, his adventures and other people's suffering, almost invariably connected—that he told with the air of an amiable ghoul."—**Junot Díaz**

The Diaries of Auberon Waugh. It's in my bathroom, and it's always good for a giggle.
—**J. K. Rowling**

The series of Don Camillo stories, by the modern Italian author Giovanni Guareschi, collected in three volumes. The stories are set in a small Italian town and involve three protagonists: the local priest Don Camillo; the mayor Peppone; and the church's Christ statue, which Don Camillo consults regularly for advice and which answers. Don Camillo and Peppone clash constantly in words and occasionally with their fists. But the two of them are joined by a common sense of humanity. The Don Camillo stories range from gut-wrenchingly tragic to hilarious. Whenever I start the next story in Guareschi's collection, I never know in advance whether it will make me cry or laugh.—**Jared Diamond**

Spilt Milk, by the Brazilian novelist Chico Buarque. A deathbed monologue about class, race, love, and political history has no right to be this funny.—**Katherine Boo**

I love humor and for this reason I've always enjoyed Mark Twain. He was without a doubt the funniest writer who ever picked up a pen.
—**John Grisham**

St. Aubyn takes the prize. I don't think I would be able to define a work of literature as great if it didn't make me laugh at least a little. **Michael Chabon**

Houellebecq and St. Aubyn are both making me laugh, but the St. Aubyn is more intentionally funny. And Christopher Hitchens's memoir, *Hitch-22*. There's a line in there that goes something like, "By that time, my looks had declined to such a degree that only women would go to bed with me."
—**Jeffrey Eugenides**

Jennifer Finney Boylan's endlessly witty *Stuck in the Middle with You* made me laugh out loud over and over again; it's about her experience as a transgender parent, who started off as her children's father and ended up as their "Maddy"—not quite a mom, but definitely no longer a dad.—**Andrew Solomon**

I've been reading a nonfiction cartoon called *Couch Fiction*, by a British psychoanalyst, Philippa Perry. The book is simply the best single volume on analysis I've ever read, and takes us through one man's analysis and his attempts to resolve a range of problems with his mother and his girlfriend. It's done with images and speech bubbles by Junko Graat; it's constantly charming and always deeply accurate and thought provoking.
—**Alain de Botton**

James McBride

What are you reading at the moment?

You Are Not a Gadget, by Jaron Lanier.

Are you a one-book-at-a-time person?

More or less. Though at times, I will gobble anything within range.

What's the best book you've read so far this year?

The Rise and Fall of the Third Reich, by William Shirer. All 1,100 pages, and I wish there were more. Just finished it. I should've read it years ago.

If you had to name a favorite novelist, who would it be?

Toni Morrison. Morrison is like John Coltrane. She can play anything. She plays off the horn, like Coltrane did. She busts through the form. Coltrane's music demanded listening. Morrison's work is the same. It simply demands attention. There is no living author like her.

Care to call out your nominees for most overlooked or underappreciated writer?

That's a long list. At the top would have to be Paul Monette, author of *Becoming a Man*. He was a superbly gifted writer who died during the AIDS epidemic that deprived us of a generation of talent. I've often thought to myself, if they took the graphic sex scenes out of that book, it could be required reading in public schools. But maybe I'm dreaming. Anzia Yezierska, *Bread Givers*. Henry Roth, *Call It Sleep*; Carlo Levi, *Christ Stopped at Eboli*; and the British writer John Wyndham (*The Chrysalids*), whose deep

---

James McBride is the author of *The Good Lord Bird*, *The Color of Water*, *Song Yet Sung*, and *Miracle at St. Anna*.

imagination and challenge to religious zealotry should serve as a template for any young sci-fi writer. *The Chrysalids* is a children's book, by the way.

What kinds of stories are you drawn to?

Anything that involves David and Goliath.

Any you steer clear of?

Corny, unbelievable novels; political books; stories by super-duper mountain-climber types who spend thousands snowboarding or traversing high peaks and writing books about it while they could be digging water wells in Peru someplace, helping somebody. I usually just go to the part of those books where the guy dies. I don't know if that's a good thing or not. Probably not. I avoid pulp fiction. I dig spy novels. I read more history books than anything else. Leon Litwack's books on slavery are favorites, especially *Been in the Storm So Long*. I read a bit of Nietzsche when I travel. I'd like to see a book that tells us who those people are on bikes who wear those funny little uniforms and ride all over the road.

Which book has had the greatest impact on you?

Probably the Bible, because it was hammered over my head so much.

What book made you want to write?

Kurt Vonnegut's *Welcome to the Monkey House*.

In what ways does your music-playing influence or inform your writing?

Only in a structural sense. I'm not one of those who can listen to music and write. I need the door closed. Windows shut. Facing the wall. No birds tweeting, views of nature, and so forth. A clean office, devoid of funk, without open books and dirty coffee cups and papers strewn around, would drive me bananas. If anything, I prefer traffic and sirens. But in a structural sense, jazz demands that you negotiate the road ahead with certain restrictions—tempo, harmony, chords, and so on—and that's a good template for the working writer. You can't write just anything. Your story needs structure. Jazz sets out a kind of road map that you're supposed to follow, but there are limits. If you're playing a solo in the key of B flat and play, say, an F sharp or B natural, you better have a good reason for it—or be Charlie Parker. You can make it work, of course, but remember this: Even though you're driving the car, you may not know the exact route home. You'll get there somehow. If you trust the music, and stay within the parameters, within that framework, you'll get home.

Same with writing. That's why I say writing is an act of faith. But my way may not be the best way.

What books might we be surprised to find on your shelves?

That's tough, because I just moved and most of my books are in boxes. It took three guys several hours to move those books. I peeked inside one box, and here's what I found: *Encyclopedia of Disability*, entire volumes. *The Polish Jewry: History and Culture* (published by Interpress, various authors); part of the Marvel Comics Civil War series; and the first three volumes of the new black Spider-Man in hardback, and I'm waiting for the fourth to come out. A couple of hillbilly joke books in there too.

Do you ever read self-help? Anything you recommend?

My self-help books are generally restricted to cars. I started with John Muir's *How to Keep Your Volkswagen Alive* and now have the service manuals to most of the cars I've owned: 240 Volvo, Honda, Ford, etc. Jane Bryant Quinn's *Making the Most of Your Money* works for me, though she's not fond of cars. Several books on jazz arranging and technique, most notably Oliver Nelson's *Patterns for Improvisation*.

If you could require the president to read one book, what would it be?

I'm convinced that anyone who takes that job doesn't need advice from me on anything. It would only make their life worse. But if I had to force him to read something, it would be *My Way of Life*, a pocket-reader version (edited by Walter Farrell) of the *Summa Theologica* of St. Thomas. God's wisdom comes in handy when you're the leader of the free world. I got that as a gift from the late Lt. Gen. William J. McCaffrey. His son, Gen. Barry McCaffrey, was a leader of American forces in the Persian Gulf war. The father, Gen. William McCaffrey, was a commander in the all-black 92nd Division in Italy. He understood what it meant to send men into harm's way. I admired him greatly.

Did you identify with any literary characters growing up?

Not really. My mother was more interesting and mysterious than any literary character I'd ever come across.

Who were your literary heroes?

Toni Morrison (*The Bluest Eye*) got me out of bed, Richard Wright (*Black Boy*) got me to school on the bus, but Harper Lee (*To Kill a Mockingbird*) helped me sleep at night.

Disappointing, overrated, just not good: What book did you feel you were supposed to like, and didn't?

I'm not good enough to say anybody is overrated. But I'll say this: When pop singers and Hollywood stars write children's books, it usually means there's a lot of good trees dying for nothing.

Do you remember the last book you put down without finishing?

I put down *A Year of Days*, by Episcopal Bishop Edmond Lee Browning, every night without finishing it. I've been reading one page a day for three years. You're supposed to read only one page at a time. As for lousy books, there are plenty. But I'd rather see kids reading lousy books than obeying the television like drones.

If you could meet any writer, dead or alive, who would it be?

I already met my hero: Kurt Vonnegut. I wanted to know if he liked Louis Armstrong better than Richard Wagner. I can't remember the answer. He poured me a drink, and we sat up listening to music. I left his house walking on air, soused, having drunk his liquor and smoked his filterless cigarettes. I asked him why he smoked filterless cigarettes, which are stronger and worse for you. He said, "More value."

If you could be any character from literature who would you be?

Spider-Man. If that doesn't count, George Smiley, from John le Carré's early work. Smiley understands. Smiley takes it across the face. Smiley's got a job to do. Smiley's got a broken heart. Smiley can take it.

What book have you always meant to read and haven't gotten around to yet?

Harriet Beecher Stowe's *Uncle Tom's Cabin*.

Anything you feel embarrassed never to have read?

I've never read the great Russian writers. Fact is, I just don't have any great interest in Russia or Russian culture or Russian history. None at all. Who knows why. I suppose we're all allowed to be dumb here once or twice.

What do you plan to read next?

John le Carré's *A Delicate Truth*.

James Patterson

What's the best book you've read so far this year?

I spent several eventful and exhilarating summers at a mental hospital outside Cambridge, Massachusetts. I was working my way through school there—honest. But I do love crazy people. Crazy authors especially: William Burroughs, Jean Genet, Ken Kesey, Sylvia Plath, Cormac McCarthy. Maybe that's why *Where'd You Go, Bernadette* is my favorite novel so far this year. It's funnier than a season's worth of *Modern Family*, *Curb Your Enthusiasm*, and *Justified* episodes; it's also the most original and imaginative fiction I've read since *The Invention of Hugo Cabret*.

If you had to name a favorite novelist, who would it be?

I'm much more comfortable writing about "favorite" books than I am proclaiming "the best" of anything. I'm afraid I have to talk "favorites"—plural—though. Gabriel García Márquez, James Joyce, and Günter Grass are important to me because their writing made it crystal clear that I wasn't capable of the write stuff. Those three dream-killers are still among my favorites. So is George Pelecanos in the thriller-mystery game. Also Richard Price, who seems to remember every good line and phrase he ever heard. This was even true in his first novel, *The Wanderers*, which made me sick with envy way back when I was young, carefree, and more susceptible to jealousy.

Who do you consider the best thriller writers of all time?

There's that gnatty "best" word again. Soldiering on, I love Pelecanos. Also Nelson DeMille, Michael Connelly, James Lee Burke, Dennis Lehane,

James Patterson is the author of many books, including the Alex Cross novels, which include *Kiss the Girls* and *Along Came a Spider*; the Women's Murder Club novels; and the Michael Bennett series.

Walter Mosley, Don Winslow, and Richard Price, of course. As one-offs, *Night Dogs*, *The Ice Harvest*, *Marathon Man*, *Different Seasons*, and *Cutter and Bone* are among my "besties." I believe that thrillers should thrill—and most don't, at least not for me. I also don't think that thriller writers need to play by the constricting rules of realism. Sometimes I come across reviews carping that a certain thriller isn't very "realistic" or that such and such a scene "would never happen in real life." Makes me think of an art critic accusing Klee or Chagall of not being very realistic.

Who is your favorite overlooked or underappreciated writer?

Let's assume that I've overlooked most of the good ones myself, but I'm a fan of *Mrs. Bridge* and *Mr. Bridge*, by the late Evan S. Connell. It was Connell, and also Jerzy Kosinski (*Steps*, *The Painted Bird*) who first made me aware of the power of short, very concise and witty chapters. (At least I got the short part right.) Frederick Exley's *A Fan's Notes* is another overlooked beaut. Also Edward St. Aubyn's *Patrick Melrose Novels*. And George Saunders's *CivilWar-Land in Bad Decline*. A troubling sidebar is that for every George Saunders found, there are a dozen others, not just overlooked, but undiscovered.

What kinds of stories are you drawn to? Any you steer clear of?

I avoid the same kinds of books that I do people—long-winded, sanctimonious, goody-two-shoes, self-important, mean-spirited. Well, maybe not mean-spirited when it comes to books.

What books might we be surprised to find on your shelves?

I'm not entirely sure who "we" is. Some people would be surprised, I guess, to find *Train Dreams*; *Caravaggio*; *Swerve*; *What We Talk About When We Talk About Anne Frank*; *Poems: 1962–2012*, by Louise Glück, on my bookshelves. Others might be surprised that I enjoy so-called chick lit. And kids' books by the baker's dozen. I was surprised to find *11/22/63* in my stacks. Aren't I supposed to be mad at Stephen King?

Do you ever read self-help? Anything you recommend?

I'm a believer in literal self-help rather than help by others. I try to avoid self-appointed experts for hire.

Of the books you've written, which is your favorite?

Ah, which of my babies? Well, my current passion is the books I write to get more kids reading (that's your kids and grandkids, dear reader)—the Middle School series, *I Funny*, Maximum Ride, *Treasure Hunters*. I'm proud to have created Alex Cross, the Women's Murder Club, Michael Bennett, the Private series. Jeez, enough with the self-serving lists.

Of the films based on your books, which is your favorite? What made it so good?

Sadly, I feel my books have been better than the movies made from them. I'm a total movieholic, so that state of affairs is more depressing to me than it ought to be. My current paranoid theory is that I'm a victim of "caricature assassination" in certain Hollywood quarters—"Oh, that airport author has another best-selling page-turner." True story: When *Along Came a Spider* was in galleys, I got a large offer from a studio. All I had to do was change Alex Cross into a white man.

Describe the best letter you've ever received from a reader.

I get hundreds of very sweet, heartfelt letters from parents thanking me for getting their kids reading. Each one absolutely makes my day—make that my week. Many, many women thank me for getting their husbands reading, or reading again. Occasionally, a husband thanks me for getting his wife reading, but that's rare.

What book has had the greatest impact on you personally? Professionally?

Tristram Shandy shivered my timbers as a grad student, and woke me out of my zombie state about the glorious possibilities for breaking the rules whenever I damn well felt like it. Mix first person and third person? Sure, if it helps the story. Sentence fragments? Hell, yes.

If you could require the president to read one book, what would it be?

It seems to me that Barack Obama is sufficiently well read. The president might consider E. M. Forster's *Two Cheers for Democracy* or even Tina Fey's *Bossypants*, which would have helped him surround himself with people who don't think they know everything about everything: being poor, being wealthy, getting sick, getting old, fighting a war. If it matters to anybody, I voted for Mr. Obama.

Did you grow up with a lot of books? What are your memories of being read to as a child?

It's all getting a little dim back at the far end of the tunnel—but I recall that my mother and father read a lot, mostly best sellers. But the better ones— Gore Vidal, Herman Wouk. I don't remember being read to as a kid, or actually being a child at all. Some friends suggest that I never was a child.

Do you have a favorite childhood literary character or hero?

Peter Pan. I loved Peter Pan. Still love Peter Pan. Peter Pan is the only ride that I enjoyed at Disney. And I'm pretty sure that I wrote the Maximum Ride books for kids—starting with my own beloved Jack—because of my affection as a child for Peter Pan.

Disappointing, overrated, just not good: What book did you feel you were supposed to like, and didn't? Do you remember the last book you put down without finishing?

I put down at least a book or two a week. I also walk out on scads of movies, and even Broadway plays. I believe it's the sane thing to do. I'm not a big *Gatsby* fan, and unfortunately I never got into *Don Quixote*, even though I thought I would love the book.

If you could meet any writer, dead or alive, who would it be? What would you want to know?

I'm fascinated by the idea of James Joyce, but I doubt we would have much to talk about. I'd like to have a lunch with Bill Clinton. Maybe a drink with Hunter Thompson. Just one—or two. Dinner with Angelina Jolie would be nice. Does she write?

If you could meet any character from literature, who would it be?

Jesus. Somewhere in his late twenties or very early thirties. Pre-Crucifixion. I would advise against the experience on the cross. I would suggest he talk to his Father about it. Lay out his own well-reasoned point of view. Maybe mention that I was negative about crucifixions as object lessons.

Jonathan Lethem

What are you reading at the moment? Are you a one-book-at-a-time person?

I'm all over the place right now, happily. In my office I tend to be racing through short books—Russell Hoban's *Turtle Diary* and Edward St. Aubyn's Melrose books and Lydia Millet's *Magnificence* just now, while at the bedside table and on trains and airplanes I'm grinding away at monsters over a period of months, if not years: Robert Musil's *Man Without Qualities* and Karl Ove Knausgaard's *My Struggle*. I've been trending to these galactic structures lately—last summer I had my head broken open by Doris Lessing's *Four-Gated City* and so now appear doomed to read the Martha Quest novels—backwards. I also recently noticed how many unfinished novels have been important to me: Musil's, Kafka's, Mervyn Peake's Gormenghast trilogy, Christina Stead's *I'm Dying Laughing*. Reading around in Ellison's *Three Days Before the Shooting . . .* ; I bet I'd like that thing in Salinger's safe.

What's the best book you've read so far this year?

I just devoured in succession two spanking-new studies of great artists, both terrific reading experiences, brain-expanding but embracing, too: Claudia Roth Pierpont's *Roth Unbound* and T. J. Clark's *Picasso and Truth*. Both hit their very tricky targets. They'll be with me for a good long time.

If you had to name a favorite novelist, who would it be?

I hate this question. My favorite letter is *D*, which gives me Dostoyevsky, Dickens, Dick, Delany, and DeLillo. Unless it's *S*, which gives me Stead,

---

Jonathan Lethem is the author of *Motherless Brooklyn*, *The Fortress of Solitude*, *Dissident Gardens*, and *Chronic City*, among other books.

Spark, Salter, Saramago, and others. I could go to a desert island with *D* or *S*, I think.

Care to call out your nominees for most overlooked or underappreciated writer?

Every writer I'm reading and loving seems underappreciated to me—then you mention the name and people say either, "Everyone reads them!" (Charles Portis, Dawn Powell) or, "You're being willfully obscure!" (Ronald Hugh Morrieson, Anna Kavan). That said, this is a major sport for me—I bore my friends with this all the time—so let's go: Laurie Colwin. Iain Sinclair. James Tiptree Jr., Stanley Elkin, and Stanley Ellin. And . . . But I'll stop. I'd also champion the familiar-but-taken-for-granted: the greatness of Shirley Jackson, Elizabeth Bowen, Brian Moore, Thomas Berger. The stories of Bruce Jay Friedman.

What books might we be surprised to find on your shelves?

I notice other people are surprised to see so much of a certain kind of postwar British novelist: Anita Brookner, Penelope Fitzgerald, L. P. Hartley et al. They're not surprising to me. I think people who haven't read them imagine they're cozy books, but they're not—despite their relatively traditional form, they're often unsettling.

Do you ever read self-help? Anything you recommend?

As a kid I used to compulsively reread Alan Watts's *Wisdom of Insecurity*. I didn't think of that as self-help at the time, but I think of it that way now. It's still the help I need.

What are your favorite Brooklyn stories? And now that you're at Pomona College, your favorite books about California?

Two merciless little novels—Paula Fox's *Desperate Characters* and L.J. Davis's *A Meaningful Life*—bring to life the South Brooklyn I knew as a child in the early '70s. Apart from that, however, I don't much seek out books about Brooklyn; I'm more turned on by what Brooklyn grain I detect (or imagine I detect) in the voices of certain Brooklyn-born writers who leave the place largely unexplored as a subject: Robert Stone, Gilbert Sorrentino, Maurice Sendak.

As for California, I read Raymond Chandler long before I'd been here. I breathed in the atmosphere of those books before I even understood Chandler was writing about real places rather than conjuring a zone where his stories could be enacted. Now that I'm here, I see his books—and Ross

Macdonald's—as making a deep stratological survey of the place, in the manner of John McPhee.

Did you identify with any literary characters growing up? Who were your literary heroes?

Starting at about eleven, with *Alice in Wonderland* and Lewis Carroll, I began identifying with the writer—or what I've learned now to call "the implicit author"—of a given fiction, rather than with the characters directly. Possibly some would say this explains a deficit of heroes in my stories.

Disappointing, overrated, just not good: What book did you feel you were supposed to like, and didn't? Do you remember the last book you put down without finishing?

An invitation to air one's limitations? Sure, I'll bite. Based on other things I like, people keep insisting I read Bulgakov's *Master and Margarita*. Each time I try, I discover an allegory of Russian politics, both labored and coy, starring Lucifer and a black cat—just about what I'd least wish to read in the world.

If you could meet any writer, dead or alive, who would it be? What would you want to know?

I know I should use my time machine to go deep-canonical, but the prospect of trying to navigate a dinner party with Herman Melville, Charlotte Brontë, and Honoré de Balzac—figuring out what I could say to them, or what they could say to each other—is beyond my capacities as a bon vivant. Instead, I think I'd want to hang out with three guys I just missed out on knowing, a group more "relatable" to twentieth-century me—Don Carpenter, Philip K. Dick, and Malcolm Braly. They're all, as it happens, semi-outlaw types with Marin County connections, so they'd probably have a good time if thrown together. And I could flatter myself and claim I've been implicated in the revival of each of their posthumous careers, so we'd have something to raise a glass or spark a joint to. I'd be thrilled to let them know they're in print.

What book have you always meant to read and haven't gotten around to yet? Anything you feel embarrassed never to have read?

In the matter of putting things down unfinished, I'm too old now not to do it all the time, when something's not working. No harm, no foul, just mutual détente. As for the classics unread, in that too I try to leave shame out of my game. The existence of vastly more great books than I can ever hope to read is a primary locus of joy in this life, and weight on the scale in favor of human civilization. What's weird is that I've already doubled back on myself—rereading those classics to which I gave giddy short shrift in my teenage years, I find them as mysterious as if they were new. What good does it do a fifty-year-old to go around feeling as if he's read *The Red and the Black* or *Malone Dies* when he did it as a high school freshman? I often bear false confidence—I'll reference these things in conversation, or with students—then open the book and wonder who it was that actually read it. Not me.

What do you plan to read next?

I've got a beautiful stack right here: Hilton Als's *White Girls*, Tao Lin's *Taipei*, Jamie Quatro's *I Want to Show You More*, the new compendiums of William Gaddis's and Italo Calvino's letters. And *Daniel Deronda*, which, you know, I always meant to read and never got around to. I hear it's good.

Jhumpa Lahiri

What are you reading at the moment? Are you a one-book-at-a-time person?

I'm reading the poems of Patrizia Cavalli, whom I've had the great pleasure of meeting in Rome. I adore her personally and I love her poems. She describes desire like no one else. I'm thrilled that a bilingual edition of her poetry, in Italian and English, will be published this fall in the United States. I'm also reading the letters of Cesare Pavese and Pasolini's *Teorema*, which was conceived both as a novel and a film. The combination of poetry, fiction and either letters or the diary of a writer I admire is ideal.

What's the best book you've read so far this year?

Lovers, a novel by a French writer named Daniel Arsand. I read it first in the English translation, then in Italian. It's a harrowing love story with rich historical context. But it's free of bulk, of weight, of all the predictable connective narrative tissue. I found it incantatory, transcendent. It inspires me to tell a story in a different way.

If you had to name a favorite novelist, who would it be?

Thomas Hardy. Ever since I first read him, in high school, I've felt a kinship with his characters, his sense of place, his pitiless vision of humanity. I continue to reread him as often as I can. The architecture of his novels is magnificent, and the way his characters move through time and space is remarkably controlled. The world he creates is absolutely specific, as is the psychological terrain. In spite of the great scope of his work, its breadth and

Jhumpa Lahiri is the author of *Interpreter of Maladies*, *The Namesake*, *Unaccustomed Earth*, and *The Lowland*.

complexity, the prose is clean, straightforward, economical. No scene, no detail, no sentence is wasted.

And your favorite short story writers?

William Trevor, Mavis Gallant, Gina Berriault, Flannery O'Connor, Alice Munro, Andre Dubus. Also Joyce, Chekhov, Cheever, Malamud, Moravia. I recently discovered the work of Giorgio Manganelli, who wrote a collection called *Centuria*, which contains one hundred stories, each of them about a page long. They're somewhat surreal and extremely dense, at once fierce and purifying, the equivalent of a shot of grappa. I find it helpful to read one before sitting down to write.

What immigrant fiction has been the most important to you, both personally and as an inspiration for your own writing?

I don't know what to make of the term "immigrant fiction." Writers have always tended to write about the worlds they come from. And it just so happens that many writers originate from different parts of the world than the ones they end up living in, either by choice or by necessity or by circumstance, and therefore, write about those experiences. If certain books are to be termed immigrant fiction, what do we call the rest? Native fiction? Puritan fiction? This distinction doesn't agree with me. Given the history of the United States, all American fiction could be classified as immigrant fiction. Hawthorne writes about immigrants. So does Willa Cather. From the beginnings of literature, poets and writers have based their narratives on crossing borders, on wandering, on exile, on encounters beyond the familiar. The stranger is an archetype in epic poetry, in novels. The tension between alienation and assimilation has always been a basic theme.

What kinds of stories are you drawn to? Any you steer clear of?

I am drawn to any story that makes me want to read from one sentence to the next. I have no other criterion.

Any books we would be surprised to find on your shelves?

Almost all the books I have on my shelves now are in Italian. I have been reading predominantly in Italian for over a year. I read more slowly as a result. But also more carefully, less passively.

Do you ever read self-help? Anything you recommend?

Literature has always been and will forever be my only form of self-help.

Did you identify with any literary characters growing up? Who were your literary heroes?

I identified with orphans, like Anne of Green Gables, or pioneers, like the characters of Laura Ingalls Wilder, or children who slipped in and out of different worlds and dimensions, like the siblings in *The Lion, the Witch and the Wardrobe*. And of course there was the writer, Jo, in *Little Women*. I loved the brother and sister in *From the Mixed-Up Files of Mrs. Basil E. Frankweiler*, who run away from home and survive among works of beauty. I never go to the Metropolitan Museum of Art without thinking of them.

What books have you enjoyed reading with your own children? Any you're especially looking forward to reading together with them?

My husband and I have been reading to our children every night for the past ten years (our eldest is now eleven). We take turns, alternating nights. I love rereading and sharing the books I read and loved as a child, such as the Pippi Longstocking series by Astrid Lindgren and everything by Roald Dahl. And I've loved discovering new books with them. Last summer we read a great series together called *The Incorrigible Children of Ashton Place*, by Maryrose Wood. These days I also like to read to my children in Italian, which they can now follow. We just read some beautiful fables adapted by Italo Calvino, and another collection of very brief and amusing stories by Gianni Rodari, called *Le Favolette di Alice*. They're about a tiny little girl who keeps finding herself temporarily trapped inside of things, like pockets, ink bottles, birthday cakes, and soap bubbles.

If you could meet any writer, dead or alive, who would it be? What would you want to know?

The idea of meeting writers of the books I've read doesn't interest me. That is to say, I wouldn't go out of my way. If the book is alive to me, if the sentences speak to me, that's enough. A reader's relationship is with the book, with the words, not with the person who created it. I don't want the author to explain anything to me or to interfere. Still, I wish I'd met Edward Gorey before he died, if only to salute his brilliance.

If you could be any character from literature who would you be?

I'd like to be Sebastian Flyte from *Brideshead Revisited*, but only during the early chapters, before things start to go downhill. I've always wanted to dress for dinner.

What do you plan to read next?

I'm planning to read the travel essays of Antonio Tabucchi.

I tend to think of the reading of any book as preparation for the next reading of it. There are always intervening books or facts or realizations that put a book in another light and make it different and richer the second or the third time.
—**Marilynne Robinson**

There is so much to read, and time is so short! I am seventy, but I have not yet reached the age when rereading gives more pleasure than the surprise of a new story or a new writer.
—**Isabel Allende**

Reading is rereading just as writing is rewriting. Any worthwhile book took many, many drafts to reach completion, and so it would make sense that the first time the reader works her way through the volume it's more like a first date than a one-time encounter. If the person was uninteresting (not worthwhile) there's no need for a repeat performance, but if they have promise, good humor, hope, or just good manners, you might want to have a second sit-down, a third. The joy of reading is in the rereading; this is where you get to know the world and characters in deep and rewarding fashion.
—**Walter Mosley**

I'm rereading *The Portrait of a Lady*, which I do every few years to remind myself that there really is such a thing as elegance, in life and in prose—and to remember how much devastation can unfold around it. I am moved by Henry James's ineffable sadness, the belief that human experience is full of loss and that high morals don't stand a chance. I don't entirely agree with that point of view, but I find it galvanizing.
—**Andrew Solomon**

I reread [Janet] Malcolm's *Psychoanalysis: The Impossible Profession* just to remind myself how nonfiction is supposed to be done. I love how ominous her writing is. Even when she is simply sketching out the scenery, you know that something wonderful and thrilling is about to happen.
—**Malcolm Gladwell**

[The book I most like rereading is one] I've had for over fifty years called *The Armed Forces Officer*. It was written by Brigadier S. L. A. (Slam) Marshall. After World War II he was commissioned to review the actions of our soldiers and provide a historically based book of guidance for army officers. It is one of the finest leadership books I've ever read and was given to every officer back then. It was always with me and is right in front of me now. It once went out of print, and I was able to persuade the Pentagon to reissue it with a new cover and an update. The book has received more updates and can now even be found on Amazon. Right next to it is *The Professional Soldier*, by Morris Janowitz. It was published in 1960, two years after I became an officer. It is a sociological analysis of the military officer at that time. I learned that the average senior army officer was white, a West Pointer, rural, and an Episcopalian from South Carolina. I nailed one out of five. In my early years in the army, my focus was on learning about and understanding my chosen profession. I was studying to be a good lieutenant. And, of course, the Bible.
—**Colin Powell**

Richard Dawkins

What's the best book you've read so far this year?

I've been reading autobiographies to get me in the mood for writing my own and show me how it's done: Tolstoy (at one time my own memoir was to have been called, at my wife's suggestion, *Childhood, Boyhood, Truth*); Mark Twain; Bertrand Russell; that engaging maverick Herb Silverman; Edward O. Wilson, elder statesman of my subject. But the best new book I have read is Daniel Dennett's *Intuition Pumps and Other Tools for Thinking*. A philosopher of Dennett's caliber has nothing to fear from clarity and openness. He is out to enlighten and explain, and therefore has no need or desire to language it up like those obscurantist philosophers, often of "Continental" tradition, for whom obscurity is valued as a protective screen, or even admired for its own sake. I once heard of a philosopher who gushed an "Oh, thank you!" when a woman at a party said she found his book hard to understand. Dennett is the opposite. He works hard at being understood, and makes brilliant use of intuition pumps (his own coining) to that end. The book includes a helpful roundup of several of his earlier themes, and is as good as its intriguing title promises.

Who are your favorite contemporary writers and thinkers?

I've already mentioned Dan Dennett. I'll add Steven Pinker, A. C. Grayling, Daniel Kahneman, Jared Diamond, Matt Ridley, Lawrence Krauss, Martin Rees, Jerry Coyne—indeed quite a few of the luminaries that grace the *Edge* online salon conducted by John Brockman (the Man with the Golden Address Book). All share the same honest commitment to real-world truth,

Richard Dawkins is the author of many books, including *The God Delusion*, *The Selfish Gene*, and *An Appetite for Wonder*.

and the belief that discovering it is the business of scientists—and philosophers who take the trouble to learn science. Many of these "Third Culture" thinkers write very well. (Why is the Nobel Prize in Literature almost always given to a novelist, never a scientist? Why should we prefer our literature to be about things that didn't happen? Wouldn't, say, Steven Pinker be a good candidate for the literature prize?)

You have written several books on science and secularism. What other books on the subject would you recommend?

Look at the list of those who obsessively attack Sam Harris and you'll get an idea of what a dangerously effective writer he is: clear, eloquent, penetratingly intelligent, suffers no fools. Much the same could be said of Christopher Hitchens, and the attacks on him have increased now he is no longer around to fight back. Less well known, but very good in their different ways, are J. Anderson Thomson's *Why We Believe in God(s)*, a psychologically informed analysis of what J.L. Mackie called "The Miracle of Theism," and Sean Faircloth's *Attack of the Theocrats!*, a chillingly well-researched unmasking of the contemporary political threat to America's noble secular tradition.

You were born in Kenya and spent your early childhood there. What kinds of books did you read while growing up in Africa?

The greatest novel to come out of Kenya is, in my admittedly limited opinion, one of the great novels of the English language, and it is lamentably neglected by literary connoisseurs: Elspeth Huxley's *Red Strangers*, a saga sweeping through four generations of a Kikuyu family, based on the author's sympathetic and lifelong familiarity with that tribe. Beginning before the coming of the white men, she takes us readers into the Kikuyu world and mind so successfully that when the British finally arrive, we find their ways as quaint and alien as if they were invading Martians. We feel at home in an economy pegged to the goat standard (as I put it in my introduction to the Penguin reprint of the book), and we share the tribal indignation that rupees cannot, as promised, be "changed into goats." Huxley's descriptive powers rival Steinbeck's, with the added subtlety that her metaphors and imagery are drawn from the Kikuyu mind. The pasture "gleamed like a parrot's wing." A felled tree "tottered like a drunken elder."

I was much too young to read this literary tour de force during my African childhood, though I have read it many times since and am proud of my achievement in persuading Penguin Books to restore it to print. However, just as Elspeth Huxley immersed herself in Kikuyu life to produce her masterpiece, Geraldine Elliot listened to the folk tales of the Ngoni people further south (where I lived after my family moved from Kenya), and she produced a beautiful series of children's books which I adored. *The Long Grass Whispers*, *Where the Leopard Passes*, and others are fables of animal wiles and trickery, a kind of African Brer Rabbit and Brer Fox. Kalulu the rabbit is the cunning hero of most of the stories, perennially outwitting Nkandwe the jackal, Fisi the hyena, Nyalugwe the leopard, and others. The names of the characters are actually species names in the local family of languages, one of which I knew as Chinyanja, so that was an added bond.

Did you identify with any fictional characters as a child? Who was your literary hero?

I didn't know children were expected to have literary heroes, but I certainly had one, and I even identified with him at one time: Doctor Dolittle, whom I now half identify with the Charles Darwin of *Beagle* days. This gentle, kindly naturalist, who could talk to nonhuman animals and commanded godlike powers through their devotion to him, is nowadays unfashionable—and even banned from libraries—because of suspected racism. Well, what do you expect? Hugh Lofting was writing in the 1920s, and the ubiquitous racism of England at that time can be seen in so much fiction, including Agatha Christie, Sapper (*Bulldog Drummond*), and many other popular writers for all ages. This is not to excuse it, but Lofting's racism was paternalistic rather than malign and, in my opinion, sufficiently outweighed by the admirable anti-speciesism of all his books.

What book has had the greatest impact on you?

The obvious, and true, answer is Darwin's *Origin*, but I didn't read the book itself until after its message had changed my life by secondary routes. So I'll go, less obviously, for a work of science fiction, Fred Hoyle's *Black Cloud*. In many ways a deplorable book (the hero, with whom we are supposed to identify, is obnoxious, aggressively rude, sexist, and a terrible role model for scientists), I nevertheless learned more science from it, at a formative age, than one ever expects from a work of fiction. It was *The Black Cloud* that first pumped my intuition about information theory and the idea of the arbitrariness of the medium by which information is apprehended. I understood, too, the potential difficulty of separating out individuals from the group in which they are embedded. Is a beehive a colony or a superorganism? If human brains were joined telepathically by high-speed data transmission links, would we become one massive individual? The plot engagingly illustrates the way in which discoveries are simultaneously made more than once in radically different ways. But above all the novel bequeathed to me the haunting idea of "the Deep Problems" of existence and origins, questions which the human mind was never evolved to understand.

What books would you recommend to an aspiring scientist?

Both Peter Medawar and James Watson have written books on this. Called, respectively, *Advice to a Young Scientist* and *Avoid Boring People*, these are not their authors' best books, but they offer memorable hints for success in the vocation of science. Watson, in particular, has a list of quirky imperatives such as "Don't take up golf"; "Work on Sundays"; "Hire spunky lab helpers"; and "Avoid being photographed."

In general, what kinds of stories are you drawn to?

I'm not an aficionado of science fiction, but I've already appreciated a novel that pumps scientific intuition. Arthur C. Clarke and Isaac Asimov, too, exemplify that kind of good science fiction, unlike slack-jawed fantasy where the writer dreams heedlessly away without respecting the decent constraints of science. Another first-class example of the right sort of science fiction is Daniel F. Galouye's *Dark Universe*. Here the intuition being pumped concerns mythology and the origins of religion. A people who, for reasons that emerge, lost light at some remote part of their history and now live in perpetual darkness, retain "light" in their language but only in mythic allusions to a lost paradise from which they have fallen. They worship things like "Great Light Almighty," "Oh, thank Light," "For Light's sake!," and their pantheon includes demonic figures who engineered the fall from Light's grace. The demons are called Strontium, Cobalt, and the arch-devil Hydrogen Himself. Go figure, as Americans say.

I also enjoy social satire of the Evelyn Waugh, Aldous Huxley, Kingsley Amis, Michael Frayn kind. Witty observation of the way people are and the way they talk, the sort of sharply penetrating perceptiveness that makes me want to run into the street and hug somebody with sheer delight.

What books might we be surprised to find on your shelves?

Depending on how naïvely literalistic you are, you might be surprised to find the Bible. The King James Version, of course, and not so much on my shelves as continually off my shelves, because I open it so often: sometimes to quote it, sometimes for sheer literary pleasure—especially Ecclesiastes and the Song of Songs.

If you could require the president to read one book, what would it be? And the British prime minister?

I'd take the following two books, hand one to each of them, then ask them to swap books so they end up reading both: Carl Sagan's *Demon-Haunted World* is the best antidote I know to superstition and pseudoscience. Not that either Obama or Cameron are superstitious or supernaturalists, but they need to develop a less obsequious attitude to their constituents who are. Robert Axelrod's *Evolution of Cooperation* is salutary for anybody involved in settling disputes and trying to foster cooperation. Indeed I wrote in my foreword to the revised edition: "The world's leaders should all be locked up with this book and not released until they have read it. This would be a pleasure to them and might save the rest of us. *The Evolution of Cooperation* deserves to replace the Gideon Bible."

Disappointing, overrated, just not good: What book did you feel you were supposed to like, and didn't?

Pride and Prejudice. It must be my prejudice, and I am not proud of it, but I can't get excited about who is going to marry whom, and how rich they are.

If you could meet any writer, dead or alive, who would it be? What would you want to know?

Sorry to be boringly predictable, but Shakespeare. Who are you? And how did a humble country boy like you become the greatest genius, and part creator, of our beloved English language? Might you have been even better if you'd studied at Oxford or Cambridge?

What book have you always meant to read and haven't gotten around to yet? Anything you feel embarrassed not to have read?

Ah yes, David Lodge's Humiliation game. I'd be champion at that. There are so many, but I'll say *War and Peace*.

What do you plan to read next?

War and Peace. Oh dear, I set myself up for that, didn't I?

In seventh grade, for some perverse reason, I decided to read the entire *World Book Encyclopedia*. I got about fifty pages into the first volume before moss started growing on my eyelids.

—Carl Hiaasen

Everything by Ernest Hemingway.

—John Irving

Most contemporary political memoirs, including mine, *My American Journey*.

—Colin Powell

I was trained to consider "disappointment" of this sort a character flaw of my own, a failure to comprehend, to appreciate what others have clearly appreciated. My first attempt at reading, for instance, D. H. Lawrence was a disappointment—I wasn't old enough, or mature enough, quite yet; now, Lawrence is one of my favorite writers, whom I've taught in my university courses many times. Another initial disappointment was Walt Whitman, whom I'd also read too young (I know, it's unbelievable, how could anyone admit to have been "disappointed" in Walt Whitman? Please don't send contemptuous e-mails).

—Joyce Carol Oates

Finnegans Wake. Can't finish it. Just can't. It was required reading in one of my college classes, and I'm a pretty good crammer, so I'd planned on pulling an all-nighter, but I couldn't get past page twenty. I attributed it to lack of sleep and have tried several times since then—but fully awake, I couldn't get past page ten. If that makes me lowbrow, so be it.

—Jeanette Walls

I don't enjoy Jonathan Franzen, although I mean to. I couldn't finish *The Corrections* and thought *Freedom* was hilariously overrated. Maybe I am just bitter because it was such a gigantic success. I couldn't read *The Shipping News*, but I pretended to love it because we had the same agent when it came out. It drove me crazy, but I later forgave the author everything for those later great, life-changing short stories.

—Anne Lamott

I'm not a big fan of the Twilight series. I can't get past the premise, which is that a group of wealthy, sophisticated, educated, highly intelligent, centuries-old vampires, who can do pretty much whatever they want, have chosen to be . . . high school students. I simply cannot picture such beings sitting in a classroom listening to a geometry teacher drone on about the cosine. I have more respect for vampires than that.

—Dave Barry

Sometimes I put books down that are good but that I see too well what the author is up to. As you practice your craft, you lose your innocence as a reader. That's the one sad thing about this work.

—E. L. Doctorow

Sting

What's the best book you've read so far this year?

I enjoyed Hilary Mantel's *Bring Up the Bodies*, almost as much as I enjoyed its predecessor, *Wolf Hall*. Her portrait of Thomas Cromwell is complex and largely sympathetic to a character that is usually cast darkly and exclusively as Henry VIII's "muscle." I enjoyed Nathaniel Philbrick's treatment of the American War of Independence in *Bunker Hill* for similar reasons, a well-researched story proving to be more nuanced and compelling than a well-established myth.

If you had to name a favorite novelist, who would it be?

Mark Twain, for the perfect combination of plot and character in *Huckleberry Finn*.

What kinds of stories are you drawn to?

I like personal dramas set within the sweep of historical events: Colum McCann's *TransAtlantic* and *Let the Great World Spin*, or Ian McEwan's *Sweet Tooth*.

We have to ask about Nabokov. How does it feel to have turned on a generation of junior high schoolgirls to *Lolita*? Are you a Nabokov fan?

Is that true—that my appalling rhyme led a mass migration to the linguistic cosmos of Nabokov? I don't think so, but then, they could have gone to worse places.

Sting is an award-winning singer, songwriter, and human rights activist. He is the author of *Broken Music: A Memoir*.

In what ways do the books you read figure into the music you write?

Songwriting is of course a very different art to that of the novelist—condensing sometimes large ideas into rhyming couplets seems to be the opposite process.

But it is interesting to me how often a novel will begin with a quote from a poem or a song, so the territories do overlap to some extent. My favorite songs are narrative songs, short stories that can be recounted in three minutes. My favorite novels are extended songs. What is *One Hundred Years of Solitude* if not an opera? And a grand one at that!

You've written a memoir, *Broken Music*. What was that experience like for you—the writing itself, and the publication and reception of the book?

I began to realize while writing and remembering that memory is a neural muscle, and once you begin to stretch it, it grows to accommodate everything that has ever happened to you, often things you might prefer to forget. But the abiding emotions that sustained me through the process were gratitude and forgiveness; to use the newly developed muscle otherwise is largely a waste of time. I think people were surprised that I wrote almost exclusively about my early life, before the distorting lens of fame and success, and the well-worn clichés of celebrity.

What books might we be surprised to find on your shelves?

The complete works of P. G. Wodehouse, for their innocent escapism.

Do you ever read self-help? Anything you recommend?

A self-help book? Isn't that an oxymoron?

What book has had the greatest impact on you?

Probably Bulgakov's *Master and Margarita*, a delicious and disruptive satire of Soviet Russia. I hear a dead man was put on trial in Moscow only this past summer; Woland would have loved it!

If you could require the president to read one book, what would it be?

Meditations, by Marcus Aurelius—Stoicism and the limitations of power. "When you wake up in the morning, tell yourself: The people I deal with today will be meddling, ungrateful, arrogant, dishonest, jealous and surly. They are like this because they can't tell good from evil. But I have seen the beauty of good, and the ugliness of evil, and have recognized that the wrongdoer has a nature related to my own—not of the same blood or birth, but the same mind, and possessing a share of the divine."

Did you grow up with a lot of books?

We only had two in the house, an illustrated Old Testament and volume one of *Encyclopaedia Britannica*. I was well versed in everything from "aardvark" to "azimuth," but little else. The public library became a sort of refuge. I never throw a book away now. I have kept every dog-eared paperback I have ever read. Books are the only things I'm acquisitive about. And no, I don't lend my books . . . join the library!

Do you have a favorite childhood literary character or hero?

I imagined myself as Jim Hawkins in *Treasure Island*, an innocent among thieves and cutthroats. It must have been the first book I ever read from start to finish, with unforgettable characters, Long John Silver, Blind Pew, Ben Gunn . . . The Black Spot still terrifies me.

What books are on your coffee table?

Albert Camus: *Solitude and Solidarity*, a beautiful and evocative portrait of the man and the writer, edited by his daughter Catherine, and Ellen von Unwerth's *Fräulein* . . . Well, what did you expect?

Disappointing, overrated, just not good: What book did you feel you were supposed to like, and didn't? Do you remember the last book you put down without finishing?

I'm no critic. It's hard enough writing a book without some opinionated parvenu dismissing your work because he wasn't in the mood or is too daft to catch your drift. Mind you, anything with the word "Code" in the title, I will avoid like the plague!

If you could meet any writer, dead or alive, who would it be? What would you want to know?

I'd like to ask Shakespeare if he composed while walking, or was he entirely sedentary?

What do you plan to read next?

I'm weighing *My Lunches with Orson* against Daniel C. Dennett's *Intuition Pumps and Other Tools for Thinking*.

Any plans to write another book?

Oh yes! I definitely want to give it another crack!

Reading Through Tears

The last book that made me cry? That's easy: the winner of the Yale Younger Poets prize, Eduardo Corral's collection, *Slow Lightning*. When I finished that book I bawled. Wise and immense, but peep for yourself: "Once a man offered me his heart and I said no. Not because I didn't love him. Not because he was a beast or white— I couldn't love him. Do you understand? In bed while we slept, our bodies inches apart, the dark between our flesh a wick. It was burning down. And he couldn't feel it."—**Junot Díaz**

That is a very rare occurrence. I remember tearing up the first time I read Nabokov's description, in *Speak, Memory*, of his father being tossed on a blanket by cheering muzhiks, with its astonishingly subtle foreshadowing of grief and mourning.—**Michael Chabon**

My own book *Canada* made me cry the last time I read it. If it was any good, it should've. Beyond that, the very last book that made me cry was more than one poem in James Wright's collected poems, *Above the River*.
—**Richard Ford**

The honest answer is *The Casual Vacancy*. I bawled while writing the ending, while rereading it, and when editing it.—**J. K. Rowling**

The South Beach Diet.—**Jeffrey Eugenides**

I was on holiday years ago with *Corelli's Mandolin*. Rendered inconsolable and had to be put to bed for the afternoon.—**Emma Thompson**

I don't want to read any book that makes me cry. I get all the gloom I can stand from newspaper headlines.
—**Carl Hiaasen**

I'm not sure I ever cried while reading a book.—**John Grisham**

I'm not usually one for leaving tear stains in the margins, but in recent weeks I caught myself sobbing twice— while reading a Saunders story and a forthcoming book by my friend David Finkel. Finkel's first book, *The Good Soldiers*, followed a battalion charged with carrying out George W. Bush's "surge." The new book follows some of those veterans as they struggle to reintegrate themselves into American life, and it's devastating.
—**Katherine Boo**

I read Jeremy Adelman's biography of Albert O. Hirschman early this year and was deeply moved by it. I finished that book with tears in my eyes.—**Malcolm Gladwell**

I cried reading Mary Berg's diary of hunger in the ghetto in Warsaw. More recently and trivially, I cried when I read through my own book of essays and realized: thank God, it's done.—**Nicholson Baker**

I'm always close to tears reading Judith Kerr's delightful children's story, *The Tiger Who Came to Tea*. It tells of a tiger who turns up, quite unexpectedly, at teatime at the house of a girl called Sophie and her mother. You'd expect them to panic, but they take the appearance of this visitor entirely in their stride—and their reaction is a subtle invitation for us to approach life's unexpected challenges with resilience and good humor.
—**Alain de Botton**

Andrew Solomon

What are you reading at the moment? Are you a one-book-at-a-time person?

I'm rereading *The Portrait of a Lady*, which I do every few years to remind myself that there really is such a thing as elegance, in life and in prose—and to remember how much devastation can unfold around it. I am moved by Henry James's ineffable sadness, the belief that human experience is full of loss and that high morals don't stand a chance. I don't entirely agree with that point of view, but I find it galvanizing. I've also read a good bit of William James for research recently. I tend not to think that brevity is the soul of wit, and neither do the James brothers, so reading them in sequence makes me feel like a houseguest at a very congenial house.

What's the best book you've read so far this year?

Christian Caryl's *Strange Rebels* argues convincingly that the problems of the twenty-first century were all hatched in 1979, and looks particularly at the move away from secularism and the welfare state; it's a bold and illuminating take on our time, and its analysis of militancy seems particularly relevant as we look to Syria. On a lighter note, I loved Cécile David-Weill's *Suitors*, a charming comedy of manners set at a country estate in the South of France, apparently one of the few places in the world where anyone still has enough manners to make a comedy about.

Andrew Solomon is the author of *Far from the Tree* and *The Noonday Demon*.

If you had to name a favorite novelist, who would it be?

I have a soft spot for George Eliot. She achieves scope without ever sacrificing her devastating precision. Her psychological insight accumulates through perfectly observed details, without a trace of pomposity. The way she assembles multiple portraits is one of my great inspirations as I try to construct my own nonfiction. Virginia Woolf is my other favorite. I feel as if she is writing not simply about the mind, but about my mind. Her books are as visceral to me as music. I find that Woolf, like chocolate, requires rationing; I could easily become emotionally obese if I let myself consume her work too often.

Care to call out your nominees for most overlooked or underappreciated writer?

Rose Macaulay, for her wistful humanity and her glorious sense of humor. There is a scene in *The Towers of Trebizond* in which the narrator realizes that she has copied the wrong sentence out of her Turkish phrase book and has accidentally been soliciting the attention of a hotel guest when she merely wished to explain that she didn't speak the language; it ranks among the best comic scenes in fiction. Emma Lazarus, for her humanitarian passions. She wrote the poem on the Statue of Liberty ("Give me your tired, your poor"), but we've largely forgotten the sedate beauty of her other work, including the prose poems *By the Waters of Babylon*. Rumer Godden, who is incorrectly categorized as a children's writer, and who writes with so much understatement that readers can miss the depth of her insight and her vivid grace. *An Episode of Sparrows* was reissued, and I find it quietly transporting.

You recently earned a doctoral degree in psychology from Cambridge. What were the best books you read during the course of your research?

I was studying motherhood, and I started with D. W. Winnicott, progenitor of the theory of the "good enough mother." Winnicott presumed that mother-infant interactions were reciprocal and satisfying to both. "The most remarkable thing about a mother," he observed, "is her ability to be hurt so much by her baby and to hate so much without paying the child out, and her ability to wait for rewards that may or may not come at a later date." Winnicott sees this selflessness as a hallmark of successful mothering. The book that influenced me the most was Rozsika Parker's *Torn in Two*, published in the United States as *Mother Love, Mother Hate*. Parker's book argues that competent mothering requires two conflicting impulses—to protect and nurture the child, and to push the child out into the world—and suggests that ambivalence is the engine of achieving these dichotomous objectives. Her book notes that we have stigmatized the pushing away and sentimentalized the clinging, and that in doing so, we have denied basic truths about motherhood, causing mothers who experience ambivalence to see themselves as bad mothers when ambivalence is in fact a healthy, necessary state.

What kinds of stories are you drawn to? Any you steer clear of?

I like the long and associative, and read a lot of neo-Proustian stuff. I tend to be put off by action stories—by anything that is about sports, physical danger, or machines. My four-year-old son, however, loves stories about sports, physical danger, and especially machines. So I may be revising my point of view.

What books might we be surprised to find on your shelves?

Every Peanuts anthology ever. I played Linus in my summer camp production of *You're a Good Man, Charlie Brown* and have been addicted to the comic strip ever since. I read them when I'm stressed out, and they serve as something of a security blanket.

Do you ever read self-help? Anything you recommend?

I'm never clear on how "self-help" differs from "help." Books help; they've helped me to understand love, taught me empathy, and given me courage. Even when they merely entertain, they help. For a delicious analysis of the extremely unhelpful self-help industry, see Jessica Lamb-Shapiro's forthcoming *Promise Land*.

What's the last book that made you laugh out loud? That made you cry? And the last book that made you angry?

Jennifer Finney Boylan's endlessly witty *Stuck in the Middle with You* made me laugh out loud over and over again; it's about her experience as a transgender parent, who started off as her children's father and ended up as their "Maddy"—not quite a mom, but definitely no longer a dad. Louise Erdrich's *Painted Drum* made me cry: "And when it happens that you are broken, or betrayed, or left, or hurt, or death brushes near, let yourself sit by an apple tree and listen to the apples falling all around you in heaps, wasting their sweetness. Tell yourself that you tasted as many as you could." *Cracked*, by James Davies, made me furious. Davies argues against psychopharmacology by proposing that all medical approaches to depression, bipolar illness, and schizophrenia are tainted by profit and are therefore ipso facto fraudulent. But everything is tainted by profit; a farmer profited from growing the chicken I ate for dinner last night, but its deliciousness is not a fraud. Davies's book, like Irving Kirsch's *Emperor's New Drugs*, Robert Whitaker's *Anatomy of an Epidemic*, and Daniel Carlat's *Unhinged*, embraces a smug populism that will keep people from taking medications that could save their lives.

If you could require the president to read one book, what would it be?

It would behoove the president to read *Random Family*, Adrian Nicole LeBlanc's searing masterpiece of relentless close-up journalism. No other book I've read charts so clearly the trajectory of poverty and its corrosive compulsions. It's impossible to read it and not become a more empathetic person. The president could use its lessons on the quadrant of society that we've largely abandoned.

Did you identify with any literary characters growing up? Who were your literary heroes?

Prince Andrei Bolkonsky, of course. Sebastian Flyte. I suffered under the misapprehension that I was an Old World aristocrat manqué, rather than a middle-class, striving, and slightly affected New Yorker descended from peasants.

What books have you most enjoyed reading (or rereading) with your children?

We've been reading *Winnie-the-Pooh*, and I am trying to nail the voices of Pooh and Eeyore and Owl half as winningly as my father did. We have a bit of a Moomintroll addiction. And then there are Carl Sandburg's *Rootabaga Stories*, by which I remain as wholly captivated in adulthood as I was in childhood. We're entranced by Tim Egan's recent Dodsworth series about a nattily dressed indeterminate animal (badger? woodchuck?) traveling the world with his hapless, ill-behaved duck.

Disappointing, overrated, just not good: What book did you feel you were supposed to like, and didn't? Do you remember the last book you put down without finishing?

Oliver Sacks relates fascinating case histories and he writes fluently, but he treats his subjects with a tinge of the ringmaster's bravado—an underlying tone of, "Hey, if you think that's weird, wait until you get a load of this one!" It is possible to have clinical rigor without such voyeuristic emotional deficits.

If you could meet any writer, dead or alive, who would it be? What would you want to know?

The J writer, or Yahwist, of the Torah. I'd want to ask him what he intended to be literal and what he intended to be figurative. And I'd point out that confusion around this question has had a toxic effect on the rest of history.

If you could be any character from literature who would you be?

Godot. I rather like the idea that everyone is waiting for me.

What book have you always meant to read and haven't gotten around to yet? Anything you feel embarrassed never to have read?

Moby-Dick.

What do you plan to read next?

Moby-Dick. But I've said that before.

Right now I'm looking right at Mary Gaitskill's *Bad Behavior*; the new Diane Keaton autobiography; *Having It All*, by Helen Gurley Brown (research); and *The Consolations of Philosophy*, by Alain de Botton —all in various states of having-been-read-ed-ness.—**Lena Dunham**

My current audiobook (Yes, they count; of course they count; why wouldn't they?) is *The Sisters Brothers*, by Patrick deWitt. It was recommended by Lemony Snicket (through his representative, Daniel Handler), and I trust Mr. Snicket implicitly. (Or anyway, as implicitly as one can trust someone you have never met, and who may simply be a pen name of the man who played accordion at your wedding.)—**Neil Gaiman**

Shalom Auslander's *Hope: A Tragedy*. His last book, *Foreskin's Lament*, really made me laugh.—**David Sedaris**

Raylan, by Elmore Leonard, one of my writing heroes. There is nobody better at lowlife dialogue. And also, by the way, not a cooler guy on the planet.—**Carl Hiaasen**

I'm reading *Zona*, the latest book by one of my favorite contemporary writers, Geoff Dyer. The premise of the book sounds immensely boring—an essay on Andrei Tarkovsky's film *Stalker*—but fortunately, like most of Dyer's works, it isn't about anything other than the author: his obsessions, his fears, his encroaching (and always endearing) feelings of insanity.—**Alain de Botton**

The Summer of 1787, by David O. Stewart. As I grow older, I am increasingly fascinated by our founding fathers. The challenges they faced and the compromises they made, good and bad, to create a nation have inspired us and people around the world. I wish today's political leaders, especially in Washington, would show the courage and willingness to fight for what they believe in, but possess an understanding of the need to compromise to solve the nation's problems. They all need to go off and read *1787*.—**Colin Powell**

Mary Poppins, by P. L. Travers. *Dancing to the Precipice*, by Caroline Moorehead. *Bring Up the Bodies*, by Hilary Mantel. I've always got two or three on the go.—**Emma Thompson**

The Priceless Gift: The Love Letters of Woodrow Wilson and Ellen Axson Wilson, edited by Eleanor Wilson McAdoo, and *Woodrow Wilson: Life and Letters*, volumes one and two, by Ray Stannard Baker. (Research for my next novel.)—**Joyce Carol Oates**

Moonraker, Ian Fleming, 1955.—**Michael Chabon**

Right now I'm shuttling between *The Map and the Territory*, by the French novelist Michel Houellebecq, and *The Patrick Melrose Novels*, by Edward St. Aubyn, which everyone I know seems to be reading. Houellebecq's known for being a provocateur. He'll say things like "Life was expensive in the west, it was cold there; the prostitution was of poor quality." He says a lot of depressing, un-American things I get a big kick out of.—**Jeffrey Eugenides**

Malcolm Gladwell

What's the best book you've read so far this year?

There have been many. I loved Jonathan Dee's new novel, *A Thousand Pardons*. The best science book I read was Adam Alter's *Drunk Tank Pink*, which is a really provocative look at how much our behavior is contextually determined.

Which writers do you find yourself returning to again and again—reading every new book and rereading the old?

Did I mention Lee Child? The two contemporary writers whom I consider as role models are Janet Malcolm and Michael Lewis. I reread Malcolm's *Psychoanalysis: The Impossible Profession* just to remind myself how nonfiction is supposed to be done. I love how ominous her writing is. Even when she is simply sketching out the scenery, you know that something wonderful and thrilling is about to happen. Lewis is tougher, because what he does is almost impossible to emulate. *The Big Short*, one of the best business books of the past two decades, was about derivatives. I read Lewis for the same reasons I watch Tiger Woods. I'll never play like that. But it's good to be reminded every now and again what genius looks like.

Your new book is in part about underdogs. Who are your favorite underdog writers—underappreciated, yet to be recognized, or altogether forgotten?

The most influential thinker, in my life, has been the psychologist Richard Nisbett. He basically gave me my view of the world. Years ago, he wrote a book called *The Person and the Situation* with Lee Ross. If you read that

---

Malcolm Gladwell is the author of *The Tipping Point*, *Blink*, *Outliers*, *What the Dog Saw*, and *David and Goliath*.

book, you'll see the template for the genre of books that *The Tipping Point* and *Blink* and *Outliers* belong to. That book changed my life. A few years ago, I learned that it was out of print and had been out of print for some time—which broke my heart. (Thankfully there's a new edition.)

Who are your favorite social science writers? Anyone new and especially smart we should pay attention to?

I mentioned Adam Alter, who is a psychologist at New York University. I also really like Adam Grant, who is a psychologist at Penn and the author of *Give and Take*. What really excites me as a sports fan, though, is all the smart sports books coming from an academic perspective: *The Sports Gene*, by David Epstein; *The Numbers Game*, by Chris Anderson and David Sally; and *The Wages of Wins* and *Stumbling on Wins*, by Dave Berri and others.

Many a book is now touted as *The Tipping Point* for X or Y, or generally Gladwellian. What do you make of the many imitators and homages?

I'm flattered, naturally. Although I should point out that it is sometimes said that I invented this genre. I did not. Richard Nisbett and Lee Ross did.

What books, to your mind, bring together social science, business principles, and narrative nonfiction in an interesting or innovative way?

Can I return again to Michael Lewis? Bringing together social science and business principles is easy. Doing that and telling a compelling story is next to impossible. I think only Michael Lewis can do it well. His nonbusiness books like *The Blind Side*, by the way, are even better. That book is as close to perfect as a work of popular nonfiction can be.

Did you identify with any fictional characters as a child? Who was your literary hero?

In my mid-adolescence, my friend Terry Martin and I became obsessed with William F. Buckley. This makes more sense when you realize that we were living in Bible Belt farming country miles from civilization. Buckley seemed impossibly exotic. We used to go into Toronto and prowl the used-book stores on Queen Street looking for rare first editions of *The Unmaking of a Mayor* and *God and Man at Yale*. To this day I know all the great Buckley lines. Upon coming to Canada for a speech, for example, he is asked at the border for the purpose of his visit:

Buckley: I have come to rid Canada of the scourge of socialism.
Guard: How long do you intend to stay?
Buckley: Twenty-four hours.

In southern Ontario farming country when I was growing up, we considered that kind of thing deeply hilarious.

In general, what kinds of stories are you drawn to? Any you steer clear of?

I don't think I will ever write about politics or foreign policy. I feel like there is so much good writing in those areas that I have little to add. I also like to steer clear of writing about people whom I do not personally like. My rule is that if I interview someone, they should never read what I have to say about them and regret having given me the interview.

What's the last book to make you laugh out loud? To cry? And the last book that made you angry?

I read Jeremy Adelman's biography of Albert O. Hirschman early this year and was deeply moved by it. Hirschman wasn't just a man with a thousand extraordinary adventures (fighting fascists in Spain, smuggling Jews out of France, writing *Exit, Voice, and Loyalty* and a handful of other unforgettable books). He was also wise and decent and honest. I finished that book with tears in my eyes.

What books might we be surprised to find on your shelves?

I have—by conservative estimate—several hundred novels with the word "spy" in the title.

If you could require the president to read one book, what would it be?

The new Lee Child, of course! It might be nice for him to escape for a few hours to a world where one man can solve every one of the world's problems with nothing but his wits and his fists.

Disappointing, overrated, just not good: What book did you feel you were supposed to like, and didn't? Do you remember the last book you put down without finishing?

I feel terrible for saying this. But I started reading *The Cuckoo's Calling* before I knew it was by J. K. Rowling, and I couldn't finish it. Is there something wrong with me?

If you could meet any writer, dead or alive, who would it be? What would you want to know?

Shakespeare's wife, of course. So I could settle this whole thing once and for all.

If you could meet any character from literature, who would it be?

I'd like to go for a long walk on the Hampstead Heath with George Smiley. It would be drizzling. We would end up having a tepid cup of tea somewhere, with slightly stale biscuits. I would ask him lots of questions about Control, and he would evade them, gracefully.

What book have you always meant to read and haven't gotten around to yet? Anything you feel embarrassed not to have read?

I have never read any Tolstoy. I felt badly about this until I read a Bill Simmons column where he confessed that he'd never seen *The Big Lebowski*. Simmons, it should be pointed out, has seen everything. He said that everyone needs to have skipped at least one great cultural touchstone.

What do you plan to read next?

Something with the word "spy" in the title.

Scott Turow

What book is on your night stand now?

I'm loving Adam Johnson's *The Orphan Master's Son*, set in North Korea. The novel won this year's Pulitzer but, more important, comes with the enthralled recommendations of writer friends. Like most readers, I'm inclined to rely on the word of people in my life whose tastes I respect.

What was the last truly great book you read?

When I noticed that Patti Smith's *Just Kids* had won the National Book Award for nonfiction in 2010, I ranted about contemporary culture, so celebrity-besotted that we were now giving vaunted literary prizes to rock stars. Then I read the book. It is profound and unique, a perfectly wrought account of what it means to give your life to art and to another person. I expect it to be read with wonder for a long time.

What's your favorite literary genre? Any guilty pleasures? Do you like to read other legal thrillers?

I read little nonfiction, but I have no boundaries about the fiction I relish. The only unfailing criterion is that I can hitch my heart to the imagined world and read on. Yes, I enjoy the novels written by lawyer friends, but regard that as a busman's holiday.

Scott Turow is the author of *Presumed Innocent*, *Innocent*, and *Identical*, among other novels. His works of nonfiction include *One L* and *Ultimate Punishment*.

What's the best book about the law ever written?

A Theory of Justice, by John Rawls. It's not beach reading, but I don't know of a more lucid articulation of the intuitions many of us share about what is just. Among works of fiction, Melville's *Billy Budd* would be my first choice, especially in the present day, when the sexual undertones that once dared not speak their name are so apparent.

And the best book about Chicago?

Although the eponymous protagonist of Saul Bellow's *Herzog* wanders through many locales, the extended sections of the novel set in Chicago are remarkable for their vividness, humor, and idiosyncratic insights. All of Bellow's writing about Chicago was accomplished with such energy that you have to wonder if he had his finger in an electric socket.

What book has had the greatest impact on you?

Probably *The Count of Monte Cristo*, which I read at age ten. Its account of prison escape, sword-fighting, and long-nurtured revenge transported me, and somehow inspired the thought that if it was this exciting to read a book, then it had to be even more thrilling to write one, to live the experience for years instead of days, and to feel the whole adventure come to life within you. Such is the wisdom you get from ten-year-olds. But now and then, there are days when it turns out he had it right.

Who are the writers you most admire?

Living? Ian McEwan and Cormac McCarthy lead by a thimble's width in a very close race. Le Carré and Ruth Rendell are the writers of suspense I most cherish. And among those no longer walking among us, I prize Tolstoy, Dickens, Bellow, Graham Greene, Hemingway, Tillie Olsen, and everybody's all-star, Shakespeare.

If you could require the president to read one book, what would it be?

The *Book Review* actually posed the same question to me before President Obama took office, and I find, demonstrating Hobbes's eternal wisdom about consistency, that my answer would no longer be the same. In 2008, I recommended a book about the *Vasa*, the seventeenth-century Swedish warship that sank on its maiden voyage, killing more than one hundred sailors, because no one dared tell the king the boat wasn't seaworthy. These days I think I would choose Malraux's *Man's Fate*, for that novel's nuanced meditation on the great personal costs and redeeming value of political idealism.

Describe your reading habits. Paper or electronic? Do you take notes?

Because I spend so much time traveling, I tend to do most of my reading on the same iPad on which I write. For me, it's words, not paper, that matter most in the end. This practice has had the additional benefit of greatly reducing the time I spend storming through the house, defaming the mysterious forces who "hid my book."

Read more than one book at a time?

I'm often sampling more than one book, as I'm deciding what I'll devote myself to next.

Listen to audiobooks?

Audiobooks are generally reserved for poetry. How neat is it to listen to Philip Levine on the way to the grocery store?

You've been the president of the Authors Guild since 2010. How has that experience changed the way you think about, select, buy, and read books?

Not a lot. Naturally, I'm more committed to books written by the authors on the guild's board, a very gifted bunch. And although I shop like mad on Amazon, I buy books there only as a last resort, as a lame protest against some of the company's book-selling practices.

What were your favorite books as a child?

Black Beauty, by Anna Sewell, remains a star-dusted memory, because my mom read it aloud to my sister and me at night for months. I was no more than seven.

Do you have a favorite character or hero?

John Updike's Harry Angstrom, a.k.a. Rabbit, who gropes toward personal grace through four novels only to whiff in the end. After I finished *Rabbit at Rest*, I wrote Updike a fan letter telling him that I didn't understand how he found the strength to get up every day to write a book so sad, especially about a character whom Updike knew and revealed with such amazing intimacy. It was like sending a dear friend to the gallows. But Updike's intricate rendering of Rabbit over the course of thirty years is a profound achievement.

Disappointing, overrated, just not good: What book did you feel you were supposed to like, and didn't?

I may be the only person in captivity who wasn't persuaded by *The Remains of the Day*, which I regarded as largely a parlor trick with the passive voice. I also have had a violent reaction against a couple of Toni Morrison's novels, which I deemed deliberately opaque.

Do you remember the last book you put down without finishing?

I do that so often I have a term for it—I say I "read at" a book. That is seldom a comment on the quality of the work, more the sign of a wandering mind. I've been known to come back to a book months or years later and finish it with enormous enthusiasm. The last one in that category was *The Tiger's Wife*, by Téa Obrcht.

If you could meet any writer, dead or alive, who would it be? What would you want to know?

I adore the company of other writers, because they are so often lively minds and, frequently, blazingly funny. And of course we get each other in a unique way. (That's probably a common feeling in all professions; certainly I know many lawyers who are bored by anybody who isn't an attorney.) But I haven't found my friendships with other writers to be especially revelatory about the literary process. Overall, I hold to the saying that "writers are better read than met," meaning only that what makes them fascinating is on the page and not on their sleeves. Still, I'm full of regret at the moment that my relationship with Dutch Leonard went no further than a couple of notes back and forth, just so I could have paid tribute in person. And it would have been a revelation to hang out around Shakespeare in close quarters between 1604 and 1606. How does one human write *Othello*, *King Lear*, and *Macbeth* inside three years, not to mention a few sonnets that will be read forever? It would almost be like watching the earth and heavens created in seven days.

What do you plan to read next?

Well, let me tell you what's queued up: *Dom Casmurro*, by Joaquim Maria Machado de Assis, a classic of Brazilian literature, which I'm taking up because I'm headed to the country; *Case Histories*, by Kate Atkinson; *Swamplandia!*, by Karen Russell; and *Revelation Space*, by Alastair Reynolds, one of those books I'm returning to because of my son's rapturous endorsement.

Donna Tartt

What are you reading at the moment? Are you a one-book-at-a-time person?

I've always got a dozen books going, which is why my suitcases are always so heavy. At the moment: Am greatly enjoying the Neversink Library reissue of Jean Cocteau's *Difficulty of Being*, since my copy from college is so torn up the pages are falling out. Am also loving Rachel Kushner's *Telex from Cuba* and Gilbert Highet's *Poets in a Landscape*, a charming appreciation of Catullus and Propertius and the Latin poets. (I love almost all the reissues of the New York Review Books Classics—at the Corner Bookstore, uptown, they shelve them all together, and I always make a beeline for that shelf the instant I set foot in the store.) On the table by my bed: *Byron: The Last Journey*, by Harold Nicolson; *Horse, Flower, Bird*, by Kate Bernheimer; Barry Paris's biography of Louise Brooks; and *Rifleman: A Front-Line Life*, by Victor Gregg with Rick Stroud. I always have a comfort book going too, something I've read many times, and for me at the moment that comfort book is Raymond Chandler's *The Big Sleep*.

What's the best book you've read so far this year?

I certainly haven't enjoyed anything more than *The Unquiet Grave*, by Cyril Connolly, which I went back and reread sometime early this year. I've loved it since I was a teenager and like always to have it to hand; when I lived in France, years ago, it was one of only six books I carried with me—but

---

Donna Tartt is the author of the novels *The Goldfinch*, *The Secret History*, and *The Little Friend*.

because of its aphoristic nature, usually I only read bits and pieces of it, and it's been many years since I read the whole thing start to finish.

Who are your favorite novelists?

The novelists I love best, the ones who made me want to become a writer, are mostly from the nineteenth century: Dickens, Melville, James, Conrad, Stevenson, Dostoyevsky, with Dickens probably coming first in that list. As far as twentieth-century novelists go, I love Nabokov, Evelyn Waugh, Salinger, Fitzgerald, Don DeLillo; and of the twenty-first century, my two favorites so far are Edward St. Aubyn and Paul Murray.

What's the best thing about writing a novel?

I love having an alternate life to retreat into and to lose myself in. I love being away from the world so long—so far out from shore. Eleven years.

The hardest?

Honestly, there are so many hard things about writing a novel that it's hard to pick just one, but I particularly hate having to try to formulate an answer when someone asks me: What's your book about?

What kinds of stories are you drawn to? Any you steer clear of?

I'm not very interested in contemporary American realism, or books about marriage, parenting, suburbia, divorce. Even as a child browsing at the library I distinctly remember avoiding books that had the big silver Caldecott award sticker on the front, because I loved fairy tales, ghost stories, adventures, whereas the Caldecott prize stories often had a dutiful tone that tended more toward social issues. Those things were not my cup of tea, even when I was small, and I knew it—although if something's written well enough, anything goes. To paraphrase Nabokov: all I want from a book is the tingle down the spine, for my hairs to stand on end.

Do you ever read self-help? Anything you recommend?

I was a great fan of the now defunct Loompanics press, which published such self-help classics as *The Complete Guide to Lock Picking* and *How to Disappear Completely and Never Be Found*.

What books might we be surprised to find on your shelves?

See above.

How do you organize your own personal library?

Not very well, I'm afraid. But I know where everything is.

Do you keep books or give them away?

Keep them. But I give lots of books as gifts.

If you could require the president to read one book, what would it be?

I wouldn't dream of requiring the president to read a book; he's far too busy, and besides, I think we probably wouldn't enjoy the same books.

Did you identify with any literary characters growing up? Who were your heroes?

As a child I adored Huckleberry Finn and Peter Pan. As a teenager: Franny Glass. In my twenties: Agatha Runcible.

If you could meet any writer, dead or alive, who would it be?

This to me is the most interesting question on the list, as it's something I spend a great deal of time thinking about every day. Just because you love a writer's books doesn't necessarily mean they would be great company. I'd love to meet Oscar Wilde, because they all say he was so much more wonderful in person than on the page. From reading the journals of Tennessee Williams, I'm almost positive that if Tennessee and I had ever met, we would have been friends. And if it was a dinner date? Albert Camus. That trench coat! That cigarette! I think my French is good enough. We'd have a great time.

Disappointing, overrated, just not good: What book did you feel you were supposed to like, and didn't?

I don't like Hemingway. And I know I don't love *Ulysses* as much as I am supposed to—but then again, I never cared even one-tenth so much for the *Odyssey* as I do for the *Iliad*.

Do you remember the last book you put down without finishing?

Definitely I do, but impolitic to say.

If you could be any character from literature, who would you be?

This is a hard question, because so many great characters from literature come to bad ends. Mrs. Stitch, from *Scoop*, driving around madly in her tiny motorcar, looks like she's having a lot of fun, though. So does Tom Ripley.

What book have you always meant to read and never gotten around to yet? What do you feel embarrassed never to have read?

I'm looking at Shelby Foote's three-volume history of the Civil War on my shelf—somehow I've never managed to read the whole thing. And I've never read most of the novels of Thomas Hardy, although I don't feel embarrassed about it. Even though I love a lot of his poetry, his novels are just too sad for me.

What will you read next?

Lord Rochester's Monkey, by Graham Greene. And—now that it's out—*Doctor Sleep,* by Stephen King.

Stories I'm Drawn To (Continued)

I like stories about people who have to go into darkness for a good reason and then have to figure out how to deal with the darkness that seeps into their souls. It's a variation on the noble cause, I guess. I avoid stories that explain the villain and why he acts out. It's just not that interesting to me. I like the bargain that good cops make. Like a law of physics, they go into darkness; darkness goes into them. They have to decide how to prevent it from destroying them.
—**Michael Connelly**

I think "experimental fiction" is a synonym for "Give me a break," and I've never been able to warm to sci-fi. Other than that, I'm an omnivore.
—**Anna Quindlen**

Sad to say, I do like a bit of action. I get impatient with love; I want fighting. I don't like overrefinement, or to dwell in the heads of vaporous ladies with fine sensibilities.
—**Hilary Mantel**

I love just about any kind of story as long as it is well told, makes an emotional impact, and holds an elusive sense of mystery. That said, it has been many years since I've read fantasy or science fiction.
Khaled Hosseini

Anything that involves David and Goliath.
—**James McBride**

I like stories where people suffer a lot. If there's no suffering, I kind of tune out. After reading Karl Ove Knausgaard's memoir, *My Struggle*, I was shocked to discover that people suffer in Norway as well. Good for them! *Skal!*
—**Gary Shteyngart**

Ann Patchett

What's the best book you've read so far this year?

Anthony Marra's *A Constellation of Vital Phenomena*. And all the books I mention below. It's been a great year for reading.

Describe your ideal reading experience (when, where, what, how).

In the best-case scenario, I know nothing about the book, and reading it is my sole obligation. For example, I read J. K. Rowling's *The Casual Vacancy* as a pile of paper because I was going to interview her. I thought that book was brilliant. When it came out and got such middling reviews I was mystified. I felt so lucky to have had my own experience with it. I recently read Donna Tartt's novel *The Goldfinch* the same way, eight hundred pieces of paper and no explanation of what was coming. I stayed on the couch for three days and did nothing but read. People have such high expectations for Donna's novels because they come around so rarely, and she knocked this one out of the park.

Is there anything that especially inclines you to pick up a particular book—are you swayed by covers, titles, blurbs, reviews, what your best friend has to say?

I'm swayed by everything, which is why it's nice to read a book as a pile of paper every now and then. A well-written rave review always catches my

---

Ann Patchett is the author of *Bel Canto*, *State of Wonder*, *The Patron Saint of Liars*, and *Truth and Beauty*, among other books.

attention. Baz Dreisinger's review of Jim McBride's *The Good Lord Bird* was so convincing that I went straight to the bookstore and bought myself a copy. I'm pleased to report that McBride deserved every bit of the praise. I also read two great reviews by Barbara Kingsolver this year—one of Karen Joy Fowler's *We Are All Completely Beside Ourselves* and the other of Elizabeth Gilbert's *The Signature of All Things*. I thought that Kingsolver, who loved both books, was right on the money.

How has owning a bookstore changed your approach to deciding what to read?

If I'd done this interview two years ago, I'd be telling you how much I was enjoying rereading *The Ambassadors*. Parnassus has made me a very current reader. I read a lot of galleys. I read the books of the people who are coming to the store. I miss having time for James, but I'm also enjoying myself immensely.

Please take a moment to herald your favorite overlooked or underappreciated writer.

Geoffrey Wolff! I asked Vintage to put *A Day at the Beach* back in print so I could take it with me on book tour in November. I'm a big fan of all of Wolff's work, but this is the best book of essays I know. I've become a very convincing bookseller, and I plan to sell the hell out of this one.

What's the best book you've ever received as a gift?

Living Room, an out-of-print book of photographs by Nick Waplington. The photographer Melissa Ann Pinney gave it to me years ago. It's still the book I want to show everyone who comes to my house. And the illustrator Barry Moser is a great friend, and the books of his that he's given me over the years would be the first things I would grab if the house were on fire (assuming my husband and dog were already outside).

Tell us about your favorite memoirs.

Edwidge Danticat's *Brother, I'm Dying* is probably my favorite. I also love her new novel, *Claire of the Sea Light*. She's so smart and such a beautiful writer. She knows exactly how to break my heart and put it back together again. Patti Smith's *Just Kids* reminded me of what it felt like to be young and want so much to be an artist and live a meaningful life. And then there's Moss Hart's *Act One*. *Act One* is one of the best things about owning a bookstore. I can sell *Act One* to people all day long.

What book has had the greatest impact on you?

After I read *Charlotte's Web*, I became so obsessed with pigs that my step-father got me one for my ninth birthday. It was because of that pig that I became a vegetarian. That's impact.

Did you grow up with a lot of books? What are your memories of being read to as a child?

I grew up in a house full of books. My memories are of my parents reading, but not of them reading to me. I don't mean that critically. They loved books. I wanted to read what they were reading. I read *Humboldt's Gift* when I was fifteen because my mother had just finished it. After that, it was all Saul Bellow all the time. I read *Humboldt* again a few months ago, and I was amazed by how clearly I remembered it. Nobody writes like that any-more—maybe Michael Chabon.

Disappointing, overrated, just not good: What book did you feel you were supposed to like, and didn't? Do you remember the last book you put down without finishing?

Do you mean today? I get so many galleys—at my house, at the book-store—there are books stacked up everywhere that people want me to read. I probably quit reading a couple books a week. I have to love a book, or at least have an enormous sense of obligation toward a book, in order to keep going.

If you could meet any writer, dead or alive, who would it be? What would you want to know?

I'd want to see my friend Lucy Grealy again. I'd want to know how the afterlife was treating her, if there was anything or everything about this world she missed. She'd say to me, "My God, how did you get here?" And I would say, *"The New York Times Book Review* told me I could meet any writer, living or dead, and I picked you!" Then I imagine there would be a great deal of hugging and dancing around.

If you could meet any character from literature, who would it be?

Mowgli and his crowd. We could invite Charlotte the spider and Wilbur the pig over, make it a talking-animal party.

What's next on your reading list?

J. Courtney Sullivan came to read at Parnassus, and I gave her a copy of Jeannette Haien's *The All of It*. She sent me Edna O'Brien's *The Country Girls Trilogy* in return. I very much want to read that. Also, Rachel Kushner's *The Flamethrowers*. And the new Doris Kearns Goodwin; that's a must. I'm a Doris Kearns Goodwin completist.

What to Read on that Desert Island

Moby-Dick, Ulysses, and *How to Build a Working Airplane Out of Coconuts.*
—**Michael Chabon**

The King James Bible. *Anna Karenina*. And a how-to book on raft-building.
—**Jeffrey Eugenides**

Collected works of Shakespeare (not cheating—I've got a single volume of them); collected works of P. G. Wodehouse (two volumes, but I'm sure I could find one); collected works of Colette.
—**J. K. Rowling**

This is a question that always kills me. For a book lover this type of triage is never a record of what was brought along but a record of what was left behind. But if forced to choose by, say, a shipwreck or an evil *Times* editor, I'd probably grab novels that I'm still wrestling with. Like Samuel R. Delany's *Dhalgren* (which in my opinion is one of the greatest and most perplexing novels of the twentieth century) or Toni Morrison's *Beloved* (to be an American writer or to be interested in American literature and not to have read *Beloved*, in my insufferable calculus, is like calling yourself a sailor and never having bothered to touch the sea) or Cormac McCarthy's *Blood Meridian* (so horrifyingly profound and compellingly ingenious it's almost sorcery). Maybe Octavia Butler's *Dawn* (set in a future where the remnants of the human race are forced to "trade" genes—read: breed involuntarily—with our new alien overlords). Or Gilbert Hernandez's *Beyond Palomar* (if it wasn't for *Poison River* I don't think I would have become a writer). To be honest I'd probably hold a bunch of these books in hand and only decide at the last instant, as the water was flooding up around my knees, which three I'd bring. And then I'd spend the rest of that time on the desert island dreaming about the books that I left behind and also of all the books, new and old, that I wasn't getting a chance to read.
—**Junot Díaz**

Amy Tan

What's the best book you've read so far this year?

Richard Ford's *Canada*. I've loved all his books, from the characters to the parenthetical sentences. His voice always sounds so casual, as if the narrator is working it out in his head for the first time. There's quiet intensity, an easy familiarity with the character. You know the habits in how the character thinks, what he might take into account. The narrator is more observational than judgmental, and forgiving in that way. It has much to do with a need to be rewarded for doing more, or compensated for following the rules or recognized as better for working harder. It's not simple greed. It's about a sense of self before and after you've taken the wrong road to a land of diminishing opportunity.

Describe your ideal reading experience (when, where, what, how).

I've often fantasized I would get a lot of writing done if I were put in prison for a minor crime. Three to six months. Incarceration would be good for reading as well. No e-mail, no useless warranties to get steamed about, no invitations to fund-raisers. But until I commit the necessary minor crime, I would choose a twelve-hour flight. Time flies by fast with a good book. Two benefits. I do have to pick the right-length book matched to destination. It's terrible to have twenty pages left and then be told to put your seat in an upright position. That happened when I read *The Immortal Life of Henrietta Lacks*.

Amy Tan is the author of *The Joy Luck Club, The Kitchen God's Wife, The Hundred Secret Senses, The Bonesetter's Daughter, Saving Fish from Drowning,* and *The Valley of Amazement,* among other books.

Who are your favorite novelists?

My favorite anything is always relative to the context of present time, place, and mood. When I finish a book and want to immediately find another by the same author and no other, that author is elevated to my favorite. In the past, they have included: Louise Erdrich, Vladimir Nabokov, Javier Marías, Richard Ford, Ha Jin, Annie Proulx, Arthur Conan Doyle, F. Scott Fitzgerald, D. H. Lawrence, Jamaica Kincaid—many, many others.

Do you have a favorite classic work of Chinese literature?

Jing Ping Mei (*The Plum in the Golden Vase*). The author is anonymous. I would describe it as a book of manners for the debauched. Its readers in the late Ming period likely hid it under their bedcovers, because it was banned as pornographic. It has a fairly modern, naturalistic style—"Show, don't tell"—and there are a lot of sex scenes shown. For years, I didn't know I had the expurgated edition that provided only elliptical hints of what went on between falling into bed and waking up refreshed. The unexpurgated edition is instructional.

Who are the best Chinese and Chinese-American writers working today?

I've read Chinese novels only in translation, which limits how well I can judge who is "best." I've read work by the early feminist writers Wang Anyi, Zhang Jie, and Cheng Naishan (who died recently). You have to understand how radical their novels and short stories were at the time they were published. They included notions of suffering, thwarted love, the Cultural Revolution, a forlorn look at the past, and a nostalgic Shanghai. A love story could have been seen as criticism of the Cultural Revolution. I also admire Yan Geling's stories. Beneath beauty and idealism is cruelty and ill intent. I've read a couple of Mo Yan's novels, which also could be judged as a less patriotic view of the Great Leap Forward. When he won the Nobel Prize in Literature, there was a flurry of criticism accusing him of being an apple polisher to the party for not speaking up for another Nobel laureate who was in prison, the dissident Liu Xiaobo. Then came the bashing of Mo Yan's work for its crude literary style and subjects. With prizes, I've observed, literary merit is often a sliding scale based on the author's political actions—or inaction.

Among Chinese-American writers, two immediately come to mind: Yiyun Li and Ha Jin, with their particular mix of displaced characters, circumstances, and past. Their stories often have tragedy, but rise above that. They elicit discomfort and compassion—good and necessary conditions that change me, as any writing is capable of doing by putting me in unfamiliar situations and magnifying the details I would have overlooked.

Please take a moment to herald your favorite overlooked or underappreciated writer.

For years, I have been heralding the work of Rabih Alameddine, a Lebanese-American writer. His prose is gorgeous, his approach irreverent, and the ideas in his stories are sometimes comical or fantastical, but always deadly serious—very relevant to understanding the complex history behind multiple holy wars today. In Italy and Spain, his books are best sellers. He has full-page profiles in major newspapers, has garnered prizes, is a darling of literary festivals, and has won acclaim from international writers. In the United States, he's hardly known. Why is there a geographic divide in literary appreciation?

What kinds of stories are you drawn to? Any you steer clear of?

I'm open to reading almost anything—fiction, nonfiction—as long as I know from the first sentence or two that this is a voice I want to listen to for a good long while. It has much to do with imagery and language, a particular perspective, the assured knowledge of the particular universe the writer has created.

I don't steer clear of genres. I simply haven't steered myself toward some of them. I haven't sought out much science fiction since the days when my husband and I read aloud H. P. Lovecraft while sitting around the campfire on backpacking trips. In those days, I would also read aloud gruesome passages from *Bear Attacks*. We enjoyed scaring ourselves witless in the wilderness, where there were, in fact, many bears. These days, I simply read the news and all the horror stories about the House of Representatives.

What books might we be surprised to find on your shelves?

A lot of books on animal cognition and behavior—crows, ravens, dogs, and even ants. I'm a sucker for dog training books as well. And I collect antiquarian books on biology. One is a four-volume set, *The Science of Life*, by sci-fi writer H. G. Wells; his son G. P. Wells; and Julian Huxley, a biologist and also a prominent eugenicist.

What's the best book you've ever received as a gift?

On December 7, 1999, I left the bedside of my editor Faith Sale, just before she was removed from life support. We had been like sisters. Two hours later, Stephen King called and asked my husband, Lou, and me to meet him at his hotel room. It was his first public foray after being nearly killed by a van six months before. He gave me an advance reading copy of *On Writing*. A couple of years before, we had talked about the question no one asks us in interviews: language. He had been thinking of doing a book on writing, and I had said, "Do it." He now asked me to look at the dedication. It was for me. We then went to see the premiere of *The Green Mile*, about a man on death row who can heal people, including those dying of cancer. That night was both enormously sad and gloriously uplifting.

What book has had the greatest impact on you?

Probably the Bible. My father was a minister, and I heard verses every day. I memorized big whacks of passages to earn progressive levels of pins. The repetitive rhythms of the Bible were inscribed in my writing brain from childhood. (And it may account for my tendency to start sentences with "and.") Many of my stories also relate to undoing handed-down beliefs, whether they come from religion, society, or mothers. And my writing sensibility was also warped by a steady dose of gothic imagery, often related to religious sins or virtue: David braining Goliath, Samson's bloody head missing a lock of hair, a stinking corpse arising to be kissed by relatives.

If you could require the president to read one book, what would it be?

I would never require anyone to read any book. That seems antithetical to why we read—which is to choose a book for our personal reasons. I always shudder when I'm told my books are on required reading lists.

Did you grow up with a lot of books? What are your memories of being read to as a child?

Books were luxuries. We had the *World Book Encyclopedia*, donated Reader's Digest Condensed Books, inspirational books by Billy Graham, Bibles in foreign languages, and my favorite, a book on a high shelf called *Psycho-pathia Sexualis*. One Christmas I received an Italian book of Chinese fairy tales. All the sages, gods, and mortals looked like Italian movie actors and actresses. I recently unearthed it.

My mother and father didn't read fiction books, at least not in English. But for one year, my father read to my brothers and me bedtime stories, a page a night from a book called *365 Stories*, covering the daily life of happy American kids with minor dilemmas. The fiction books I read on my own came from the library. From the age of six, I carefully chose five or six every two weeks, working my way through the ones I could reach on progressively higher shelves. Fairy tales were favorites. I crossed a threshold of reader pride after finishing *To Kill a Mockingbird*. And I made it a point to read banned books, like *The Catcher in the Rye*, which led to counseling sessions with a youth minister, who told me such books would give me sinful feelings. That incident solidified feelings I have about the power of books and one's helplessness without them.

Do you have a favorite childhood literary character or hero?

Jane Eyre remains a favorite. Her truthfulness sometimes made me laugh. And her loneliness and need to make her own way mirrored my feelings. The Little Prince is another lost soul I clung to. Pippi Longstocking was a bit too cheerful.

Which writers inspire you?

When I first started writing short stories, I read collections by Amy Hempel, Mavis Gallant, Alice Munro, Molly Giles, Flannery O'Connor, Eudora Welty, Richard Ford, Mary Robison, Chekhov, and many others. And then I read Louise Erdrich's *Love Medicine*, with its strong multiple voices. The stories were bound by community and mutual loss. That later became a model for the structure of *The Joy Luck Club*.

These days, any book that astonishes me can either inspire me or make me feel I should give up writing. Coetzee's *Disgrace* made me feel the latter.

If you could meet any writer, dead or alive, who would it be? What would you want to know?

Emily Dickinson. I would be her nursemaid, her quiet companion on walks in the woods. I imagine that anything she spotted—feathers, tea leaves, a hole in a fence—would lead her to utter something profound about human emotions in a lifetime of expectation.

If you could meet any character from literature, who would it be?

I would not want characters to come to my world. They'd lose their special qualities, the perfect amount of what I should know about them. On the other hand, I could go to theirs because they would not have any preconceptions of who I was. I'd like to hang out with the Cheshire cat, learn how to disappear, and speak in smart illogic. He would look exactly like his pen-and-ink illustration by Tenniel. I'd be rendered in pen and ink, too. That would be required for entering a pen-and-ink world with its particular dimensional strangeness.

Do you miss playing with your old band, the Rock Bottom Remainders?

I deeply miss our founder, Kathi Kamen Goldmark. But I have a feeling the Remainders will go on like the sequels of novels. We are already banding together at the Miami Book Fair to do our first annual reunion.

What's next on your reading list?

I've just started two books. One is dark, *Weights and Measures*, by Joseph Roth. It fits the mood of what I feel is happening in the United States—the dangerous shifts, the disintegration of what held the country together, the moral demise of politicians, moneylenders, and heroes.

The other is more hopeful: *My Beloved World*, by Sonia Sotomayor. I'm grateful for her wisdom and compassion on the Supreme Court. In June, Justice Sotomayor invited my husband and me to have a private lunch with her in her chambers. This was right when the justices began deliberations over the major cases. We talked about our mothers' fears, about publishing, translations, snorkeling, adopted kids, and cultural self-identification—all sorts of things, except the cases. I've read the first ten pages of her memoir and know already that it's like a continuation of the conversation we had.

Bryan Cranston

What's the best book you've read so far this year?

Lyndon Johnson and the American Dream, by Doris Kearns Goodwin. Real insight on the thirty-sixth president from someone who knew him well.

Describe your ideal reading experience (when, where, what, how).

While shooting in Portland, Oregon, I got the pleasure of discovering Powell's Books, an enormous old bookstore (which I hope still exists) and stayed there the entire day. I just curled up in a comfy chair and read. They had a cafe in the store that I frequented. What joy. I suppose it helped that it was a rainy day. Rain creates a Pavlovian response in me to relax with a good book. I find that peace at our beach house, and created a cozy nook just for that purpose. I admit that I am driven to work and have to remind myself that reading is not an indulgence or a luxury. I have to improve that aspect of my life.

You recently recorded the audiobook version of Tim O'Brien's *The Things They Carried*. Are you a fan of the book? Did performing it aloud change your perception of it?

The main reason I agreed to do the audiobook was because I had wanted to read that book and never got around to it. So I thought, why not commit to this and then I will be guaranteed to read it? These questions have exposed an uncomfortable condition, in which I can make time for reading books if

---

Bryan Cranston is an actor best known for his starring roles on the television series *Breaking Bad* and *Malcolm in the Middle,* and is the winner of three Emmy awards and a Golden Globe award.

it's "work related" but not for just my own personal pleasure. . . . I need to see a shrink.

What was the experience of recording a book like for you? How was it different from the theater, film, and television work you've done?

I found narrating an audiobook very challenging, a task exacerbated by my suspected—but undiagnosed—mild dyslexia. Still, the experience was rewarding for the discovery that one, I did it; and two, that I won't do another one; and three, that the strength of the story got me through the long recording sessions. It's a real talent to convey emotions through your vocal choices and it takes real stamina. There are far better actors doing that work than myself.

Do you draw inspiration for your theater, television, and film projects from the books you read?

A) Yes. The three main tools in an actor's toolbox are personal experience, research, and imagination. Richly drawn literary characters plant seeds in our brains for future reference. When developing a character we will unwittingly pull from those memories to form a whole character. . . . Then we selfishly claim them as original.

B) And vice versa. Anna Gunn, my wife on *Breaking Bad*, gave me a beautiful hardcover of *The Dangerous Book for Boys*. A perfect book to flip through to get back in touch with the little boy within. It inspired me to create a concept for a TV show. . . . Stay tuned.

You recently portrayed Lyndon Johnson at the American Repertory Theater in Cambridge in the play *All the Way*, a production that is headed for Broadway. Did you read any books on Johnson, aside, I presume, from Doris Kearns Goodwin, to prepare for the role? What books in particular informed your portrayal?

In addition to Goodwin's book, I plunged into Robert Caro's *Master of the Senate*, Mark Updegrove's *Indomitable Will*, and Michael Beschloss's *Taking Charge*. And I must admit being curious about the new book, Roger Stone's *The Man Who Killed Kennedy: The Case Against LBJ*, but I think I'll save that for after the run of the play.

Of all the characters you've played across different media, which role felt to you the richest—the most, perhaps, novelistic?

Breaking Bad's Walter White. The depth of this tragic story made it feel like the character reached Shakespearean level.

What kinds of stories are you drawn to? Any you steer clear of?

I like mysteries, thrillers, and adventures best. I haven't been interested in very many science fiction novels.

What books might we be surprised to find on your shelves?

After my confession of not being attracted to sci-fi, one might be surprised to see the collection of Philip K. Dick's short stories. Love those.

What book has had the greatest impact on you?

Nonfiction: *The Road Less Traveled*. Fiction: *Moby-Dick*.

If you could meet any writer, dead or alive, who would it be? What would you want to know?

The *Wizard of Oz* novelist, L. Frank Baum . . . If he really was a racist as is rumored. And if so, how could he write such a heartfelt story? Were the Munchkins a metaphor? Did he have the Wicked Witch of the West killed off because he hated green people?

What's next on your reading list?

After *All the Way* is up and running, I will transition into reading a Dalton Trumbo biography by Bruce Cook. I have once again succumbed to perusing books for occupational purposes. But I love baseball and I'm eager to read *The Art of Fielding*. It's on my bed stand right now, taunting me.

I usually read at night, in the bed, before falling asleep. In the summertime, I love to read on the porch in a rocker under a ceiling fan.—**John Grisham**

Every evening by my living room fireplace in a splendid Eames chair, giving thanks to my bad back for excusing this extravagant purchase.—**P. J. O'Rourke**

I love to pick up a book, read two pages, and shake my head with wonder and gratitude that I'm going to be covered for the ten or so days I've got this book to which I will keep returning. Two pages into *The Poisonwood Bible*, *Middlemarch*, and *In the Garden of Beasts*, I said, "I'm in."—**Anne Lamott**

I like to read at the beach, but the beach always turns out to be too relaxing, and I fall asleep after two pages. So I wind up doing most of my actual reading at night in bed, where I sometimes get through as many as three pages before I fall asleep.—**Dave Barry**

I like to read in my own house, in any of the rooms I always mean to paint or otherwise improve and never do. Every detail is so familiar to me that it makes almost no claim on my attention. I read whenever I can, when I am not preparing to teach, or writing. **Marilynne Robinson**

The book creates the experience. If I'm loving something, I suddenly discover large chunks of reading time that I wasn't aware of having. But I will say there's nothing like being stuck in a middle seat on a long flight that begins with a two-hour delay. In a situation like that, a few years ago, I'd brought along a new novel that critics were wild about and that I was certain I would enjoy. It was so boring and dead that after fifty pages I just closed it and stared at the seat-back tray and suffered, resenting the author and psychoanalyzing the critics.
—**Jonathan Franzen**

I am not picky—if possible I would like to read in Rome or Paris, but since that's usually not an option, I like to read in bed.—**Caroline Kennedy**

I travel a lot, and having a good book on airplanes and in airports transforms tedium into treasured time. The other day, I was stuck at O'Hare for eight hours, but I had a prepublication copy of a riveting memoir, *A House in the Sky*, by Amanda Lindhout, about being kidnapped in Somalia. A few of the other travelers were having loud hissy fits, complaining that we were being treated horribly, and I had to bite my tongue to keep from shouting out: "We got food and clean water! You all don't know how good we have it!"—**Jeannette Walls**

Reading is still my favorite pastime. It kicks writing's butt. You learn so much more from reading than you do from writing, although writing pays slightly more. I start reading at four p.m. and continue way into cocktail hour, which begins at four thirty.—**Gary Shteyngart**

My most recent, best reading experience was a vacation last summer that involved reading feverishly in a friend's sixteenth-century stone cottage in the Corrèze, and doing the same in a cheap but airy hotel room overlooking the Corniche in Marseille. At home, I dedicate occasional whole days to reading as if I'm a convalescent. The ideal place for this is the bath, where the body floats free. Books go a little wavy, but they're mine, so who cares.
—**Rachel Kushner**

Michael Connelly

Tell us about your favorite book of the year.

I think I'll go with nonfiction and pick *Act of War: Lyndon Johnson, North Korea, and the Capture of the Spy Ship Pueblo*, by Jack Cheevers. I worked with Cheevers in the early '90s. He was a very good reporter then, and all those skills are on display in this page-turner, which jumps between high politics in Washington and the gripping high-seas journey of the spy ship in 1968. This book held me like *Flyboys* and *Lost in Shangri-La*.

When and where do you like to read?

I mostly read on airplanes and right before sleep. I admit my reading time is limited because I can write in the situations and places where people usually read. But reading is the fuel—it's inspiring—so I try to keep the tank full. What happens most of the time is, I binge read. I will put aside a day or two to do nothing but read. I did that recently with Stephen King's *Doctor Sleep*.

Of the books you've written, which is your favorite?

I know I am supposed to say *The Gods of Guilt* here, since I just wrote it, but my favorite will probably always be *The Last Coyote*, because it was the first book I wrote as a full-time author, and I think the improvements were more evident to me than in the transitions between other books. But don't

---

Michael Connelly is the author of many books, including *The Black Box*, *The Drop*, *The Fifth Witness*, *The Reversal*, *The Scarecrow*, *The Brass Verdict*, *The Lincoln Lawyer*, and the Harry Bosch series.

confuse "favorite" book with "best" book. I am not sure I could pick a book that I would say is my best. I hope I haven't written it yet.

You've said that your mother introduced you to crime fiction. Which books got you hooked?

She was into P. D. James and Agatha Christie, and I liked it, but I would not say I got hooked in until I started reading John D. MacDonald, who was writing about the place where I was growing up. His character Travis McGee kept his boat, the Busted Flush, at the Bahia Mar Marina in Fort Lauderdale. I worked there while in high school, and my boss was named in a couple of the novels. They also kept a slip open for the Flush. I thought that was pretty cool.

Who's your favorite fictional detective? And the best villain?

It's got to be Philip Marlowe as the detective. He had an unmatchable mixture of sardonic humor, weariness, and resolve. I'll go with Francis Dolarhyde from Thomas Harris's *Red Dragon* as the villain. He remains in the shadow of Hannibal Lecter, but I find him more realistic and a reminder that these sorts of killers are more banal than genius. That makes them scarier.

You covered crime for the *Fort Lauderdale News* and *Sun-Sentinel* and for the *Los Angeles Times*. What did reporting teach you about storytelling?

That it's all about momentum. Momentum in writing means momentum in reading. There is a prevailing school of thought that something good must take time, sometimes years to create and hone. I have always felt that the books I have written fastest have been my best—because I caught an unstoppable momentum in the writing.

What's the best thing about writing a book?

There is a great freedom to it. You set your own hours and pace, you write without anyone looking over your shoulder and telling you what to do. It either happens or it doesn't, but when it does there is an amazing sense of fulfillment to it. It's like improvising jazz on a piano or saxophone. What comes out may have roots in something else, but you've made it yours.

The hardest or least rewarding?

The gamble you take with everything you write. Not knowing if what you created with that freedom to improvise is worth the paper you print it out on. You can put a good chunk of yourself and your time into something and only you may love it in the end.

What kinds of stories are you drawn to? And what do you steer clear of?

I like stories about people who have to go into darkness for a good reason and then have to figure out how to deal with the darkness that seeps into their souls. It's a variation on the noble cause, I guess. I avoid stories that explain the villain and why he acts out. It's just not that interesting to me. I like the bargain that good cops make. Like a law of physics, they go into darkness; darkness goes into them. They have to decide how to prevent it from destroying them.

What books might we be surprised to find on your shelves?

I'm not sure what would be surprising. Maybe the complete collection of Patrick O'Brian's Aubrey-Maturin novels. *The Public Burning*, by Robert Coover? That's one of my favorite novels of all time.

Who is your favorite overlooked or underappreciated writer?

There's a guy who writes about the Panhandle in Florida named Michael Lister. I like his stuff a lot. There's a new practitioner of the LA crime novel named P. G. Sturges. He's really good, too, with his stories about the Short-cut Man.

President Clinton gave you some nice publicity when he was photographed reading one of your early novels. Which of your books would you recommend to President Obama?

The Closers, because I think it's the book that underlines Harry Bosch's belief that everybody counts or nobody counts.

Disappointing, overrated, just not good: What book did you feel you were supposed to like, and didn't? Do you remember the last book you put down without finishing?

Too many to list here, and I am not that impolitic anyway—at least with writers still living. But I have to say I am an impatient reader. My time to read is too short, so I only give a book—any book—a short leash. It's got to draw me in quickly. It doesn't matter to me who wrote it, what the pedigree is, or what the critics say. If I'm not in the car, buckled in, and riding with the story by the second chapter or so, I'm probably going back to the shelf for something else.

If you could meet any writer, dead or alive, who would it be? What would you want to know?

I'd like to ask Raymond Chandler about chapter thirteen of *The Little Sister*. It describes a drive around 1940s Los Angeles, and it still holds up as a description of the city right now. Beautiful. I'd ask him how he pulled that off. And I'd tell him that that short chapter of his was what made me want to become a writer. I'd also ask him whether it takes a tortured life to produce something like that. I'd say, Ray, can a writer be happy and still be good at it?

What book do you think everybody should read before they die?

The Giving Tree, by Shel Silverstein.

What do you plan to read next?

Four Days in November: The Assassination of President John F. Kennedy, by Vincent Bugliosi. I've been sitting on this one for a long time. This is the time to read it.

Neil deGrasse Tyson

Who are your favorite science writers? Anyone new and good we should be paying attention to?

In no particular order: Dava Sobel, Timothy Ferris, Cornelia Dean, Bill Bryson, and Michael Lemonick. And I just recently discovered the delightfully irreverent books of Mary Roach. I take this occasion to note that Agnes M. Clerke, writing in the late nineteenth century and the turn of the twentieth, was one of the most prolific science writers in any field, although her specialty was astrophysics, then a male-dominated area. Her titles include *The Concise Knowledge Library: Astronomy* (1898), *Problems in Astrophysics* (1903), and *Modern Cosmologies* (1905).

If a parent asked you for book recommendations to get a child interested in science, what would be on your list?

Kids are naturally interested in science. The task is to maintain that innate interest, and not get in their way as they express it. Early on, my favorite children's book was *On the Day You Were Born* (1991), written and illustrated by Debra Frasier. I'm often asked by publishers whether I will ever write a science-based children's book. My answer will remain no until I believe I can write one better than Frasier's. It hasn't happened yet, and I don't see it happening in the foreseeable future. Also, I remain impressed how fast the Dr. Seuss Cat in the Hat's Learning Library series updated Tish Rabe's book *There's No Place Like Space: All About Our Solar System* (1999, 2009) to reflect the official 2006 demotion of Pluto to "dwarf planet" status.

Neil deGrasse Tyson is the director of the Hayden Planetarium at the American Museum of Natural History, the host of *Cosmos: A Space-Time Odyssey*, and the author of *The Pluto Files*, among other books.

What are the greatest books ever written about astronomy?

Because the field of study changes so rapidly, any book that's great in one decade becomes hopelessly obsolete by the next. But if I am forced to pick one, it would be Carl Sagan's *Cosmos* (1980). Not for the science it taught, but for how effectively the book shared why science matters—or should matter—to every citizen of the world.

And your favorite novels of all time?

Jonathan Swift's *Gulliver's Travels* (1726). I often find myself reflecting on the odd assortment of characters that Lemuel Gulliver met during his travels. We're all familiar with the tiny Lilliputians, but during his voyages he also met the giant Brobdingnagians. And elsewhere he met the savage humanoid Yahoos and the breed of rational horses—the Houyhnhnms—who shunned them. And I will not soon forget the misguided scientists of the Grand Academy of Lagado beneath the levitated Island of Laputa, who invested great resources posing and answering the wrong questions about nature.

What kinds of stories are you drawn to? Any you steer clear of?

Not enough books focus on how a culture responds to radically new ideas or discovery. Especially in the biography genre, they tend to focus on all the sordid details in the life of the person who made the discovery. I find this path to be voyeuristic but not enlightening. Instead, I ask, After evolution was discovered, how did religion and society respond? After cities were electrified, how did daily life change? After the airplane could fly from one country to another, how did commerce or warfare change? After we walked on the Moon, how differently did we view Earth? My larger understanding of people, places, and things derives primarily from stories surrounding questions such as those.

What books might we be surprised to find on your shelves?

I have multiple shelves of books and tracts on religion and religious philosophy, as well as on pseudoscience and general fringe thinking. I'm perennially intrigued how people who lead largely evidence-based lives can, in a belief-based part of their mind, be certain that an invisible, divine entity created an entire universe just for us, or that the government is stockpiling space aliens in a secret desert location. I find this reading to be invaluable in my efforts to communicate with all those who, while invoking these views, might fear or reject the methods, tools, and tenets of science.

What book has had the greatest impact on you?

George Gamow's *One, Two, Three . . . Infinity* (1947) and Edward Kasner and James Newman's *Mathematics and the Imagination* (1940) are both still in print. I have aspired to write a book as influential to others as these books have been influential to me. The closest I have come is *Death by Black Hole: And Other Cosmic Quandaries* (2007), but while I think it succeeds on many educational levels, I'm quite sure it falls short of what these authors accomplished. For me, at middle-school age, they turned math and science into an intellectual playground that I never wanted to leave. It's where I first learned about the numbers googol and googolplex (a googolplex is so large, you cannot fully write it, for it contains more zeros than the number of particles in the universe). It's also where I learned about higher dimensions and the general power of mathematics to decode the universe.

If you could require the president to read one book, what would it be?

I'd like to believe that the president of the United States, the most powerful person in the world, has time to read more than one book. But picking just one book reveals my bias: *Physics for Future Presidents*, by Richard A. Muller (2009) is, of course, already conceived for this purpose. The president's science adviser has traditionally been a physicist. Parting the layered curtains of science reveals that there's no understanding of biology without chemistry, and there is no understanding of chemistry without physics. Informed people in government have known this from the beginning. And all of engineering derives from the laws of physics themselves. So the physics literacy of a president is a good thing, especially since innovations in science and technology will drive the engines of twenty-first-century economies. Failure to understand or invest wisely here will doom a nation to economic irrelevance.

What books have you most enjoyed sharing with your children?

The last book that I read to both of my kids, at the same time, was Carlo Collodi's *The Adventures of Pinocchio* (1883). At the time, they were both old enough to read on their own, but I nonetheless invited them to hear my recitation, in four or five sittings. Only when you read the original book do you realize how much of an undisciplined, stubborn, trouble-making truant Pinocchio actually was—complete with him squashing Jiminy Cricket, reducing him to a mere smudge on the wall, killing his short-lived spiritual adviser early in the story. The book served as an excellent example of how not to behave as a child. And it further served as a reminder of how Hollywood, or Disney in particular, can denude fairy tales of their strongest messages.

If you could meet any writer, dead or alive, who would it be? What would you want to know?

Oscar Wilde. Anyone who could pen the phrase "We are all in the gutter, but some of us are looking at the stars" gets a seat at my dinner table. Also, I've been intrigued by the breadth of topics that interested Edgar Allan Poe. In particular, his prose poem of speculative science called "Eureka" (1848), which lays out basic tenets of modern cosmology, seventy years before cosmology even existed as a subject of study. For all we know, their best-known works are only the tip of an iceberg of mental processing and thoughts that engaged them daily. These would surely be thoughts that would emerge during a nice meal I might have with them, over a good bottle of wine.

If you could be any character from literature, who would you be?

I'd be Thomas Stockmann, the medical doctor in the 1882 Henrik Ibsen play *An Enemy of the People*. And I'd handle the situation a bit differently. I'd alert the townspeople of the problem with their public baths in such a way that they would welcome the news rather than reject it. This requires sensitivity to how people think and an awareness of what they value in life and why. The town might then have been compelled to fix the problem rather than view the messenger and his message as their enemy. When I first read the story, I was astonished that educated adults would behave in such a manner and was prepared to discount the whole story as a work of unrealistic fiction. I would later see actual people—including those in power—behave in just this way on all manner of scientific topics, instilling within me the urge to become the doctor's character and make everything OK.

What book have you always meant to read and haven't gotten around to yet? Anything you feel embarrassed never to have read?

Although I'm not actually embarrassed by this, I tend not to read books that have awesome movies made from them, regardless of how well or badly the movie represented the actual written story. Instead, at cocktail parties, I've always found it a bit awkward when I'm not up-to-date on all the latest novels and other written works that get reviewed in *The New York Review of Books*. That means I'm not only not reading the hottest novels, I'm not even reading the reviews of the novels themselves.

What do you plan to read next?

Four books that I just acquired from an antiquarian bookseller—short monographs by the philosopher, mathematician, and social activist Bertrand Russell: *Justice in War-Time* (the 1924 printing), *Mysticism and Logic and Other Essays* (1932 edition), *Common Sense and Nuclear Warfare* (1959), and *Has Man a Future?* (1961). It's always refreshing to see what a deep-thinking, smart, and worldly person (who is not a politician) has to say about the social and geopolitical challenges of the day.

I wanted to be Meg Murry, the admittedly geeky heroine of *A Wrinkle in Time*, by Madeleine L'Engle. I loved how she worked with others to fight against an unjust system and how she fought to save her family against very long odds. I was also captivated by the concept of time travel. I keep asking Facebook's engineers to build me a tesseract so I, too, could fold the fabric of time and space.—**Sheryl Sandberg**

Once I'd banished King Arthur, and I was nine or ten, the characters I lived through were the two leading men in *Kidnapped*, the strait-laced young David Balfour and the weathered desperado Alan Breck. The lessons I learned through David were that you had to leave home, go out into the world, and become your own man; and you must not despise any unlikely role models you might meet. I didn't find any similar story to teach me about being a woman.—**Hilary Mantel**

Horton. He's the one who heard a Who and hatched an egg. I was a big Dr. Seuss fan when I was very young— I had *The Sneetches* and *Horton Hatches the Egg* memorized before I started kindergarten, and much to the dismay of my friends, I can still recite big chunks of them.—**Jeannette Walls**

I've always strongly identified with Toad from *Frog and Toad*. Especially in the story in which he won't get out of the river because he doesn't want anyone to see him looking funny in his bathing suit—and thereby attracts the attention of the nearby lizards, dragonflies, field mouse, etc.—he's so completely the ridiculous instigator of his own problems. —**Curtis Sittenfeld**

Peter Pan. I loved Peter Pan. Still love Peter Pan. Peter Pan is the only ride that I enjoyed at Disney. And I'm pretty sure that I wrote the Maximum Ride books for kids—starting with my own beloved Jack—because of my affection as a child for Peter Pan.—**James Patterson**

Starting at about eleven, with *Alice in Wonderland* and Lewis Carroll, I began identifying with the writer— or what I've learned now to call "the implicit author"—of a given fiction, rather than with the characters directly. Possibly some would say this explains a deficit of heroes in my stories.—**Jonathan Lethem**

I imagined myself as Jim Hawkins in *Treasure Island*, an innocent among thieves and cutthroats. It must have been the first book I ever read from start to finish, with unforgettable characters, Long John Silver, Blind Pew, Ben Gunn. . . . The Black Spot still terrifies me.—**Sting**

As a child I adored Huckleberry Finn and Peter Pan. As a teenager: Franny Glass. In my twenties: Agatha Runcible.—**Donna Tartt**

Tintin is my favorite children's book hero, or maybe it's Captain Haddock. Tintin was willing to walk around on the bottom of the sea, trusting the two detectives to crank his air pump. Nobody can draw Tibetan mountainsides like Hergé. In the morning, in bed, I sometimes raise my fist and cry, "Action Stations!"—as Haddock did when he was startled awake from a doze.—**Nicholson Baker**

E. L. Doctorow

What's the best book you've read recently?

Well, it could be Herodotus's *The Histories* in the Landmark edition published by Pantheon. Herodotus is spectacular—part historian, part investigative reporter and inveterate storyteller. Or maybe *Mind and Cosmos*, by Thomas Nagel, an intense philosophical takedown of neo-Darwinism and scientific materialism. It's a brave contrarian book. Reminds me of Wittgenstein's remark: "Even if all our scientific questions are answered, our problem is still not touched at all." Another best is Don DeLillo's *Cosmopolis*. A beautiful conceit runs this novel—an epic journey by limo across midtown Manhattan. And then his new story collection, *The Angel Esmeralda*. DeLillo has a consummate comprehension of the world. And then Harold Bloom's *The American Religion*, which argues that our domestic Christian religions are more Gnosticism than Christian. Mormonism in his view is the religious future of this country. And I'm recently into *From Eternity to Here*—the physicist Sean Carroll's fascinating book about time. Time confounds the physicists. They ask why it goes only one way. And finally, if a reread qualifies, I'm going again through Seamus Heaney's translation of *Beowulf.* Here's a book that can be sung.

When and where do you like to read?

At my desk. Or out of doors in the backyard when the weather's fine.

E. L. Doctorow is the author of many books, including *The Book of Daniel, Ragtime, Loon Lake, World's Fair, Billy Bathgate, The March*, and most recently, *Andrew's Brain.*

As a rereader, what books do you find yourself returning to again and again?

Montaigne. Chekhov. They never fail you. Montaigne is the most honest memoirist in the world: He didn't try to construct a narrative of his life; he just went wherever his thoughts took him, diving into his own mind and setting down its reflections and feelings for everyone to see. A kind of experiment in self-portraiture under a white light—published under the title *Essais*, or *Essays*. As for Anton Chekhov, no one puts life onto the page as Chekhov does. He defies critical analysis—the prose seems artless, as if he just splashes out the sentences. I recommend the five short novels including *The Duel* and *Three Years* in the translations of Richard Pevear and Larissa Volokhonsky. But the truth is, I've never read any translation of Chekhov in which that rigorously judicious mind didn't come through.

You were involved in theater while in college and were a script reader in Hollywood. How did those experiences inform your approach to story-telling?

Yes, I was heavily involved in acting at Kenyon College. I find that astonishing now. Who was this boy playing Edgar in *King Lear*, and Joe Bonaparte in Clifford Odets's *Golden Boy*? At the time, I intended to write for the theater, you see, and so needed experience onstage to understand what actors went through. And when you are cast in a role as I was as Gloucester's good son, you read the text intently, obsessively, as you might not read it as, say, an English major. And so you learn how the play is put together, how it's constructed, and how it flows forward and maintains its tension, and how character is rendered. You feel its heartbeat. And with Shakespeare, you say the words aloud and hear the music of the language, the rhythm of the meter, and that stays with you; you are in a sense given the English language as a present. So that was valuable no matter what form my writing took—because I did drift away from theater when I took up the writing of novels.

As you say, I worked as a reader for a motion picture company—not in Hollywood, but here in New York, where the publishers were. The studios were in the hunt for books that could be filmed. I read scripts, yes, but mostly novels in galleys, and that was encouraging because I saw how many bad books were being published. It was very useful to realize that simply because something was in print didn't necessarily mean that it should have been. But there were some great moments in that job: I remember finding on my desk a first-draft partial manuscript of Saul Bellow's *Henderson the*

Rain King. It was under option by Columbia Pictures, and I urged them to pick up the option. Of course they didn't. But Bellow was important to me—I'd read his *Adventures of Augie March* in college, and it was in the nature of a revelation, the freedom in that narrative—that there were no rules for the writing of a novel except as you made them up.

Some months later the finished *Henderson* was published, and I found the first third of the book disappointing. It was somehow less than it had been in manuscript. Bellow had neatened things up; he'd met some formal obligations of the story, but in so doing he'd flattened the life out of it. I found that instructive.

You spent your early years as an editor at the New American Library and the Dial Press. What are your fondest memories of working in publishing? What has been the most significant change you've witnessed in the field?

At New American Library, a mass-market reprinter, we were publishing books with a price of fifty or seventy-five cents or a dollar and a quarter for a huge novel, and distributing them in great numbers all over the country. Or we'd buy a good first novel that had sold maybe two thousand copies in hardcover, and print a hundred thousand and put it in every airport and railroad and bus station in the country. That was wonderfully satisfying work. NAL's list was eclectic—publishing Mickey Spillane, but also Faulkner; Erskine Caldwell's *Tobacco Road*, but also Susanne K. Langer's *Philosophy in a New Key*. We published The Signet Classic Shakespeare, of which I was the house editor, and a science list which fell to me to handle. It was all very exciting, reading these books, bidding for the reprint rights, entertaining proposals, and dealing with the likes of Ayn Rand and Ian Fleming. But the game changed with the advent of the trade paperback. Trade publishers were now keeping the reprint rights for lists of their own. And so the mass-market business changed, and some of the reprinters went to what they called "originals"—genre products like thrillers, romances, and so on. You can still find good classic public-domain titles at the big paperback houses like NAL, but they're not freely distributed as they used to be—they are mostly on educational lists so far as I can tell.

I moved over to Dial, a trade publisher, in the mid-1960s, and it was a very exciting place to be—not only because this was the '60s but because your most creative juices were required just to keep that house in business. I was editing Mailer, James Baldwin. I published William Kennedy's first novel, Ernest J. Gaines, Thomas Berger, and a book by Joan Baez. But also a hoax called *Report from Iron Mountain*, a satirically inspired, dryly written presumed government study claiming that peace was not only unattainable but undesirable. This was during the Vietnam War, you see. The book was covered on the front page of *The New York Times* and hit the bestseller list.

Conglomeration—the acquisition of houses by large corporations—is the story of how things have changed. Trade publishing was never purely a business. How could it be when a house's prime assets were the tastes of its editors? You floated the consequential books with the money you earned with the commercial things on your list. Publishing was a cottage industry. People loved to be in it and took its low salaries in return for its creative excitements. A house's balance sheet could veer from good to dismal and back again from year to year. That's because it didn't offer products that were endlessly the same, like breakfast cereals or automobile tires. The hunches of its editors were very hard to quantify on a balance sheet. Now, wanting publishing to be a business like any other, the big conglomerates naturally like to increase their profit margins from one year to the next. There's a pressure on editors to sober up and produce books that earn their keep. Oddly the conglomerates have more money to play with, and so, perversely, they may be less daring, less freewheeling. This is not true of the best of them, of course. Good books are still published with vigor and are still major acts of the culture, but the corporate ethos makes it probably not as much fun.

Which books might we be surprised to find on your bookshelves?

The Oxford Study Bible. And mysteries and thrillers: Simenon, but not Agatha Christie. That Swedish couple of forty or fifty years ago, Maj Sjowall and Per Wahloo. Of the current practitioners, John Sandford and Lee Child. Two very skilled and smart writers.

Which novels have had the most impact on you as a writer? Is there a particular book that made you want to write?

I think the books I read as a child made me want to write: Stevenson's *Treasure Island* and *Kidnapped*; C. S. Lewis's *Out of the Silent Planet* and *Perelandra*; Mark Twain's boy books, and his *Connecticut Yankee in King Arthur's Court*; Jack London's *Call of the Wild* and *White Fang*; Dickens's *David Copperfield*, *Great Expectations*, and *A Tale of Two Cities*; Conan Doyle's Sherlock Holmes stories; Victor Hugo's *Hunchback of Notre Dame* and *Les Misérables*. Poe's detective and horror stories; the Horatio Hornblower sea novels of C. S. Forester; all the Oz books; and in middle school, *Mario and the Magician*, by Thomas Mann, and Kafka's *Metamorphosis*. For starters.

If you could require the president to read one book, what would it be?

He's a reader and doesn't need my instruction. On the other hand, if I could require Republican members of Congress to read one book it would be Keynes's *The General Theory of Employment, Interest and Money*.

What does your personal book collection look like? Do you organize your books in any particular way?

No, they may track my life—as a child, as a student, as an editor, and as a writer—and I think of them as precious objects, but they're like life in not being organized. Though I did at one point put some of my books together on one shelf—the works of the poets I read in college—Thomas Hardy, Gerard Manley Hopkins, Yeats, Eliot, Auden, Frost, Wallace Stevens, A. E. Housman. And also the books of poets who've been friends of mine—James Wright, Galway Kinnell, Philip Levine.

Disappointing, overrated, just not good: What book did you feel you were supposed to like, and didn't? Do you remember the last book you put down without finishing?

Sometimes I put books down that are good but that I see too well what the author is up to. As you practice your craft, you lose your innocence as a reader. That's the one sad thing about this work.

I'd love to read a concise, nonhysterical biography of Michael Jackson. I just want to know everything about him.—**David Sedaris**

The Playboy of the Western World, the second volume of Nigel Hamilton's biography of JFK and sequel to *Reckless Youth*.—**J. K. Rowling**

I really wish Michelle Alexander, who wrote *The New Jim Crow*, about African-American men in prisons, would write a sequel, focusing on the plight of women. There are tens of thousands of women doing decades for nonviolent offenses, and the abuse they suffer behind bars is virtually a given. Given Alexander's skills and audience, an exposé on the subject would have a critical impact.—**Dave Eggers**

I wish my mom would let me type and edit her journals from when she was my age, but she doesn't trust me that they're a fascinating account of the inner life of a young artist in 1970s SoHo. I also wouldn't mind reading Bill Murray's memoirs or an instructional guide to getting dressed by Chloë Sevigny.—**Lena Dunham**

A great biography of John von Neumann, the most important mathematician of the twentieth century.
—**Sylvia Nasar**

I'd like somebody to write a book that really told the truth about life now. Leo Tolstoy but with drive-through windows.—**Nicholson Baker**

The poet Charles Simic says there should be a book called *The History of Stupidity*. He says it would be the world's longest book: an encyclopedia. I don't think he plans to write it, but I wish that someone would.
—**Francine Prose**

I'm waiting for the day when Rush Limbaugh's pharmacist writes a book.—**Carl Hiaasen**

Could someone please write a book explaining why the Democratic Party and its allies are so much less effective at crafting a message and having a vision than their Republican counterparts? Kurt Eichenwald! Mark Bowden! John Heilemann and Mark Halperin! I'll preorder today.—**Ira Glass**

A definitive history of bohemianism, that ever-present undercurrent of antinomian thought and behavior wearing funny clothes. It should start with Petronius and his Satyricon hipsters. And I'll bet ancient China and Pharaonic Egypt had beatniks too.—**P. J. O'Rourke**

Dave Barry: The Greatest Human Ever.—**Dave Barry**

A work of such brilliant prose, such imaginative powers, such sweep, such flair, with such an irresistible story and riveting characters that simply by reading it attentively one could understand those discoveries of molecular biology, neuroscience, psycholinguistics, "philosophy of mind," and "string theory" in the way that their discoverers/creators understand them.—**Joyce Carol Oates**

My worst book. I wish someone would write that one so I won't have to.—**Jeffrey Eugenides**

Chang-rae Lee

What's the best book you've read recently? And your vote for best book of the last year?

Two first fictions dazzled me in the last couple of years, the novel *Mr. Peanut*, by Adam Ross, and *Battleborn*, a story collection by Claire Vaye Watkins. *Mr. Peanut* is a hybrid wonder, being at once a detective story, an arch gloss on that genre, and a bravura romance, totally upended, that employs the possible murder of one's wife as a means of revealing the manifold facets of truest, desperate love. All this is driven by the edgy sparkle of the prose, which acts not only as a mirror or lens but as an accelerant, lighting up every layer of his characters' consciousnesses to a degree that feels almost dangerous. Watkins's *Battleborn* is equally potent even though the stories range widely in setting, time, and voice, the modalities coming at you with a ferocity and intelligence that seems like a magic trick. But there's nothing artificial about these stories, for as you read them an indelible picture begins to emerge of a certain sensibility, maybe borne from the desert West—toughened, resourceful, both hellbent and eternally hopeful.

When and where do you like to read?

I'll read pretty much anywhere and anytime, but for a while now I've really enjoyed reading on flights, especially the longer hauls, when I'm unplugged from everything and can completely immerse myself in the world of a book and submit happily to its rhythms, perspectives, ideas. Turns out that a good book has an analgesic effect, too, momentarily relieving the special torture of flying (unfortunately, I'm most often in coach).

Chang-rae Lee is the author of *Native Speaker*, *A Gesture Life*, *Aloft*, *The Surrendered*, and *On Such a Full Sea*.

Are you a rereader? What books do you find yourself returning to again and again?

Lately I've been rereading books that I hadn't read since high school and college, novels like *Lord Jim* and *The Brothers Karamazov* and *Women in Love*, big, complex works which I found arresting and difficult then and find arresting and difficult now, though perhaps for different reasons. Reading Lawrence, for example, is sometimes cringe-inducing, for a certain gaseousness and the interminable-feeling meditations on morality and desire that I ate up as a profundity-seeking undergraduate. And yet there's an irrepressible life force and iconoclastic urge that's artistically inspiring.

Who is your favorite novelist of all time? And your favorite novelist writing today?

Naming a "favorite" is always impossible—how can I choose from writers as great and varied in their approaches as Flaubert, Dostoyevsky, Joyce, Borges (who didn't write novels)? Still, I've always had a love for American novelists, particularly Hemingway and Bellow and Styron and Updike. I'll also decline to name a living favorite, though I'll say Don DeLillo is probably one of a handful of living writers I try to read from the moment he publishes anything. Like any DeLillo fan, I have my favorites from his oeuvre, but his approach in all of his works is so very particular and uncommon, and always carries the mark of his hard-stamped language. I admire fearless writers.

What kinds of stories are you drawn to? And how would you describe the kinds of books you steer clear of?

I suppose people might consider me a "loose" reader, as I seem willing to read anything of quality thinking and prose. I'm not doctrinaire. I see the field of writing as filled with these wondrously rich phenomena of language and form. In my teaching, I try to expose my students to the widest range of aesthetic possibilities, so I'll offer them stories from Anton Chekhov to Denis Johnson, from Flannery O'Connor to A. M. Homes, and perhaps investigating all that strange variation of beauty has rubbed off on me. Or perhaps that's why I enjoy teaching literature.

What kinds of characters draw you in as a reader? And as a writer?

Like most people, I'm fascinated by characters who are completely flawed personalities, riven by anguish and doubt, and are psychologically suspect. Wait a minute—basically that's everybody, isn't it, in life and on the page? As a writer, I'm drawn to characters who, for one reason or another, seem to find themselves desperately out of joint, alienated but not wanting to be, and ever yearning to understand the rules of the game.

On Such a Full Sea is your first dystopian novel. Are you a fan of dystopian fiction? Do any books in particular inspire you?

I'm not automatically drawn to tales because they're dystopian. The classics from Orwell and Huxley, and contemporary works by McCarthy, Atwood, and Ishiguro are excellent because they expose our condition, certain possibilities of human expression and conduct, and not just because they're set in some imagined or futuristic realm. The altered context of these realms should surely be diverting, but it's how the context forms and deforms the characters that compels me as a reader. Otherwise it's just fancy scenery and essentially repetitive episodes.

Though _On Such a Full Sea_ is set in the United States, you began your research in China. What led you to change the setting?

Glimpsing, for the umpteenth time, an abandoned residential area of Baltimore from my seat on the Amtrak train. I intended to write a social-realist novel about the factory towns of the Pearl River Delta, but on seeing that neighborhood yet again I was struck by an odd, idle notion: why not have the people of a small city in China, say, one that was environmentally fouled, come over and resettle this forlorn place? Of course such a thing could never happen now, but the idea seemed less implausible when I considered it in the context of a very different future, a future when America was in significant decline. That was the moment that I began musing about a different novel, thinking of the details of that future society. And so those details evolved from there, Baltimore becoming "B-Mor," a specialized labor settlement/facility that produces pristine fish and vegetables for an elite "Charter" class, and a whole set of characters emerged.

What might we be surprised to find on your bookshelves?

Lots of cookbooks. My friends would tell you that I like to cook and eat. But I rarely use the recipes, and if I do I seem to have a pathological urge to revise them until they're altered profoundly. I hope not disfigured. I suppose this comes from equal parts egomania and laziness (for not wanting to go out and forage for the ingredients, or follow the prescribed manner of cooking). I simply like to look at the pictures, to be honest, which spur my appetite and make me imagine what might soon appear on the table.

What were your favorite books as a child?

I didn't read the canon of classic children's books, at least not until I became a father and read to my own children. No doubt this was because my parents were new to the country and not comfortable speaking English and didn't read to me at night. I didn't speak English myself until the first grade. I read lots of books in elementary school—I remember winning a prize for reading the most books one year—but I can't recall a single title. What I do remember finding enduringly fascinating were some of my father's books—he was a psychiatrist who also hoped to be an analyst—and he had all the works of Sigmund Freud. *The Interpretation of Dreams, Civilization and Its Discontents, Totem and Taboo,* etc. I couldn't understand any of it. But I could glean something from *Three Case Histories* and *Studies on Hysteria,* which featured patients like the Rat Man and the famous Anna O., whom I considered to be story characters. I loved reading about these very anxious people with all kinds of fascinating ailments and tics, even if I didn't really understand why they were fascinating. I suppose someone might say this was my literary "primal scene."

Which novels have had the most impact on you as a writer? Is there a particular book that made you want to write?

In high school, when I was just beginning to realize how much I loved literature and was earnestly writing my first poems and stories, I adored *Dubliners* and *A Farewell to Arms* as well as *Leaves of Grass* and *Let Us Now Praise Famous Men.* But I was perhaps most taken and inspired by Kerouac's *On the Road.* I loved the ecstatic riffs of that novel, the sense of wild possibility and bohemian grittiness, which for a buttoned-up good immigrant boy secretly yearning for something different was deeply seductive stuff. It wasn't just the depicted lifestyle that captivated me, but the revelatory passion displayed by this cast of dreamers, who to me were desperate to connect with something bigger and more beautiful, who wanted to be great artists of this life.

If you could require the president to read one book, what would it be?

Shouldn't every leader read Shakespeare's *Julius Caesar,* for its studies in the dangers of tyranny and betrayal and hubristic ambition, as well as the power and limits of rhetoric? Of course it's also a pleasure to read, chock-full of great speeches and sweet turns of phrase that seem to comment on every facet of human existence. In fact, the title of my new novel is taken from a famous speech by Brutus, which is a marvel of metaphoric vitality and persuasion.

What books are you embarrassed not to have read yet?

Being both a long-lapsed Confucian and Christian, the *I Ching* and the Bible. I've attempted to read both at different times in my life but have yet to succeed in getting very far through either. But I will keep trying, I think.

What book are you most eagerly anticipating reading in 2014?

No doubt the memoir of my good friend and former student Gary Shteyngart, which I'm sure will be painfully hilarious and very smart. Plus, I hear I get a nice shout-out.

I'm horrible at meeting people I admire, but if I could go back in time, I'd love to collect kindling or iron a few shirts for Flannery O'Connor. After I'd finished, she'd offer to pay me and I'd say, awestruck, my voice high and quivering, that it was on me.—**David Sedaris**

Emily Dickinson. I would be her nursemaid, her quiet companion on walks in the woods. I imagine that anything she spotted—feathers, tea leaves, a hole in a fence—would lead her to utter something profound about human emotions in a lifetime of expectation.—**Amy Tan**

Chekhov. I don't want to know anything in particular—I'd just like to carve up a pheasant with him, served with new potatoes and green beans from the garden. Then we could polish off some dodgy Crimean wine and play a few rounds of Anglo-Russian Scrabble and lose track of time and the score. If Isaac Bashevis Singer could be there, too, I think they'd get on well. And if Dorothy Parker could drop by at some point, and maybe Katherine Mansfield, and Sylvia Townsend-Warner . . . And suddenly it's a party.—**David Mitchell**

Rumi or Virginia Woolf—I love them both beyond all others. I would not be able to speak or communicate in any way while in their presence. I would sit before them, rocking autistically. There is nothing I would need to know beyond what they have written.—**Anne Lamott**

I'll have to go with the elephant in the room—William Shakespeare. I'd ask him: Dude, did you know how great you were? Were you aware at the time of the sheer incandescent beauty of, say, *Romeo and Juliet*? Or were you just scuffling along like the rest of us, trying to make a living?—**Lee Child**

The poet Jack Gilbert. (No relation, sadly.) He's the poet laureate of my marriage: my husband and I have read him aloud to each other for years, and he exerts a subtle influence over the way we understand ourselves in love. I would like to thank him for that, but I've always been too shy to write him a letter.—**Elizabeth Gilbert**

I'd love to have met Ford Madox Ford (no relation, also). Such a big, messy, compelling, brilliant character. My kind of guy (though, of course, it would probably have turned out disastrously, as many things in his life did).
—**Richard Ford**

Winston Churchill. He is one of my heroes, and when I look at all of the books he somehow had time to write, it just blows my mind. To be such a vital figure in modern history and at the same time write incredible history . . . I would love to talk to him about how he had time to be great as a leader and as a writer.
—**Arnold Schwarzenegger**

My choice would be the classical Greek historian Thucydides, who devoted the latter part of his life to a book detailing the history of the long series of wars between Athens and Sparta in the fifth century BC. If I met him, I would be curious to discover whether he was really as devoid of humor as is his book. In his entire book there is not a single sentence that could be considered remotely humorous, no less a joke.—**Jared Diamond**

I would love to meet Mark Twain. What a character! I imagine him larger than life, sexy, handsome, full of energy, a grandiose storyteller, a fantastic liar, and a man of heart and principles. I would not ask him anything in particular; I would try to get him a little drunk (it should be easy) and then sit at his feet to listen to his stories.—**Isabel Allende**

Gary Shteyngart

What's the best book you've read recently? And your vote for best book of the last year?

Middlemarch! Can you believe I read the whole thing? When I finished it I expected a Publishers Clearing House–type van to pull up to my house and some British people to pop out and present me with a medal and a case of sherry. I guess because of fiscal austerity in the UK, they don't have the budget for *Middlemarch* medals anymore.

Carl Hiaasen's *Bad Monkey* was my favorite book of 2013. He is the bard of South Florida. I've never had this much fun reading about a dismembered arm and a crazed chimp. I will read anything Hiaasen ever writes, even if it's written on the napkin of some filthy Key West crab house.

When and where do you like to read?

Reading is still my favorite pastime. It kicks writing's butt. You learn so much more from reading than you do from writing, although writing pays slightly more. I start reading at four p.m. and continue way into cocktail hour, which begins at four thirty.

Are you a rereader? What books do you find yourself returning to again and again?

I've read Nabokov's *Pnin* so many times the book no longer has a spine. Has there ever been a better novel written about a fumbling Russian émigré? I mean, like, why do I even bother?

Gary Shteyngart is the author of the novels *Super Sad True Love Story*, *Absurdistan*, and *The Russian Debutante's Handbook*. His most recent book is *Little Failure: A Memoir*.

You and your wife recently had a baby. How's that affected your reading life?

I've gone from *Middlemarch* to *Don't Bump the Glump!*, by Shel Silverstein. It's so nice to turn the pages of a real printed book with a small, sweet creature like my son, Johnny, by my side. I'm reminded of my father reading to me as a child, my head against his chest, letting the heavy Russian words thump in my ears. I only hope I generated the same kind of megawatt warmth against his skin as my son does against mine.

What kinds of stories are you drawn to? And how would you describe the kinds of books you steer clear of?

I like stories where people suffer a lot. If there's no suffering, I kind of tune out. After reading Karl Ove Knausgaard's memoir, *My Struggle*, I was shocked to discover that people suffer in Norway as well. Good for them! *Skal!*

What kinds of characters draw you in as a reader? And as a writer?

I do have a weakness for funny characters who can't shut up to save their lives. Cue Portnoy.

Do you read a lot of contemporary Russian literature? Who are your favorite Russian writers, current or classic?

Russia is a nightmarish authoritarian state, which is always good for some laughs. Satire always benefits when evil and stupidity collide, and Russia's been a head-on collision for centuries. Vladimir Sorokin is currently my favorite Russian author, a distant heir of Nikolai Gogol, who wasn't bad either.

In addition to your books and short stories, you write for *Travel & Leisure* magazine. What, for you, is the appeal of travel writing? And who are your favorite travel writers?

I love getting out of the country. My parents spent most of their lives living in the USSR, where travel to the West was impossible and Poland was as far as my mother ever got until we emigrated. Getting paid to travel seems completely insane, but there it is, one of the luckiest careers I've ever stumbled upon. As for favorite travel writers, Paul Theroux's *The Great Railway Bazaar* remains the Old Testament of the genre.

What were your favorite books as a child? Are there any in particular you look forward to introducing your son to?

When I was five, I read *The Wonderful Adventures of Nils and the Wild Geese*, by Selma Lagerlof. It was so inspiring I wrote my own version called *Lenin and His Magical Goose*, a hundred-page tome about Lenin encountering a socialist goose and conquering Finland together. It was commissioned by my grandmother, who paid for each page with a block of Soviet cheese. Even today, Random House pays me in cheese.

My son might have less Bolshevik tastes than I did growing up, so I think it's going to be all about this Seuss, MD, and his penchant for colored eggs.

Which novels have had the most impact on you as a writer? Is there a particular book that made you want to write?

See the question above.

If you could require the president to read one book, what would it be?

Definitely *Don't Bump the Glump!*, by Shel Silverstein. It's about how a great many creatures you encounter will try to eat you, even if you start out acting all bipartisan.

What does your personal book collection look like? Do you organize your books in any particular way?

No, it's a mess! Russian books, American books, architecture books. I like how they form nice colors together. It's important to talk to your books to remind them they still matter.

You've become quite an avid presence on Twitter. Are there other authors you like to follow on Twitter or elsewhere online?

So many! Among them @SalmanRushdie, @marykarrlit, @csittenfeld, @MargaretAtwood, @emilynussbaum, @CherylStrayed, @Mariobatali, @jenniferweiner, @judyblume, @JamesFrancoTV, @PGourevitch, @NathanEnglander, @plattypants (Adam Platt), @Rebeccamead_NYC, @susanorlean, @colsonwhitehead, @GilbertLiz (Elizabeth Gilbert), @JonathanAmes, @DavidEbershoff, @KBAndersen (Kurt Andersen), @SashaHemon, @jonleeanderson, @BananaKarenina (Elif Batuman), @walterkirn, @MollyRingwald, @John_Wray, @Tracy_Chevalier, @Darinstrauss, @mohsin_hamid, @michaelianblack, @JayMcInerney, @FrankBruni, @tejucole, @suketumehta, @AmyTan, @jacobwe (Jacob Weisberg), @EricAsimov, @poissel (Paul La Farge), @LukeBarr, @BretEastonEllis, @janiceylee, @askanyone (Sloane Crosley), @GarryShandling.

Disappointing, overrated, just not good: What book did you feel you were supposed to like, and didn't? Do you remember the last book you put down without finishing?

As literary fiction's foremost blurber, I will never publicly admit to disliking a book. Do you know how hard it is to write one? Every time I see a writer crying on the streets of Brooklyn, I give her a hug and nine bucks for a latte at Connecticut Muffin. We're all in this together.

What books are you embarrassed not to have read yet?

Dickens's *Bleak House*. What's wrong with me? On the other hand, I finished *Middlemarch*! So lay off me.

Rachel Kushner

What's the best book you've read recently?

Twelve Years a Slave, by Solomon Northup. An incredible document, amazingly told and structured. Tough, but riveting. The movie of it by Steve McQueen might be the most successful adaptation of a book ever undertaken; text and film complement each other wildly. I also recently read Michelle Alexander's *The New Jim Crow* and can't quit promoting it. That and *Golden Gulag*, by Ruth Wilson Gilmore, are important books that assess with deep and careful thought how we came to be a society of mass incarceration of people of color.

When and where do you like to read?

My most recent, best reading experience was a vacation last summer that involved reading feverishly in a friend's sixteenth-century stone cottage in the Corrèze, and doing the same in a cheap but airy hotel room overlooking the Corniche in Marseille. At home, I dedicate occasional whole days to reading as if I'm a convalescent. The ideal place for this is the bath, where the body floats free. Books go a little wavy, but they're mine, so who cares. Currently I'm deep in *Kippenberger: The Artist and His Families*, in this manner. It's very good. None of the usual biography clichés ("And yet his greatest disappointments were still to come. . . ."). And if you want to understand the art world, and cult of personality, it is a very instructive read.

What books do you find yourself returning to again and again?

I am a rereader. Quality is variety if you wait long enough. Barthes, Baudelaire, Benjamin, Célinc, Duras, Faulkner, Fitzgerald, Melville: There is so

---

Rachel Kushner is the author of *The Flamethrowers* and *Telex from Cuba*.

much to revisit. *Ingrid Caven*, by Jean-Jacques Schuhl, is always in rotation. I used to read *Morvern Callar*, by Alan Warner, every year—I adored that book. This past fall I reread the first two volumes of Proust (new Penguin translations). It was my third reread. I was teaching a Proust seminar at Syracuse, to MFA students of writing. To read for the purpose of leading a class called for a different way of looking at the volumes, more systematic. What I felt every week was that the system, the structure of metaphysical themes and concerns, was right there in the text, so natural to locate. In preparation I read, among other things, Edmund White's sweet and short biography of Proust and was so impressed by it. Edmund White might be a rare person of letters in an old-fashioned sense.

Who is your favorite novelist of all time?

For all time, two: Marcel Proust and Marguerite Duras.

Sell us on your favorite overlooked or underappreciated writer.

I am just getting into Zora Neale Hurston, who is possibly a much better writer than the critics and rivals who tried to erase her from history, resulting in a life in which she worked as a maid and died in a welfare nursing home. She's clever. She does something modern to the sentence. Her race politics (outlined in her memoir, *Dust Tracks on a Road*) are a bit over my head, a bit strange, but fascinating. Alejo Carpentier is so important to me that I don't know if he's famous or not, he's huge in my own private world of greats. *The Lost Steps*, *The Chase* (Sartre's favorite), *Reasons of State*—his prose is spare and baroque at the same time, brutal and comic and full of historical rage and intricate human achievement. *Kingdom of This World*, about the Haitian Revolution, is a singular work of art. Famous in the hipper poetry circles but perhaps not the wider world, Ariana Reines is something special, and her book *Mercury* is a shining achievement. I revere it.

What kinds of stories are you drawn to? And how would you describe the kinds of books you steer clear of?

I steer clear of books with ugly covers. And ones that are touted as "sweeping," "tender," or "universal." But to the real question of what's inside: I avoid books that seem to conservatively follow stale formulas. I don't read for plot, a story "about" this or that. There must be some kind of philosophical depth rendered into the language, something happening. I am often drawn to works that are significant to either the modernist project or to France in the nineteenth century or twentieth century and contemporary Latin America, and lately I read about race in America, because it's an enormous unanswered question. But I'll read about any world if it's rendered with originality, in a good-ugly or severe way. Or in a beautiful way, but free of sentimentality and predictability. And if a book is humorless, I want it to be as good as José Saramago. That about sums it up!

What kinds of characters draw you in as a reader? And as a writer?

I tend to like the complicated antihero: Charlus, from Proust. Balzac's Vautrin. Bolaño's Hans Reiter/Archimboldi, in *2666*. Shrike, from *Miss Lonelyhearts*. The Judge from *Blood Meridian*. Recktall Brown from *The Recognitions*. If I could write a character like one of those? Well. I should be so lucky.

Which books might we be surprised to find on your bookshelves?

Maybe those in my country and western section—the Larry McMurtry novels, an amazing picture book of the Grand Ole Opry, and a history of frontier prostitution lamentably titled *Soiled Doves*. Also, I have always collected books on cars and racing. I have a book that's just a glossary of terms from the world of gas dragsters, and another on the Czech-built Tatra, the most beautiful make of car the world has ever seen. And I am a completist about the photo books of the "porn auteur" Elmer Batters. If only I collected books on marijuana I could have a shelf called "Ass, Gas, or Grass: Nobody Reads for Free."

What kind of reader were you as a child?

Supposedly I went into my room with *Alice in Wonderland*, which was given to me when I was five, and didn't come out until I was done. I was an early reader but I don't think that says much. Having a child and being around them, it's apparent to me that there's some kind of clock that goes off at different times for different kids. Mine went off early, and I didn't like to sleep. So my mother let me stay up as late as I wanted looking at books, and she says I stayed up all night doing that starting at age three. My best years are way behind me.

What were your favorite childhood books? Do you have a favorite literary character?

I got all my politics and culture and my sense of the great wide world of adults from *Mad* magazine. But all other comic books literally gave me a headache. I loved *Island of the Blue Dolphins*, *Julie of the Wolves*, and the Laura Ingalls Wilder books. I still think of that moment at the end of *Island of the Blue Dolphins* when Karana is rescued and the seaman gives her a coarse dress made of denim coveralls to make her "decent." Later, fourth or fifth grade, I remember being obsessed with *My Ántonia*, by Willa Cather; devastated by the brave demise of McMurphy in *One Flew Over the Cuckoo's Nest*; and crushed out on Pappadopoulis, the bohemian Odysseus of *Been Down So Long It Looks Like Up to Me*, by Richard Fariña.

What children's books have you enjoyed discovering (or rediscovering) through your six-year-old son?

We read a lot of books that were mine when I was little, saved all these years: *Higglety Pigglety Pop!*, by Maurice Sendak. *The Wedding Procession of the Rag Doll and Broom Handle*, by Carl Sandburg, illustrated by Harriet Pincus. *The Slightly Irregular Fire Engine*, by Donald Barthelme. Tolstoy's *Fables and Folktales for Children*—so simple, and wonderful, if slightly dark. They remind me that a children's story doesn't need to pander in order to entertain. (The problem with so much recent children's literature: it panders, and yet is often inappropriate for children.) Two new discoveries that are profound works of children's literature: *Paddle-to-the-Sea*, by Holling C. Holling, and *The Animal Family*, by Randall Jarrell.

Which novels have had the most impact on you as a writer?

I studied the novels of Joan Didion and Don DeLillo, who seemed deft and worldly in a way I hoped to someday be. More recently, I have grown deeply impressed by the verve and erudition of *The Recognitions*, by William Gaddis. It is a work that, to me, fulfills the ambition to apprehend the writer's own moment as history—that is the goal, to my mind. I don't care to read about present-day America unless the writer truly has something to say about these times—uses the contemporary, rather than gets used by it. The whole idea of "offering up a mirror" is not enough. I want more.

Is there a particular book that made you want to write?

Cormac McCarthy's *Blood Meridian* is without question the book that made me want to try to be a fiction writer as an actual serious undertaking.

If you could require the president to read one book, what would it be?

Given who our president is, this is like a trick question. I have serious problems with Obama. But Obama is not poorly read; that is not his problem. He's extremely well read. He's still got a drone program. He lets bankers run our economy. Allows Guantánamo to remain open. It would be foolish to pretend I could recommend some enlightening text and he'd scratch his chin and then go for a policy makeover.

What does your personal book collection look like? Do you organize your books in any particular way?

Subject areas for nonfiction. Literature is alphabetical, except I keep poetry on its own set of shelves, but some poets go with fiction for reasons that remain mysterious to me, such as Anne Carson, Francis Ponge, Rimbaud. And I have a "hot" bookcase where I keep what I'm looking at for a novel I'm writing. On the fiction shelves, in front of more dormant areas, I place images of girls and women reading, maybe that's precious, it's just a habit that got started at some point: postcards of paintings by, for instance, Tamara de Lempicka, Gerhard Richter, Lucian Freud, and Cindy Sherman as ingénue-librarian, reaching up.

Disappointing, overrated, just not good: Do you remember the last book you put down without finishing?

I set aside books without finishing them all the time, but that doesn't mean I didn't like them. Take, recently, *Living Currency*, by Pierre Klossowski, or the *Hypnerotomachia Poliphili*, or Xenophon's *Anabasis*—I dip in, and in thirty pages I have a taste of something important that I don't have the training to really benefit from reading to completion anyhow. For years all I'd read of *Ulysses* was the first hundred pages plus the Molly Bloom soliloquy, and nevertheless I had the audacity to still consider myself an admirer of that work. Later I read the whole thing, but in that earlier time, it was much better to have read some of it than none of it.

What books are you embarrassed not to have read yet?

There are various major works I have not read—*Anna Karenina*, *The Red and the Black*, *The Betrothed*. But nothing I am embarrassed not to have yet read. Reading widely and deeply is crucial, I constantly read, but knowing every important work of literature, if you want to be a novelist, is not required and could even hinder things. A writer is someone who can ask questions and follow bold instincts of assimilation. A vast intellectual, someone incredibly erudite about the entire canon, might have more difficulty doing so.

Acknowledgments

I'd like to thank four groups of people. First, at *The New York Times*, I want to thank Sam Tanenhaus, for hiring me first as children's book editor, then as features editor, and for giving me big shoes to fill at the *Book Review*. I am hugely grateful to Arthur Sulzberger Jr., Dean Baquet, Bill Keller, Jill Abramson, and Janet Elder for their tremendous leadership, encouragement, and support at the *Times*. At the *Book Review*, I've had the pleasure and honor to work with a great team of people: Bob Harris, David Kelly, Alex Star, Jenny Schuessler, Barry Gewen, Alida Becker, Jen McDonald, Greg Cowles, Parul Sehgal, Jen Szalai, Sarah Smith, John Williams, Blake Wilson, Steve Coates, Elsa Dixler, Ihsan Taylor, Amy Rowland, Doug Sanders, Valencia Prashad, Jude Biersdorfer, Francis Mateo, Jeffrey Hanson-Scales, and our art director, Nicholas Blechman, who makes By the Book—and every issue, every week—look so distinctive.

I want to thank those who worked specifically on this book: Alex Ward, for helping shepherd this project. My terrific agent, Lydia Wills, as always. Scott Turow, a great champion of books and their authors, for writing a lovely foreword to the book. And Jillian Tamaki, the talented illustrator who creates portraits each week for the column, beautifully reproduced in the book and on its cover.

At Henry Holt, Paul Golob, whose meticulous reading and edits both awe me and put me to shame. Emi Ikkanda, mistress of organization.

Everyone I've worked with at Holt has been terrific: Stephen Rubin, Gillian Blake, Pat Eisemann, Maggie Richards, and the entire sales team. And Meryl Levavi, Rick Pracher, and Molly Bloom, who gave the book its great look and brought it out on schedule.

And at home, I want to thank my husband, Michael, and my three burgeoning readers, Beatrice, Tobias, and Theodore, for all their love, inspiration, and support—even when I had to work at night and couldn't read by their side.

Index

About the Editor

PAMELA PAUL is the editor of *The New York Times Book Review* and the author of *Parenting, Inc.*, *Pornified*, and *The Starter Marriage and the Future of Matrimony*. Prior to joining the *Times*, Paul was a contributor to *Time* magazine and *The Economist*, and her work has appeared in *The Atlantic*, *The Washington Post*, and *Vogue*. She and her family live in New York.

NE   10-14